Untying the Land Knot

Untying the Land Knot

Making Equitable, Efficient, and Sustainable Use of Industrial and Commercial Land

Edited by
Xiaofang Shen, *with* Xiaolun Sun

THE WORLD BANK
Washington, D.C.

ISBN (print): 978-0-8213-8970-6
ISBN (electronic): 978-0-8213-8924-9
DOI: 10.1596/978-0-8213-8970-6

Library of Congress Cataloging-in-Publication Data has been requested.

Cover photos: Ray Gordon. The photos were taken in mid-2009 from inside the partially completed main customs building/gatehouse at the Lekki Free Trade Zone project on the Lekki peninsula east of Lagos, Nigeria.

Contents

Boxes

Figures

Tables

Preface

Xiaofang Shen and Xiaolun Sun

A decade ago in Mozambique, following a stakeholder workshop where the need to improve access to industrial and commercial land as a means to encourage investment was a topic of discussion, a government official came up to us and said, "The Irish model was nice to know, but difficult to follow—at least for Mozambique." With less than 4 percent of the country's territory surveyed and even less registered at the time, implementing the Irish model appeared to be nearly impossible. Descriptions of the dash to the finish line do not show those at the starting point how to take the first step, and the start is sometimes the most difficult. This experience reinforced our interest in researching examples of good practices from developing countries for solving the enormous problems related to business access to renting or buying industrial and commercial land to set up their activities.

In order to create new jobs, generate more income, and modernize the economy, many countries see an urgent need to encourage industrial and commercial investment, both domestic and foreign. However, investment in many sectors cannot take place unless land, along with other basic factors of production, is available. Making land available is no simple matter in today's developing world, where land markets are underdeveloped, property rights are poorly defined, and land use management systems are incomplete or nonexistent. Many countries have comprehensive land reform plans aimed at overcoming these weaknesses, but many of the plans remain on paper only. Their implementation is typically slow.

Questions arise among policy makers: What can we do about the investment the country needs badly? Should we wait another 5 or 10 years until comprehensive land reforms are completed? Can we prioritize the areas where strong investment opportunities exist for our citizens? Can we start with a few pilots of policy and institutional change and train operational officials in the process? What can we do to generate economic results—for the local populations in particular—relatively quickly? How can we safeguard social and environmental interests in the process?

These questions have led some governments to initiate the so-called "quick win" reforms to meet the immediate need for investments and, at the same time, to accelerate the process of improving the overall system. Some of these efforts are pragmatic and innovative, allowing the governments to take one step at a time as a way to overcome the political and economic resistance typical of socioeconomic transitions. In such instances, they serve as reform "pilots" with a view to testing radical policy changes in limited geographic areas and gaining the necessary experience before extending the reform schemes to bigger areas.

Such reforms are inevitably risky. Governments make mistakes when testing new paths, and those that have succeeded have often done so only after repeated attempts. Their experience is, therefore, valuable. Governments facing similar challenges want to know what has worked and what has not.

There is also an increasing awareness within the development community that economic research lags behind the reality of reform in this area. What are the "quick win" reforms? How do they work, for investors and the broad society? What makes them different from the ad hoc solutions that tend to favor special interest groups? How do they contribute to long-term improvements in land governance? At the core is a question of how public policies complement market forces to achieve land use justice, efficiency, and transparency.

This book written from the point of view of investors, and focusing on industrial and commercial land, presents what we have learned from the developing world through years of first-hand observation and empirical research. Amid endless stories of land policy failures, we chose to look at encouraging cases, accompanied by a set of technical discussion papers, to provide a fresh look into how some pilot reforms were tested, and to various extents succeeded, in a range of countries.

The experiences and lessons learned support the argument that land policy and institutional reforms, difficult as they are politically, institutionally, and technically, are necessary if development goals are to be achieved. They further support the argument that reform is possible, even in some of the most difficult environments. Finally, they suggest that an incremental approach aimed at addressing a bottleneck issue can be helpful so long as the government keeps the long-term objectives in sight. The materials presented in this book make clear that well-designed and well-implemented reforms can make business access to land equitable, efficient, and transparent, encouraging more and sustainable investment while bringing significant benefits to all citizens.

Our research is supported by the Investment Climate Department of the World Bank Group (the International Finance Corporation, the Multilateral Investment Guarantee Agency, and the World Bank). The Investment Climate Department helps governments to implement reforms to improve their business environment and to encourage and retain investment, thus fostering competitive markets, economic growth, and job creation. Funding is provided by the World Bank Group and more than 12 donor partners working through the multidonor Foreign Investment Climate Advisory Service platform.[1]

Many individuals contributed to this book, including our colleagues in Investment Climate Advisory Services, who have encountered land-related issues while working with the governments on improving the business environment in many developing countries; land professionals who have worked with us, both globally and in specific countries, in exploring this field; and, most important, government reformers and their private sector supporters who have pioneered bold and innovative land policy reforms, often under very difficult circumstances, and who have generously shared with us their unique experiences.

Our particular thanks go to the authors of the case studies and technical papers included in this book. These individuals, whose brief biographies are found following this preface, are primarily practitioners from the public or private sector in the developing world. Their contributions are based on close observation or direct involvement in the reforms. All contributions were generously provided on a pro bono basis.

A long list of individuals, from both inside and outside the World Bank Group, gave invaluable input through comments, suggestions, and collegial exchanges at various stages of developing this book. We are particularly grateful to Tony Burns, Klaus Deininger, Gregory Ingram, Jorge Munoz, and Frank Sader, who reviewed and commented in great detail on the entire manuscript. We are most indebted to Joel Bergsman, who reviewed several versions of the book and provided indispensable advice and assistance in structuring the manuscript. Additionally, we benefited from generous input regarding the various topics from Ayse Boybeyi, Malcolm Childress, Robert Eddington, Penelope Fidas, Ivan Ford, Robert Gerrits, Michael Haroz, David Hosking, Kusisami Hornberger, Reidar Kvam, Somik Lall, Jonathan Lindsay, Robin Rajack, Harris Soled, Victoria Stanley, Patricia Steele, Deepali Tewari, Margo Thomas, and Belinda Yue. Our special thanks go to Martin Adams, Refael Benvenisti, Thomas Davenport, Russell Muir, Vincent Palmade, and Dale Weigel, who inspired us to research land policy issues.

Two institutions outside the World Bank Group provided special support for this book: the International Legal Resource Center, United States, and the Law Society, United Kingdom. We particularly thank Andreea Vesa, Sarb Bajwa, and Jacqueline Gichinga for their tireless efforts to mobilize and coordinate their members' pro bono contributions to the various parts of the book. We give our special thanks to Ezra Rosser and Alex Bernshteyn, members of the International Legal Resource Center, for their assistance in the background research. Other members of the two institutions also contributed in various ways; we could not possibly list all of them here, but we give them our heartfelt thanks.

Last but not least, we are grateful to the generous support of Investment Climate Advisory Services of the World Bank Group, without which this book would not have been possible. We owe special thanks to Cecilia Sager for her guidance and support at every stage of the research project and to Cecile Fruman and Pierre Guislain for their critical support for moving this book forward.

All opinions expressed in this book are those of the authors and do not necessarily reflect the views of Investment Climate Advisory Services, the World Bank Group, or other supporting institutions. Any errors that might be contained in the book are entirely the responsibility of the individual authors.

Note

1. Formerly known as Foreign Investment Advisory Service.

Contributors

About the Editors

Xiaofang Shen is a private sector development specialist with extensive experience in investment climate work in emerging markets. During her 22-year career with the World Bank Group she has worked in more than 40 countries across five continents, advising governments on a range of investment policy, legal, and institutional issues, with particular emphasis on matters related to business access to land. From 2005 to 2007 she headed the International Finance Corporation's China Business Environment Program, based in Chengdu, a western provincial capital. Shen holds an M.A. and a Ph.D. in political science and economic development from Johns Hopkins University, School of Advanced International Studies. Before that she studied at Smith College and Nanjing University.

Xiaolun Sun is a senior investment policy officer of the Investment Climate Department of the World Bank Group. Her areas of special interest include investment policies, business taxation, tourism development, and business access to land. In 2007–09 she worked with the Agence Française de Développement in Paris through a staff exchange program to help develop an investment climate assistance program. Prior to joining the World Bank, she was research economist at the International

Labour Organization in Geneva. She holds a B.A. in economics from Beijing University and a Ph.D. in economics from University of California, Berkeley.

About the Authors

Ahmed M. G. Abou Ali is a co-founder of Hassouna and Abou Ali, a leading business law firm in the Arab Republic of Egypt. He practiced law in the United States and Egypt in the banking and corporate sectors. He is a legal adviser to companies on mergers and acquisitions and property acquisition. He is also a legal adviser to the Egyptian government on policy reforms and privatization. Over the years, he has served as the chair of the Legal Affairs Committee of the American Chamber of Commerce in Egypt, reporter of the Committee on Profession at the Egyptian Capital Market Association, and member of the board of the Egyptian Alternative Dispute Resolution Association. He holds an LL.M. degree from Harvard Law School as well as a diploma in private law and an LL.B. in law, both from Cairo University.

Ali Beba is adjunct professor in the Business School and Associate Director of the Center for Asian Family Business and Entrepreneurship Studies, Hong Kong University of Science and Technology (HKUST). Before joining HKUST he headed the Center for Entrepreneurship of Ozyegin University in Turkey. Beba has taught in both Turkey and the United States and has led research and development projects funded by the Turkish government and international organizations. Via his Company Project Development and Implementation Center, he provides consulting and training services for nongovernmental organizations and private institutions. He graduated from the Middle East Technical University, Turkey, and received a Ph.D. from the University of Tulsa, Oklahoma.

Stephen B. Butler is principal research scientist in the International Projects Department of the National Opinion Research Center, University of Chicago. He is a seasoned consultant in international development and has advised government development agencies, international organizations, central banks, and regulatory commissions in 30 transitional and developing countries across all regions. Prior to his international development work, he was in private sector legal practice and he was an executive in housing and commercial property development. His work focuses on land reform and administration, housing and mortgage market development, and regulatory barriers to business start-up. He holds a joint J.D. and M.P.A. from the New York University School of Law and the Woodrow Wilson School of Public and International Affairs of Princeton University.

Jacqueline Coolidge has more than 25 years of professional experience with private sector development in developing and transition countries, including 15 years with the World Bank Group. She has expertise in investment policy and in legal and institutional reforms, including business access to land and construction permits. She is also experienced in results measurement, especially compliance costs for businesses with regard to licenses and regulations. She has worked extensively in Central and Eastern Europe, Eastern and Southern Africa, and the Caribbean. She has degrees from the University of Michigan, Princeton University's Woodrow Wilson School, and Johns Hopkins University.

Zaki Ghiacy is director of master planning and urban design at McBains Cooper in London. His 25-year professional career has focused on the design and implementation of large-scale complex urban regeneration and brownfield redevelopment projects. His particular interest in the social and economic development impact of urban design has led him to be a consultant for governments, banks, and international organizations in the developing world. He is a contributor to the World Bank publication, *The Management of Brownfield Redevelopment*. He has also spoken at various professional forums. He is currently part of the World Bank team of the Cities Alliance Program advising a number of Eastern European cities on urban regeneration and brownfield development.

Ray Gordon is president of the Courage Group, a firm providing consulting services in urban design, film production, marketing, graphics, and related fields. For 35 years he has worked extensively with the private sector, governments, and donor agents to promote social and environmentally friendly urban and regional development. He served as a partner in a Manhattan architectural firm and contributed to the historical restoration projects in New York City. He was also a planner with the Pratt Center for Community and Environmental Development and taught graduate courses in architecture, urban design planning, and real estate regulation at both Pratt Institute and New York University. He also lectured regularly at Columbia University's graduate architecture program.

Elizabeth Hannah has 17 years of professional experience as a transactional lawyer, specializing in land law, international arbitrations, and commercial land and property acquisitions. She has conducted legal research with a focus on access to land in Sub-Saharan Africa, including review of current legislation, legal empowerment, and capacity-building issues. She was an active participant in the Urban and Peri-Urban Forestry International Meeting, Bogotá, Colombia, organized by the Food and Agriculture Organization in 2008, and she contributed to the development of international policy guidelines on urban and periurban forestry, with a specific focus on security of tenure issues, including status of property, geographic context, issues of social cohesion and organization, and use of alternate methods of resolving land disputes. She is an English lawyer and a registered foreign lawyer with the Bar Association in Florence, Italy.

Huong Mai Huynh is project officer of the Investment Climate Program in Vietnam, the International Finance Corporation (IFC). She joined IFC in 2006 after spending two years as a program officer in the Small and Medium Enterprise Policy Environment component of the Vietnam Competitiveness Initiative, an economic growth project funded by the U.S. Agency for International Development. She also spent six years with PricewaterhouseCoopers Vietnam and was a deputy manager in Business Assurance and Advisory Services of the firm. She holds a B.A. from the Foreign Trade University in Hanoi, an M.B.A. from the International University of Japan, and a professional qualification of chartered certified accountant from the U.K. Association of Chartered Certified Accountants in Hanoi.

Uda Nakamhela is senior partner at Nakamhela Attorneys, Windhoek, Namibia. His private sector practice concentrates on rural development through community-based natural resource management, tourism and hunting concessions, and joint venture agreements between local communities and commercial operators. He also advised the government and local and international nongovernmental organizations extensively on environmental legislative and policy issues. He helped the Namibian Ministry of Environment and Tourism and local communities residing in parks to negotiate and establish cooperation and joint management agreements. He graduated from the University of Cape Town, South Africa, and holds an LL.M. degree in International Law from Washington College of Law, American University.

Lan Van Nguyen is project manager of the International Finance Corporation (IFC) Investment Climate Program in Vietnam. He joined the IFC in July 2003 and was primarily responsible for policy-related research activities; he now manages investment climate projects in Vietnam. Prior to joining IFC, he lectured at Vietnam's National Economics University, where he taught a wide range of courses in economics, research methodology, and project management. He is author of the book *Guerilla Capitalism: The State in the Market in Vietnam*. He holds a B.A. in economics from the National Economics University in Vietnam, an M.B.A. from Boise State University in the United States, and a Ph.D. in economic sociology from the University of Sunderland in the United Kingdom.

Ivan Nimac is head of the Vienna office of the Investment Climate Advisory Services of the World Bank Group. Prior to January 2010, he managed the International Finance Corporation's (IFC) Investment Climate Programs in East Asia and the Pacific Islands. Before joining IFC, he worked for the Australian Department of Foreign Affairs and Trade, was the deputy chief of mission for the United Nations Development Programme in Zagreb, and was deputy permanent representative of Croatia to the United Nations in New York. He has worked extensively in the developing world, advising national and multilateral development agencies. He holds degrees in economics, law, and international relations.

Chung-min Pang is a partner with Clove Capital in Hong Kong SAR, China. His work experience has been primarily in emerging markets spanning several continents. He joined China's Ministry of Agriculture in 1978 and participated in the early reform of the Chinese economy. In 1984 he joined the International Finance Corporation and for eight years worked on a range of industrial, agricultural, financial, and advisory projects. In 1992 he joined Salomon Brothers to lead the development of the firm's China investment banking business. He later joined Bank of America as managing director and China country manager. In 2002 he moved into private equity, continuing to focus on China.

Ezra Rosser is an associate professor at American University's Washington College of Law. He has an M.Phil. in land economy from Cambridge University, a J.D. from Harvard Law School, and a B.A. in economics and English from Yale University. He has taught poverty, housing, federal Indian, and property law. He has served as a 1665 Fellow at Harvard

University, a visiting scholar at Yale Law School, and a Westerfield Fellow at Loyola University, New Orleans School of Law. He is chair of the Poverty Section of the Association of American Law Schools, a research affiliate of the National Poverty Center at the University of Michigan, and editor of the Poverty Law Blog, http://maximinlaw.wordpress.com/.

Didier G. Sagashya is the deputy director general of the National Land Center of Rwanda, which implements comprehensive land policy and institutional reforms across the country. Prior to that he served consecutively as director of the General Inspection Department in Kigali City Council and as director of Lands, Housing, Physical Planning, Infrastructure, and Environment Protection in the district of Rwamagana in the Eastern Province of Rwanda. He holds a B.S. in civil engineering and environmental technology from Kigali Institute of Science and Technology and an M.A. in urban and regional planning from Heriot-Watt University in Edinburgh.

Lala Steyn has more than 20 years of in-field and research experience in South Africa and other African countries, focused on management and implementation of sustainable development programs and investment projects on community-owned land. Growing up in apartheid South Africa, she worked closely with nongovernmental organizations against forced removals and with community groups securing land rights in the 1980s. In 1995 she joined the Mandela government as a senior manager for the Department of Land Affairs, which was tasked with developing a land reform program for the country. In the 2000s she worked as an independent consultant on a range of sustainable development programs and projects. Recently she joined an investment bank in South Africa tasked with setting up an Education and Schools Impact Fund. She has a B.A. in politics and philosophy and an M.B.A.

Christopher Tanner is Food and Agriculture Organization (FAO) senior technical adviser on land and natural resources policy in Mozambique, where he has been leading a judicial and paralegal training program in land and natural resources laws. More recently, he led a capacity-building program for local government, rural development, and sector officers on how to implement the laws to promote a participatory model of rural development. He led the FAO team supporting the government of Mozambique in developing and implementing the 1997 Land Law; and he led a similar exercise in Guinea-Bissau in the mid-1990s. During his career in rural development he has cooperated with United Nations agencies, the World Bank, the U.S. Agency for International Development, and private sector firms. He holds a Ph.D. from Cambridge University.

Alain Traore joined the World Bank Group's Investment Climate team for Africa in March 2006. He worked as program manager for the Doing Business Better in Burkina Faso program under the International Finance Corporation (IFC), and he has worked extensively with the government of Burkina Faso on improving land administration and setting up the "one-stop shop" registry. Since September 2008, he has been providing support to other West African countries, including Senegal, Mali, and Benin, on investment climate reforms, including land market and property rights improvement. He is currently based in the IFC Dakar office. He holds a Ph.D. in private law from the University of Nancy, France.

Mathew Warnest has eight years of experience in the public and private sectors in land administration and spatial information management. He has devoted most of his career to the developing world, especially Southeast Asia and Sub-Saharan Africa. Residing in Freetown throughout 2009, he was a chief adviser to the government program for upgrading the land registration system of Sierra Leone, which was supported by the Investment Climate Facility for Africa, a multidonor-funded facility. His recent experiences include the Philippines and Rwanda, where he assisted governments in developing land sector reform programs and designing land information systems.

Songming Xu, director of Pingshan Urban Planning and Land Resources Bureau, Shenzhen, has more than 20 years of experience in real estate development, land management, and urban planning. He has researched and advised extensively on urban land market development in China. He currently leads the planning and construction of Pingshan District, Shenzhen Municipality, a flagship green city development project spearheading China's effort to create a green, low-carbon, and ecologically friendly urban environment. He has an M.B.A. from Roosevelt University, Chicago, and is a Ph.D. candidate in government and economics at Huazhong Normal University, Wuhan, China.

Abbreviations

BIA	Bureau of Indian Affairs, United States
CBNRM	community-based natural resource management
CPA	Communal Property Association, South Africa
DONRE	Department of Natural Resources and Environment
DUAT	Direito de Uso e Aproveitamento da Terra (Land Use and Benefit Right), Mozambique
EEAA	Egyptian Environmental Affairs Authority
EFTC	Egyptian Federation of Tourism Chambers
EGPC	Egyptian General Petroleum Corporation
FAO	Food and Agriculture Organization
FIAS	Foreign Investment Advisory Service
GDLRC	General Directorate of Land Register and Cadastre, Turkey
GDP	gross domestic product
GUF	Guchet Unique du Foncier (One-stop Shop for Land Registry), Burkina Faso
ICT	information and communications technology
IFC	International Finance Corporation
IT	information technology
LGAF	Land Governance Assessment Framework

LIS	land information system
LURC	land use rights certificate, Vietnam
MERNİS	Central Population Administration Information System, Turkey
MODMP	Ministry of Defense and Military Production, Arab Republic of Egypt
MOT	Ministry of Tourism, Egypt
MoNRE	Ministry of Natural Resources and Environment, Vietnam
NAPR	National Agency of the Public Registry, Georgia
NGO	nongovernmental organization
OSS	one-stop shop
PPC	Provincial People's Committee, Vietnam
RDB	Rwanda Development Board
RDLRC	Regional Directorate of Land Register and Cadastre, Turkey
SANParks	South African National Parks
SAR	Special Administrative Region
SDLM	State Department of Land Management, Georgia
SEZ	special economic zone
SME	small and medium enterprise
TAKBİS	Automation Project for the General Directorate of Land Register and Cadastre, Turkey
TDA	Tourism Development Authority, Turkey
VCCI	Vietnam Chamber of Commerce and Industry

Overview

Xiaofang Shen

> The earth had no roads to begin with, but when many people pass one way, a road is made.
>
> *Lu Xun*, Chinese writer, 1881–1936

Private sector development has been recognized as an important engine of economic growth and poverty alleviation around the world. Access to land—sometimes the best-secured, best-zoned, and best-serviced land—is a critical precondition for private investment, whether it is to build a factory, a hotel, a commercial farm, a retail center, an office building, or many other business facilities. The ability of investors to locate and develop appropriate sites in a timely and cost-effective fashion, to secure the property rights, and to use such rights as collateral for obtaining bank loans has a significant impact on their decisions to invest or not to invest in a given location.

In recent years, fast-paced economic growth and the increased investment demand for land have put considerable pressure on land use management in many developing countries. In many places, the use of land and land-related resources is already feeling the squeeze of multiple, sometimes competing, socioeconomic needs. Population growth, climate change, soil depletion, food shortage, energy crisis, and other global trends have contributed further to the short supply of land.

Consequently, many countries are struggling to balance the need for medium-term growth and employment with the need for balanced urban-rural development, resource conservation, and other long-term development goals. In some places, the rapid expansion of the modern sector has come at the cost of environmental deterioration; in others, the force of development has clashed with the well-being of those who traditionally live on the land, who are among the poorest of the poor population subject to priority help.

Moreover, governments anxious to encourage investment often find their hands tied by inadequate policy, legal, and institutional instruments. In a large part of the developing world, the land market remains underdeveloped, property rights are poorly defined, and land use planning is either incomplete or missing. In addition, land information, human capacity, and the hard and soft infrastructure needed to support coherent and effective land use are simply lacking. In such situations, business access to land is extremely constrained. Commonly, it gets mired in a protracted process or, since enforcement capacity is universally weak, proceeds unchecked. As a result, the costs of doing business are high, valuable investment opportunities are lost, and important social and environmental interests are subject to high risk.

Many governments have increased their intervention in support of business access to land in order to boost employment and growth. Some have done so through established "one-stop shops" to facilitate investors' needs; others have designated industrial zones coupled with concentrated infrastructural support; still other have gone so far as to take radical actions to acquire and consolidate the needed land on behalf of investors deemed "strategic" to the economy. The results of these interventions have been mixed at best. In many cases, they have failed, without being accompanied by determined efforts to improve the overall system. In the worst cases, government actions based on weak land governance, together with anticipated increases in land values, have created opportunities for rent-seeking behavior by those who have the power to take and allocate land and to regulate its uses. It should come as no surprise that recent Transparency International surveys have identified land as one of the most corrupt public service sectors (Transparency International 2009).

These problems have attracted the attention of policy makers and development agencies and prompted several pressing questions: Can growth and development be achieved based on more *efficient, equitable,* and *sustainable* use of land? Can different, sometimes competing, interests be balanced by involving all stakeholders, such as investors, local communities, the government, and civil society? Most urgent, can the potential conflicts be transformed into win-win situations, where investment needs are facilitated, where social and environmental sustainability is safeguarded, and where current land users are not harmed but share in the fruits of development? Addressing these and related issues is increasingly recognized as an urgent need in development policy (Deininger, Selod, and Burns forthcoming).

The Conceptual and Institutional Framework: A Multifaceted Challenge

Land, property rights, and their interactions with investment and development have long been the subject of a large literature—from Adam Smith, through Karl Marx, right up to the present. However, it is only recently that policy makers in the developing world have taken an active role in creating and strengthening land property rights for citizens and economic entities as a vital mechanism for improving the lives of the poor. According to Hernando de Soto, whose landmark work triggered the policy trend in this direction, unlocking "dead capital"—land assets that have limited use or cannot be used as collateral—provides the key to unraveling the economic potential of the developing world. As he put it, "What the poor lack is easy access to the property mechanisms that could legally fix the economic potential of their assets so that they could be used to produce, secure, or guarantee greater value in the expanded market" (de Soto 2000).

In the last few years, more broadly based empirical studies have buttressed earlier conceptual and anecdotal work and shown that the effects of land property rights are large and that the problems are widespread. A McKinsey study shows that problems related to market access to land could cost India more than 1 percent of its GDP growth annually (McKinsey Global Institute 2001). World Bank (2005) suggests, circumspectly, that rates of investment and productivity are higher on land with title than on land with no title. Most recently, various studies provide cross-country evidence that suggests a correlation between the security of land and property rights and the growth of investment and income (Knack and Keefer 1997; La Porta and others 1997; North 1990).

The importance of land goes beyond its economic impact (Deininger 2003). For many social and environmental scientists, land is an important foundation for societal well-being and stability (Bourbeau 2001; Nyamu Musembi 2007); a limited and increasingly scarce resource, the use of which must be managed with care (World Resources Institute 2005); an environment that people of all walks of life must share; and an ecosystem where altered uses in one part can upset the balance in another (Perlman 2009). It is thus generally agreed that the private possession and use of land should conform to public interests through compliance with accepted rules, regulations, and societal agreements.

The complex, multidimensional roles that land plays explain the fragmentation of both land policy and the institutional framework for land administration and land use management seen in most countries. Typically, land policies are formulated and implemented by multiple ministries (for example, lands, justice, agriculture, industry, forestry, infrastructure), development and environment agencies, national and local authorities (for example, states, provinces, municipalities, counties), and specialized agencies (for example, a property rights registry, cadastre, surveying and mapping, spatial and urban planning, transportation, public utilities). As a result, many countries have found it extremely difficult to define a holistic land policy framework, supported by all players and conducive to the general welfare.

Recognizing this challenge, the World Bank, the Food and Agriculture Organization of the United Nations, and other international development agencies have been jointly working on a comprehensive Land Governance Assessment Framework (LGAF), in an attempt to pull together perspectives on land and land policies. Five areas of concern top the list: (1) laws and institutions that govern property rights for all private citizens; (2) systems that manage land use planning, environmental protection, taxation, and other important public sector functions; (3) the management of state land assets, including proper ways to deal with expropriation, divestiture, and establishment of public infrastructure; (4) public provision of open and integrated land information; and (5) mechanisms for resolving land disputes (Deininger, Selod, and Burns forthcoming).

The effectiveness of the LGAF will need to be seen in its implementation. To formulate a holistic land policy strategy, governments will need to live up to the institutional challenge by orchestrating a complex process involving all players. Public institutions will have a critical role to play, but, in the end, how the many institutions interplay and cooperate with each other will make the ultimate difference in land governance in a given country.

The Importance of Investment Environment

Understanding the broad picture of the land reform challenge is critical to unraveling the complexities associated with investment in land. Investors seeking land appropriate for their investment projects have encountered common difficulties in accessing, securing, and developing land. Most of the problems can be traced to the fundamental weaknesses of existing land policies and land governance. Some governments anxious to attract investment have stepped up ad hoc, sometimes short-sighted, intervention that bypasses the existing systems and provides favorable treatment to investors. Such intervention creates further distortions in the system and usually benefits the few, large investors. In some extreme cases—as recently pointed out by several media publications and a specific World Bank study focusing on the problems related to rushed large-scale acquisition of agricultural land for investments—government intervention becomes counterproductive.[1]

In this context, improving the investment environment is critical. Broadly defined, investment environment refers to the general economic and market conditions that influence the decision to invest. Improving the investment environment entails improving the general conditions for the majority of investors rather than extending "special treatment" to select investors. Although some governments use special land deals as a way to attract investment, such offerings will not succeed in attracting investment on a large scale. Special deals can be made only to a few, and they can penalize most investors, especially the domestically owned small and medium enterprises, whose needs are left unattended. In today's globalized economy, no country can expect to develop a viable business sector by offering special deals, and no country can expect to attract significant foreign investment if its own citizens are not investing.

Removing the impediments to investment does not mean "all market, no regulation," a misperception sometimes held by those arguing both for and against private investment. To the contrary, healthy market competition depends on effective laws and regulations that provide equal access to land and land-related resources, respect the property rights of all players, and ensure universal compliance with the set rules and procedures for protecting common interests, including enforced land use planning and zoning regulations, environmental protection requirements, building safety standards, and, not the least important, safeguards for vulnerable social groups. Law and order make the marketplace more secure and more predictable, which is in the essential interest of investors, whose biggest fear lies in the surprises and hidden costs of doing business that they cannot anticipate.

Nevertheless, in many places, ineffective laws or inefficient institutions often stymie productive investments without producing the desired benefits for the public. They are also the source of favoritism and rent-seeking behaviors. The purpose of investment climate reform is to help governments to eliminate overly excessive and counterproductive rules and procedures that serve no legitimate purpose, while introducing efficient, enforceable, and transparent laws and regulations that facilitate the majority's business needs and safeguard vital public interests. Investment climate reforms also aim to create laws and regulations that can be used to monitor the performance of government agencies, to allow the rules and procedures to be followed by investors and regulators alike, and to enable their details to withstand public scrutiny.

Understanding the Specific Concerns of Investors

There is a preponderance of evidence from business surveys that difficulties in accessing land are among the major concerns of investors in the developing world.[2] Figure O.1 presents data offered by the Enterprise Surveys conducted worldwide by the World Bank. As seen, more than one-third of responding manufacturing firms across all regions complain about "access to land" as an obstacle to their businesses. In Sub-Saharan Africa, the share is over 50 percent, and almost half of those who complain consider the problem "major to severe."

The companies responding to the Enterprise Surveys are a representative sample of an economy's private sector. Therefore, they are mostly small and medium enterprises. The database covers both domestic and foreign firms, with the overwhelming majority of respondents being domestic. The findings of the surveys indicate that the identified problems apply equally to foreign and domestic investors (World Bank Enterprise Surveys, 2006–09).

As bad as they seem, these survey results may significantly understate the problem because they capture only existing companies—those that are already up and running. Adding to the results the unknown amount of investment that has failed to take place due to lack of access to suitable land, the overall problem can be much more serious than these data suggest.

Face-to-face interviews with investors in many countries further reveal the specific concerns of investors.[3] Those can be grouped into three broad

Figure O.1   Average Share of Manufacturing Firms Considering Access to Land an Obstacle to Their Businesses, by Region

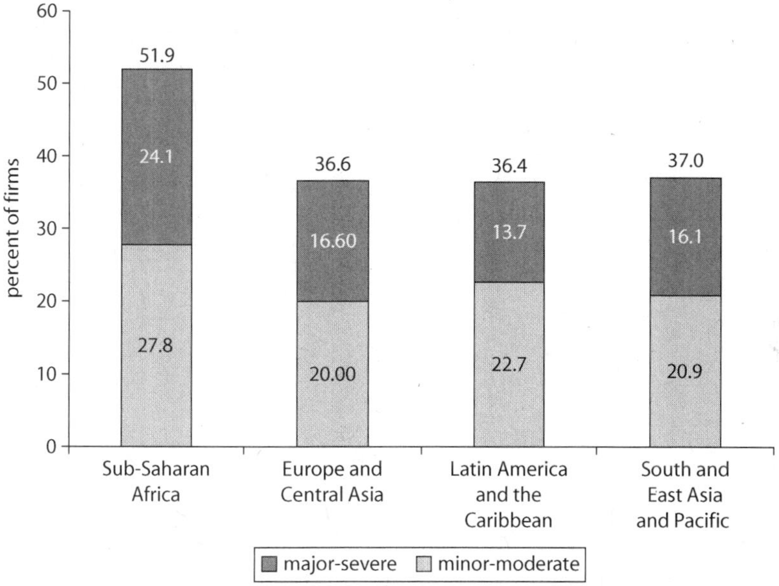

Source: World Bank Enterprise Surveys, 2006–09.

categories: limited market access to land, weak legal and administrative framework for property rights, and time-consuming and unpredictable process for site development. Figure O.2 depicts the plethora of public agencies at both national and subnational levels with which would-be investors must interact when acquiring, securing, and developing land. Navigating through this bureaucratic maze can be a Herculean task. Compared with noncommercial land users, investors usually require a higher degree of legal clarity, certainty, and administrative efficiency, as they operate in a much more open and competitive marketplace where security and timeliness are essential. If their required standards are not met, they can simply go elsewhere.

Limited Access to Land Due to an Underdeveloped Land Market

Business access to land is difficult in many countries first and foremost because market supplies of suitable land are limited. This fundamental constraint in market supply takes different forms in different regions, creating multiple challenges for investors, local communities, and governments.

Figure O.2   Investment Process Needs and Interactions with the Government

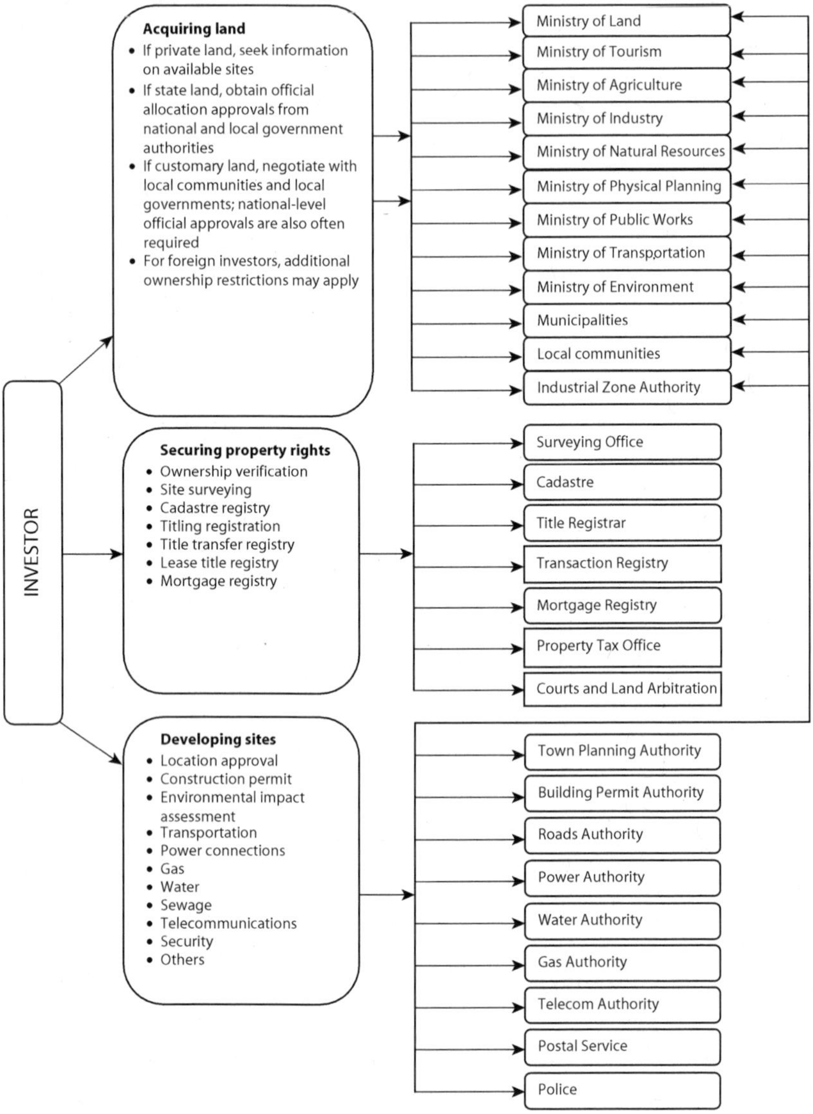

Acquiring land
- If private land, seek information on available sites
- If state land, obtain official allocation approvals from national and local government authorities
- If customary land, negotiate with local communities and local governments; national-level official approvals are also often required
- For foreign investors, additional ownership restrictions may apply

Ministry of Land
Ministry of Tourism
Ministry of Agriculture
Ministry of Industry
Ministry of Natural Resources
Ministry of Physical Planning
Ministry of Public Works
Ministry of Transportation
Ministry of Environment
Municipalities
Local communities
Industrial Zone Authority

Securing property rights
- Ownership verification
- Site surveying
- Cadastre registry
- Titling registration
- Title transfer registry
- Lease title registry
- Mortgage registry

Surveying Office
Cadastre
Title Registrar
Transaction Registry
Mortgage Registry
Property Tax Office
Courts and Land Arbitration

Developing sites
- Location approval
- Construction permit
- Environmental impact assessment
- Transportation
- Power connections
- Gas
- Water
- Sewage
- Telecommunications
- Security
- Others

Town Planning Authority
Building Permit Authority
Roads Authority
Power Authority
Water Authority
Gas Authority
Telecom Authority
Postal Service
Police

INVESTOR

Source: Author.

In many transition economies in East Asia (for example, China and Vietnam), Eastern Europe and Central Asia (for example, the Russian Federation, the Balkan states, some former Soviet Union states), and the Middle East (for example, the Arab Republic of Egypt, Jordan, and the Islamic Republic of Iran), much or even all land is owned by the state.[4]

Investors in these places often have no choice but to apply to the state for primary allocation of land. Most countries allow the lease or sale of public land to private parties, but they have yet to develop consistent and transparent criteria and procedures for determining who gets what and at what price. Some countries suffer from the lack of institutional clarity, which makes the approval process time-consuming and confusing. Moreover, the rights and obligations of the private recipients of the land are not clearly established. It is not unusual for secondary transactions of allocated land to require government approvals. As a result, access to land is at the discretion of those in power, and valuable public land assets are offered freely to some and denied to others for no clear reason.

Across Sub-Saharan Africa, market access to land is typically impeded by the fact that freehold land that can be transferred relatively easily in markets is estimated to be less than 10 percent of the total territory (see chapter 14, table 14.1). The rest of the land features a complicated tenure system combining customary and state rights (Deininger and others 2003). About 80 percent of land on the continent remains under customary use, whereas about half of the countries have national laws—either inherited from the colonial statutory legacy or enacted after their independence—that vest all land in the state. At the same time, most land transactions are informal, and this phenomenon is not only in the rural areas but also in the growing urban and periurban regions. Transactions of customary land are inherently difficult due to the lack of clear property rights and the large number of community members who may be involved. Such transactions also entail higher risk, as disputes over such land can easily arise. Governments have frequently intervened in customary land use for development purposes, taking themselves as trustees of such land. However, without showing respect for customary rights and without a sufficient system in place to compensate the customary landholders for their loss, government interventions can actually impede economic development and social justice and breed social resentment against the investment.

In other parts of the world, where there is a tradition of private ownership (Brazil, India, and Turkey) or where land has been rapidly privatized in recent decades (Hungary and Poland), investors are generally better able to access land through the market. However, even in those countries, consolidated and well-serviced land suitable for industrial and commercial development can be difficult to find. Privately held lands are concentrated in saturated urban areas or widely dispersed in periurban and rural areas without services. Informal settlements and land disputes are also common in South Asia and Latin America. In these situations, again, investors have to deal with the problems of high risk and high cost in the market. New mechanisms are sorely needed to help investors, governments, and local communities to find ways to deal with the difficulties, agree on trade-offs that are acceptable to all, and facilitate sustainable businesses and development at the same time.

Weak Legal and Administrative Framework for Property Rights and Land Transactions

Secure property rights are necessary for investors not only because they encourage business owners to make long-term investments in the land, but also because they constitute the basis for investors to obtain financing. Fixed collateral is especially preferred by banks as security for long-term finance. According to the World Bank Enterprise Surveys, globally, 73 percent of all assets that banks accept as collateral are in land and real estate properties, despite the fact that only 34 percent of all assets held by firms are in the form of land and real estate properties.

Systems for registering land titles, a public service crucial for secure property rights, are generally weak in the developing world. In recent decades, transition economies have moved aggressively to establish (or restore) property registrations to support land and housing privatization, but in many places the process is not yet complete. In the least developed regions of the world, such as in Africa, only a fraction of the land has been securely registered.

Even for properties that are registered, transactions remain difficult and subject to undue bureaucratic procedures. In Nigeria, for instance, each individual land transaction requires the governor's consent. Mortgage transactions in Lagos, the nation's financial center, average a staggering 240 days, according to a 2009 study (FIAS 2008). In Africa and elsewhere, a common complaint of investors, bankers, and lawyers is that accessing land records is time-consuming and costly, as data are poorly maintained, based in uncoordinated agencies, and sometimes simply blocked by lower-level land officers seeking additional payments. In Kenya, in 2010, a raid uncovered thousands of land files locked in the drawers of public officials hoping to collect bribes.[5] Computerization has been introduced recently in many places to deal with some of the problems, but the potential benefits from the technology cannot materialize unless radical improvements are also seen in the legal and institutional systems.

Multilayered Impediments at the Stage of Site Development

Industrial and commercial investors need to develop the site once they have acquired the land. At this stage, they need clear guidance in order to comply with relevant laws and regulations regarding zoning, environmental impact assessment, construction safety standards, and requirements needed to safeguard the public interest (Buckley, Ellis, and Hamilton 2001). Also at this stage, investors need to have their sites be properly connected with roads, power, water and sewage, telecommunications, and other infrastructural support.

Unfortunately, most developing countries still do not have adequate systems governing these needs. In many places, as requisite laws and regulations are absent or the capacity to enforce them is missing, every step in the process is subject to negotiation or, worse, arbitrary approvals. A plethora of public agencies can be involved in the process, including national and subnational regulatory authorities as well as various public utility agencies. In Turkey, according to one study, more than 20 agencies are required to give clearances at the land development stage, a major source of confusion for investors and the agencies involved as well (FIAS 2001). In Egypt, likewise, obtaining location and building permits can take more than 12 months and involve multiple authorities at both central and local levels (FIAS 1998). In Ghana, rezoning a plot for the proposed use can take more than 200 days (FIAS 2003). In Zambia, the average waiting period for power connection is 184 days (World Bank Enterprise Surveys, 2006–09). And the list goes on.

These problems have two main consequences. First, when every aspect of the process has to be negotiated, the resulting uncertainty creates high levels of risk, which, in turn, necessitate higher projected rates of return if the investment is to be attractive. This can greatly reduce the number of potential investments that would otherwise be financially viable. The second consequence is equally detrimental: the time and cost of the process discourage firms from complying with the system and encourage illegal construction, especially where governments have no enforcement capacity. Illegal construction results in chaotic development and a deteriorating environment. In a number of places, it has paved the way for disasters. As seen in China, Egypt, Turkey, and most recently Haiti, poor enforcement of construction standards can lead to a massive loss of life in cities and villages when natural disasters such as earthquakes strike.[6]

Dealing with the Problems

There are no simple solutions to the problems encountered by investors, as most such problems have deep roots in the system and fundamental improvements will take time. Moreover, land policies and management systems are complicated by a country's size, history, development level, legal tradition, and a variety of other factors. Thus, universally agreed solutions are difficult to find. It is easy to see why land policy reforms are among the most sensitive, complex, and difficult to pursue. They are frequently the last frontier for reforming countries.

Yet developing countries cannot afford to wait. Many governments under the rising pressure of job creation and income generation find it necessary to look for effective ways to bridge the gap between investors' needs and the existing land system. Many governments recognize, based on past experiences, that the failure to do so can impede investments or, worse, lead to investments that might jeopardize the goal of sustainable development entirely.

The need to use land resources more productively for growth and the need to assure maximum benefits to a majority of the people have led more and more governments to step up the effort to seek what can be characterized as "interim," sometimes called "quick win," solutions. Through this approach, the leadership tackles the problems with efforts phased in over time or places. Difficult policy changes and innovative institutional mechanisms are tested initially in limited areas or time periods in pilot programs, to be implemented on a large scale only after they have proven to be successful. In this way, governments can overcome the initial resource constraints and move forward by concentrating on prioritized areas, producing demonstrable results, and preparing the ground for a long-term and comprehensive reform process.

Interim or "quick win" reforms carry high risks. They can fail and even be counterproductive, if applied without a long-term vision of the reforms needed. Also, because the changes tested under reform pilots are new to those carrying them out, reformers need to be pragmatic and creative, often learning by doing (and by making mistakes) and adjusting approaches according to the particular challenges in each situation. Strong leadership and institutional collaboration are among the most important preconditions to success.

Case Studies

The rising need and high level of risks associated with reforming land policy have led to an increased interest among governments and donors in learning from emerging experiences. In part 1 of this book, 12 case studies illustrate the dynamics of the reform process. Some of the cases focus on reform programs initiated at the national level; others highlight the experience spearheaded by subnational leaders; still others draw attention to the achievements of individual projects. While none of the cases can claim to have resolved land issues comprehensively, each shows that progress is possible—from A to C if not (immediately) from A to Z—as long as genuine efforts are made by governments, investors, and local stakeholders. In some cases, land challenges have been turned into opportunities in very difficult situations that were considered intractable just a few years ago.

Five of the 12 cases are from Sub-Saharan Africa, where problems of accessing land are the most severe. Two cases, Burkina Faso and Rwanda, both among the least developed countries at the outset of reform, show how politically determined and carefully crafted reforms can produce relatively quick results in improving property rights for citizens, a condition critical to encouraging investment. In Burkina Faso, the creation of land "one-stop shops" initially tested in the capital city resulted in more than 100-fold increases in land title creation in three years, and the model has since been applied to other parts of the country. In Rwanda, similarly, the national leadership was able to initiate a swift, step-by-step, modernization of the land registration process, based on the vision of broad-based investment and accelerated growth across the country.

The case of Namibia shows more specifically how commercial land development can bring significant benefits to traditional land users, if appropriate legal and institutional mechanisms are put in place. In this case, the government enacted legislative reform in the mid-1990s allowing rural communities to register as "conservancies" and thus gain legal rights to the use of land and wildlife resources and, through this, to develop nature-friendly tourism businesses. The case of South Africa, in the context of the land restituted to the Makuleke community, shows that historically rooted injustice will not disappear overnight even with sweeping legal changes at the top. Efforts to build capacity at the community level and to institutionalize cooperation among the community, commercial investors, local governments, and civil society played a critical role in achieving the end result. Further, the case of Mozambique, through the experience of a joint-venture ecotourism business, suggests that, even when the law is fundamentally flawed, genuine efforts by investors and local communities to consult and cooperate with each other can turn initial conflicts into collaborations, to the benefit of all parties involved.

Beyond Africa, three cases are devoted to the issues regarding access to publicly owned land. China, an economy in significant transition, provides an example of how pragmatic approaches to dealing with the political and institutional difficulties help to improve access to state land. Using the Shenzhen special economic zone as an incubator for testing a series of new land policies, the Chinese government succeeded in attracting foreign direct investment while eventually creating an urban land market for all citizens. Vietnam, another economy in rapid transition, put domestic small and medium enterprises at the center of land policy and procedural reforms. The case shows how efforts at the subnational level to introduce small changes in the short run may create the perception of progress, diminish opposition, and lead to greater change over time. The case of Egypt, based on its special experience with the development of Red Sea tourism, further demonstrates that barriers to accessing state land can be the result of, sometimes, legitimate social, economic, and environmental considerations; however, a situation that stalemates investment is not desirable for anyone. In this case, a creative mechanism introduced at the high-level administration removed the bottleneck to investment without sacrificing the checks needed to safeguard the public interest.

The case of Turkey shows that, even in a middle-income country, partial, step-by-step solutions are sometimes necessary to overcome the challenges inherent in large, systematic improvements. Facing an overflow of land records accumulated since the nineteenth century, Turkey had an enormous and urgent need to introduce a digitized land information system integrating land registry, cadastre, land use zoning, and other data. The government approached the enormous task with a targeted pilot project as a way to produce demonstrable results, accumulate knowledge, and harness popular support.

The experience of Baja California in Mexico is one example of private investor, community, and local government collaboration in revitalizing the economy of a medium-scale area under the threat of deteriorated natural conditions for farming. By introducing integrated land use planning, community involvement, and new technologies, the strategic investor and local communities worked together to build a new aquaculture business and achieve commercial, environmental, and socioeconomic results.

Two additional cases are from the advanced economies, because they provide significant lessons relevant to many developing countries. The case of Hong Kong SAR, China, is important, because it shows how one of the world's most viable land markets has benefited from an efficient and stable land lease system responsive to the market and political changes. The case of Native American reservations in the United States provides an additional illustration of how, even in an advanced economy, historically created mistakes present challenges in developing tribal trust land that can be met only through persistent efforts, strong stakeholder collaboration, and politically sensitive approaches.

Technical Discussion Papers

While the case studies in part 1 of this book provide a rich picture of the challenges and opportunities of land-related reforms in the context of specific countries, the six chapters in part 2 provide technical discussions on the pros and cons of selected reform tools, seen both in the case studies included in this book and in the experiences of other developing and transition economies. The topics chosen—some more general than others—are all relevant to the so-called "quick win" reforms, or interim solutions, that are still under experimentation in many places but are undoubtedly gaining credibility across the developing world. As such, the purpose of the authors is not to give either final prescriptions or World Bank recommendations, but to share knowledge as part of the search for solutions.

Chapter 13 focuses on improving the allocation of state land. It highlights the benefits and practicalities of streamlining the allocation procedures, often within the existing laws, to make the process more transparent and competitive. Such procedural reforms are a first step toward achieving more consistent and transparent governance of public land. The chapter describes a common tool, called "process mapping," that many governments have used to investigate in detail the existing land allocation procedures, to reveal the overlapping and counterproductive parts, and to reengineer the system for more efficiency and transparency. The chapter further discusses the techniques of using market mechanisms, such as auctions and public tenders, to replace administrative allocation. Doing so attracts more serious investors, reduces the room for corruption, and brings higher land revenues to governments.

Chapter 14 addresses issues related to accessing customary land for business use. The chapter observes that putting customary land to investment use provides opportunities, sometimes significant ones, to the traditional landholders. However, the potential benefits cannot be derived if property rights for individuals and communities are not fully respected. The chapter also observes that a tripartite process engaging all involved parties (investors, local communities, and government agencies) is the key to finding win-win solutions. In addition, the chapter highlights the need to incorporate in the process special mechanisms to protect the weakest and most vulnerable populations, who may lack institutions to promote their basic needs. Doing so also helps create community support for the investment project, making business more sustainable.

Chapter 15 focuses on the technicality of using long-term leasing as an effective substitute for direct ownership, where privatizing public land or allowing foreign ownership is politically unacceptable. The chapter shows that lease arrangements can meet the basic needs of businesses, especially if they provide sufficient durations and clear legal rights regarding transferability, mortgage use, and properties built on the leased land. The chapter further points out the possibility for governments to use lease contracts as a venue to specify the obligations of investors to build according to maximized public interest.

Chapter 16 discusses the pros and cons of using a "one-stop shop" (OSS) to facilitate investment land procedures, an approach that has become common in many developing countries. The chapter shows that the concept of OSS can be useful if accompanied by other reforms, such as procedural streamlining and simplification, but it can become wasteful and frustrating if the many involved public agencies fail to cooperate. The chapter summarizes what it takes to ensure a useful OSS, based on a sample of one-stop shops.

Chapter 17 provides views on how to provide integrated land information to investors by introducing new information and communications technology (ICT). It observes that, in the last 10 years, such technology has become rapidly available and affordable, offering developing countries an effective tool for economic catch-up. A more integrated electronic information system allows virtual OSS for land approval procedures involving multiple agencies, benefiting both investors and the responsible agencies. However, like the physical OSS, the ICT solution works well only if the necessary political commitment and institutional collaboration are in place. Where the programs are not politically and institutionally backed, they quickly become "white elephants," wasting public resources.

Finally, chapter 18 presents the concept and principles of integrated urban design as a tool for dealing with the challenges in land use planning. This approach supplements master planning, but urges quick reactions to fast-changing development realities. Proposing a broad-brushed vision at the top and flexible, detailed planning at the district level, this approach allows governments to focus limited resources on high-priority districts, making it easier to adopt new planning concepts and technologies. Moreover, urban design requires intensive interactions among planners, urban designers, private developers, and local communities.

Many other topics that are fundamental to investment climate or general land governance are not covered. Those are, for instance, the legal and institutional issues deeply affecting land property rights and land market transactions, land valuation and taxation critical to both property owners and government revenues, comprehensive land use planning and environmental regulations essential to achieving a lasting impact on development, the paramount need to provide public infrastructure, the knotty issues related to land consolidation, the development of industrial and special economic zones, and many other important and complicated challenges facing the agenda of land governance reform. Policy debates and technical discussions on those topics exist in many studies by the World Bank and other development and academic institutions. The reader should refer to them to gain an understanding of the large context for the specific topics covered in this book.

Lessons Learned

All of this experience reveals no panacea, no neat path to a complete solution. If there is one overarching lesson to be learned, it is the importance of understanding the complexity of land issues and of dealing with potential conflicts of interest by engaging all stakeholders, strengthening institutions, and crafting win-win solutions that enlarge the pie and distribute the benefits equitably. This is the essential goal of an enabling investment environment and all development policies. This is what a good overall land governance framework aims to achieve.

The study also sheds light on some more specific messages.

First, governments have a fundamental role in supporting investment by making access to land more efficient and secure for investors. The latter include, markedly, all investors, whether they are foreign or domestic, large or small. The key to achieving the goal lies in improving the general investment policy, legal, and institutional framework applied to all, rather than relying on special treatments available for only a few.

Second, government plays an important role in safeguarding the environment, natural resources, public health, safety, and other vital public interests, when determining investment and land use policies. This requires good regulation and effective enforcement. At the same time, simple, transparent rules and procedures facilitate investment and help to improve regulatory compliance, administrative efficiency, and general land governance.

Third, land policy and administrative problems are politically and technically challenging, and dealing with them requires considerable time and resources, as well as politically sensitive changes in laws, regulations, and institutions. In this context, step-by-step and innovative approaches aimed at moving the reform process forward and demonstrating results relatively quickly are extremely useful. One lesson that stands out in all the case studies, despite the diverse contexts in which they evolved, is that pilot reforms can help governments to mitigate the political risks and minimize the resource constraints typical in the initial stages of reform.

Last but not least, piloting reforms carries risks, and "quick wins" are not necessarily "easy wins." As many of the case studies in this book show, interim solutions, or "quick win" reform schemes, require strong political leadership and have the largest impact when they serve long-term objectives and are integrated into broad reform programs. The key words are think big, start small, and move fast—backed by vision, determination, and creativeness that help the reforming governments to steer the process in the right direction.

Notes

1. "The Surge in Land Deals: When Others Are Grabbing Their Land," *Economist*, May 5, 2011, http://www.economist.com/node/18648855?story_id=1864 8855; World Bank (2010).

2. Several important business surveys conducted by the World Bank include various indicators on land access and land property rights: the Doing Business Surveys, which have been conducted annually worldwide, the Investment Climate Assessments conducted periodically in select countries, and the Administrative and Regulatory Cost Surveys conducted in some countries.

3. Between 1995 and 2009, the Investment Climate Department (including the former FIAS) of the World Bank Group conducted more than 50 diagnostic studies in 45 countries, mostly at the government's request. These studies involved in-depth interviews with business managers to gather insights into their key concerns. The following discussions draw on those studies.

4. State-owned land, in this study, includes all land owned by the national and local governments, such as ministries, municipalities, state-owned enterprises, and other public institutions.

5. Press article, *Daily Nation*, March 1, 2010 (http://www.nation, co.ke/News/-/1056/871412/-/vr51u7/-/index.html).

6. In the wake of the earthquake that hit the city of Izmit, Turkey, in August 1999, the *Guardian* reported, "Out of the two and a half million buildings making up Istanbul, around 80% were illegally or inappropriately constructed."

References

Bourbeau, Heather. 2001. "Property Wrongs." *Foreign Policy* 127 (November–December): 78–79.

Buckley, Robert, Peter Ellis, and Ellen Hamilton. 2001. "Urban Housing and Land Market Reforms in Transition Countries: Neither Marx nor Market." Paper presented at the World Bank's second "ECA Poverty Forum," Budapest, November 27–30.

Deininger, Klaus. 2003. *Land Policies for Growth and Poverty Reduction.* Policy Research Report. Washington, DC: World Bank.

Deininger, Klaus, Gershon Feder, Gustavo Gordillo de Anda, and Paul Munro-Faure. 2003. "Land Reform, Land Settlement, and Cooperatives." In *Land Reform 2003/3,* special edition: *Land Settlement and Cooperatives.* Rome: Food and Agriculture Organization.

Deininger, Klaus, Harris Selod, and Tony Burns. Forthcoming. *Land Governance Assessment Framework.* Washington, DC: World Bank.

de Soto, Hernando. 2000. *The Mystery of Capital: Why Capitalism Triumphs in the West and Fails Everywhere Else.* New York: Basic Books; London: Bantam Press/Random House.

FIAS (Foreign Investment Advisory Service). 1998. "Egypt: Reform Investment Administration and Strengthen Investment Servicing." World Bank Group, Washington, DC.

———. 2001. "Turkey: Administrative Barriers to Investment." World Bank, Washington, DC.

———. 2003. "Ghana: Administrative Barriers to Investment Update." World Bank, Washington, DC.

———. 2008. "Nigeria (Lagos and Kano): Land Market Reform Implementation; A Key Component of Improving Investment Climate." World Bank, Washington, DC.

Knack, Stephen, and Philip Keefer. 1997. "Does Social Capital Have an Economic Payoff? A Cross-Country Investigation." *Quarterly Journal of Economics* 112 (4): 1251–88.

La Porta, Rafael, Florencio Lopez-de-Silanes, Andrei Shleifer, and Robert Vishny. 1997. "Legal Determinants of External Finance." *Journal of Finance* 52 (3): 1131–50.

McKinsey Global Institute. 2001. *India's Growth Imperative.* Mumbai: McKinsey Global Institute.

North, Douglas. 1990. *Institutions, Institutional Change, and Economic Performance.* New York: Cambridge University Press.

Nyamu Musembi, Celestine. 2007. "De Soto and Land Relations in Rural Africa: Breathing Life into Dead Theories about Property Rights." *Third World Quarterly* 28 (8): 1457–78.

Perlman, Dan L. 2009. "Views of a Conservation Biologist." In *Nature-Friendly Land Use Practices at Multiple Scales*, ed. James McElfish and Rebecca L. Kihslinger. Washington, DC: Environmental Law Institute.

Transparency International. 2009. *Transparency International Annual Report 2009*. Berlin: Transparency International. http://www.transparency.org/publications/annual_report.

World Bank. 2005. *World Development Report 2005: A Better Investment Climate for Everyone*. New York: Oxford University Press for the World Bank.

———. 2010. "Rising Global Interest in Farmland: Can It Yield Sustainable and Equitable Benefits?" World Bank, Washington, DC.

World Resources Institute. 2005. *The Wealth of the Poor: Managing Ecosystems to Fight Poverty*. Washington, DC: World Resources Institute.

PART 1

Meeting the Challenges: Case Studies

Case Studies from Sub-Saharan Africa: chapters 1–5

Case Studies from Other Emerging Markets: chapters 6–10

Other Case Studies: chapters 11 and 12

CHAPTER 1

Burkina Faso: Piloting "One-Stop Shops" to Streamline Land Registry Procedures

Alain Traore

Burkina Faso is a very poor, landlocked Sahelian country. Its modern history is characterized by military coups and radical ideologies. Starting in 1983, when a revolutionary government came to power, a series of restrictive laws were passed, effectively limiting private investment and extending state control over most business activities. As part of this program, the government nationalized land in 1984.

Since 1991, the country has embarked on a comprehensive reform program. With extensive support from the World Bank, the International Monetary Fund, and other donors, it has established a good track record of macroeconomic performance and made considerable progress in its transition toward a market-oriented economy.

In spite of these reforms, however, Burkina Faso has not been able to attract significant private investment, which stagnates at around 11 percent of GDP. Although the government of Burkina Faso recognizes the importance of encouraging productive private investment for growth and has started to implement, with success, the needed reforms to this end, investors continue to find it difficult to do business in the country. According to the first publications of the World Bank's Doing Business reports,[1] the investment climate in Burkina Faso was one of the most difficult in the world. The 2006 report, for example, ranked the country 154 out of a total of 155 countries (World Bank 2005). In 5 of the 10 measurement areas covered by the Doing Business survey, Burkina Faso was among the 10 worst-performing countries in the world.

From Controversy to Reforms

The government's initial reaction to the Doing Business reports was to challenge the results and the analytical methods. Nevertheless, after extensive dialogue with World Bank Group staff, the government began to accept the validity of the data and redirected its attention from challenging the report's accuracy to implementing further reforms in order to improve Burkina Faso's attractiveness to potential private investors.

In this context, the government requested assistance from the International Finance Corporation (IFC) for efforts to improve the rankings of Burkina Faso to the top quartile of African countries. In response to this request, the IFC set up an advisory program, Doing Business Better in Burkina Faso, to facilitate reforms in four key areas that pose significant problems to private investors in Burkina Faso: procedures related to starting a business, employing workers, registering property, and enforcing contracts. The program used the Doing Business indicators to harness momentum for reform and to set a reform agenda, but extended the scope of work from the indicators to the underlying issues in order to make Burkina Faso's investment climate reforms sustainable. The Doing Business indicators were also used to measure progress.

The program started its activities in March 2006 with financial support from Switzerland.

The Initial Land Access Problems

The Doing Business reports use the procedures for registering property as a proxy for the ease of accessing land for private investment in a country. Burkina Faso ranked 148 out of 155 countries in this area in the 2006 Doing Business report (World Bank 2005). The main problems in the allocation, purchase, and transfer of land for industrial and commercial purposes, according to the conclusions of an IFC expert team that visited the country in March 2006 (IFC 2007), included the following:

- Extremely heavy administrative burden due to the multiple approvals required
- Multiple procedures in land transactions
- Lack of clarity and transparency in the procedures
- Relatively complex documents to submit
- Extremely high taxes on land transactions.

All of these combined to produce an underdeveloped land market, a very low number of official land titles, and extreme difficulties for investors seeking to access land in Burkina Faso.

The Key Players and Their Concerns

Many stakeholders are involved in the land reform program. On the one hand, the private sector had the impression that the administrative formalities had been introduced to ensure the collection of taxes—property taxes and income taxes—and not to encourage the emergence of a land and housing market. On the other hand, the public administration, including the Tax Department, justified the complexity of the procedures by pointing to the need for extreme caution in land management and concern over land speculation.

At the same time, the government was pushing for reforms because it was convinced that the development of the country should be based on market principles that would lead to the emergence of an efficient, dynamic land market and the improvement in the availability of land for economic development. To this end, a special land title operation was initiated in 2006, by the Tax Department at the instruction of the prime minister, in order to simplify and reduce the procedural costs related to obtaining land titles.

This initiative generated a lot of interest among citizens, who responded by submitting 6,190 land title requests between December 15, 2006, and December 15, 2007. Unfortunately, the public's enthusiasm was thwarted by the slow pace at which the requests were processed: only 214 titles—3 percent—were established and delivered to the landowners.

Finally, immediately after his nomination in June 2007, Prime Minister Tertius Zongo focused his attention on land issues. He wanted to implement as quickly as possible the reform measures that would facilitate investor access to land. Among these was the creation of a land one-stop shop (OSS).

The Solutions and Program Implementation

The initial task for the team of the Doing Business Better in Burkina Faso program was to build strong relationships with all of the stakeholders. The objective was to build the confidence of the program's partners before tackling reforms. In this context, the first step was to organize a workshop to validate the report by IFC land experts based on their field missions to Burkina Faso in March 2006 and to develop the program details. The discussions focused on the procedures for registering land and issuing construction permits, with the objective of reducing the time and costs of compliance.

The workshop was held on March 16, 2007, with the active participation of high-level government officials, representatives of the private sector, technical and financial partners, land and real estate professionals, as well as civil society. This workshop allowed the various stakeholders to reach consensus on most of the reforms to be implemented. Among these reforms the following were the most important:

- The creation of an OSS to bring all of the land distribution and transaction procedures under one roof
- The delegation of approval rights from the minister of finance to the secretary general of the Ministry of Finance in case the minister is absent in order to speed up the process of conferring or transferring land titles
- The possibility of obtaining land titles without having to invest in the land for industrial and commercial purposes prior to obtaining title
- The removal of certain documents or certain approvals as well as the fusion of certain procedures in the context of a request for land for industrial and commercial uses
- The progressive reduction to 5 percent of the land transfer duties and taxes and the provision of material and human resources to the responsible land administration for the control and collection of these duties and taxes.

To launch these reforms, the IFC land expert team conducted a consultation mission to Burkina Faso in January 2008 in order to prepare a detailed proposal for the creation of an OSS.

Immediately after the minister of finance received the IFC recommendations, he instructed a committee composed of his technical adviser and three officials from the Tax Department to work with the IFC program to prepare the legal documents. In March 2008 the draft documents were validated at a workshop that included the land services departments, the concerned ministries, and the private sector. On May 23, 2008, the Council of Ministers adopted the decree on the creation, attribution, organization, and functioning of the OSS.

In October 2008 the Council of Ministers nominated the director of the OSS in Ouagadougou, which kicked off implementation of the one-stop shop. With financial support from the Investment Climate Facility in addition to the IFC program,[2] work proceeded quickly with regard to finding and furnishing offices, preparing and adopting a procedures manual, and training personnel transferred from different administrations whose activities were merged into the one-stop shop. Finally, the OSS in Ouagadougou was officially open for business on March 20, 2009, followed six months later by another in Bobo-Dioulasso, the second largest city in the country.

Given that there was very little transfer of properties in Burkina Faso, the creation of the Guchet Unique du Foncier (One-stop Shop for Land Registry), or GUF, would be difficult to justify politically if it did not facilitate the delivery of the initial land titles, which was the primary concern of the population. The government, therefore, decided to empower the OSS more rapidly than IFC had recommended and conferred almost all of the administrative duties concerning land rights to the OSS the first year. At the same time, in order to improve Burkina Faso's ranking in the Doing Business report, it was suggested that certain procedures for the transfer of land titles be merged and that the payment for different services be grouped. The government followed this advice, and the number of land title procedures was reduced from eight to four in 2009 (World Bank 2008).

The Initial Results

In its first year of activities, the Doing Business Better in Burkina Faso program facilitated reforms in four areas that have a great impact on the business environment of the country. These efforts were recognized, and Burkina Faso won the World Bank Group award for being one of the fastest-reforming countries in Africa. This recognition spurred further enthusiasm in the country, which led to a raft of reforms in several areas during the second year of the program. As a result, Burkina Faso moved up its "ease of doing business" ranking from 164 to 148 in the 2009 Doing Business report and became among the world's top 10 reformers (World Bank 2008).[3]

With regard to accessing land for investment, the country made significant progress, moving up the rankings from 170 to 148 among 181 countries. Two types of reform measures could be credited for this impressive achievement:

- The first type of measures sought to speed up the land transfer process. The requirement to receive an authorization from the municipal government in order to transfer property rights was eliminated. This reduced the transfer process by 45 days. In addition, the fee to publish the government's approval was merged with the property transfer tax. This action removed another procedure in the process and simplified the payment of the associated fees and taxes.
- The second type of measures sought to reduce the costs of accessing land. The land transfer tax was reduced from 15 to 10 percent in 2007 and then from 10 to 8 percent in 2008. At the same time, with the initiation of the special land title operation in December 2007, the fees associated with the delivery of the first land title were reduced by an average of 50 percent for industrial and commercial land and 60 percent for residential land.

Apart from these measures aimed directly at improving Burkina Faso's performance in the Doing Business ranking, the country also removed investment in the land as a precondition for obtaining title for commercial purposes. This additional measure helped to ease the access of investors to credit and, in turn, helped to increase investment in the land.

In 2009 the government continued to deepen the reforms. As a result, Burkina Faso's business environment, as measured by the Doing Business report, continued to improve. The country's overall ranking moved up further, from 155 to 148 among 183 countries, in the 2010 report, and Burkina Faso figured among the top reformers in Sub-Saharan Africa (World Bank 2009). Specifically, on access to land, Burkina Faso moved up in the rankings from 163 to 114 out of 183 countries, jumping 49 places. This represents Burkina Faso's best performance in the 10 areas examined by the Doing Business report. It is the result of several reform measures, including the following:

- A table of property values was created in 2009 for different zones in the city of Ouagadougou. The Office of Registration and Taxation

(Bureau de l'Enregistrement et du Timbre) now uses this table to calculate the land transfer tax. A new table of revised values is expected
to be published in 2010. By eliminating the need to engage a government evaluator to assess the value of a property on a case-by-case basis,
the simpler procedure lowered the cost and time for transferring property in Ouagadougou.

- A desk was set up in the building of the OSS to facilitate the payment
  of transfer taxes.
- New regulations were issued that mandated a reorganization of the
  land registry and set statutory time limits for processing land registry
  requests. As a result, the time required to obtain a new land title began
  to decrease.

These reforms led to concrete results on the ground: the number of
new land titles soared from just 15 in 2006 to 2,030 in 2008[4]; the time
required to process new land title requests fell steadily from 180 days in
2006 to 59 days in 2009, and the cost of obtaining a land title dropped
from 16.2 percent of property value in 2006 to 13.2 percent in 2008–09.
The new titles are mostly for residential, rather than industrial or commercial, purposes.

A bottleneck was encountered with preparatory work related to inau-
guration of the OSS as well as internal resistance from some officials in
the fiscal administration. This led to a drop in the number of new land
titles issued in the first three quarters of 2009. The minister of finance is
paying personal attention to this issue and envisages the levy of sanctions
on uncooperative officials.

The substantial increase in the number of new land titles has also led
to strong increases in the collection of property tax revenue.

Next Steps

The IFC Doing Business Better in Burkina Faso program was initially set
up for two years, but was extended to four years because it produced
such strong results. The extended program was scheduled to end in
March 2010. However, the government was so pleased with the IFC's
assistance that it requested, and obtained, the IFC's approval to implement a second phase of the program. Conditional on obtaining funding,
the second program was scheduled to start in April 2010. The new program will pass from a Doing Business program to an Investment Climate
program. That is, the new program will focus on the implementation of

deep reforms that go way beyond what the Doing Business indicators touch upon.

More specifically, the second program will continue to support the newly created land one-stop shop through computerization and interconnection with other agencies in order to further reduce the time and cost for property transactions. In addition, the scope of the program will be expanded to accessing rural land and facilitating housing finance. Most of these activities will be pursued in partnership with other donors (for example, the Investment Climate Facility and the Millennium Challenge Account) and other IFC programs (for example, the Housing Finance Program).

In the design and implementation of the second program, close attention will be paid to the lessons learned during the first phase. Despite the overall success of the reform program and the highly positive results on the ground, the land one-stop shop did not always respect the legal time limits for processing documents. Two main factors were behind this failure:

- From the beginning, some officials in the fiscal administration opposed the creation of the land OSS. They argued that such an entity would bring no benefit and that the existing problems could be solved simply by providing them with better equipment. In spite of such resistance, the land one-stop shop was created, and some officials did not make any effort to respect the legal timeline for processing documents.
- The land OSS was overwhelmed by the scope of its responsibilities. A progressive allocation of duties would have helped it to manage its responsibilities better.

The drop in the number of land titles delivered in 2009 likely was a consequence of the slowdown in processing documents as the land one-stop shop was adjusting to its new responsibilities.

This experience serves as an important reminder that land reforms are delicate and at times difficult because they touch on the different interests of many parties. Mindfulness of these diverse parameters, patience, persistence, and continued support at high levels of government are requisites for success.

Conclusions and Lessons Learned

Motivated by a strong desire to improve its ranking in the Doing Business report, Burkina Faso started to tackle the land access problem by improving the procedures for registering property. This approach turned out to be an appropriate one, as it made an extremely complex issue, the question of land titling, more manageable by focusing the public's attention on something for which broad consensus could be established relatively easily. This allowed the country to see positive results quickly, which was a key element in rallying general support for deeper and tougher reforms in the medium to long run.

Because of Burkina Faso's revolutionary past, there was only a nascent acceptance of the concept of freehold private landownership. Most new investments had to rely on government land, which can be obtained in a three-step process that takes up to three years to complete. Meanwhile, most bank loans were not effectively collateralized by full freehold titles. For all these reasons, although the IFC program used the Doing Business report as a catalyst for reforms, the program team did not limit its activities to simplifying property transfer procedures; instead it simultaneously worked to improve the land titling process. Indeed, the program never lost sight of the ultimate goal of addressing initial land titling, the main obstacle to accessing land in Burkina Faso for industrial and commercial purposes.

The exceptional results from Burkina Faso's land reforms to date can be attributed to the combination of several factors:

- Strong political will to address problems related to accessing land for investment
- Pressure from the private sector
- The need to improve the performance of Burkina Faso in the Doing Business report
- The enthusiasm created and the momentum for reforms maintained by the Doing Business Better in Burkina Faso program
- The implementation of the special operation for delivering land titles
- The implementation of measures aimed at simplifying the procedures, rationalizing the documents, and reducing the costs for issuing land titles
- The creation of the land one-stop shop.

Notes

1. An annual report of the World Bank on business regulations in 10 areas, issued starting in 2004. It measures the time and cost of compliance in a large number of countries (181 in 2009) and ranks each country's performance in each measurement area, as well as its overall ease of doing business.

2. The Investment Climate Facility and the IFC contributed $750,000 and $26,000, respectively, for activities related to the launching of the two GUF offices in Ouagadougou and Bobo-Dioulasso.

3. Meanwhile, the number of countries covered by the Doing Business report increased from 155 in 2006 to 181 in 2009.

4. The number of land title transfers changed little: from 30 in 2006 and 37 in 2008.

References

IFC (International Finance Corporation). 2007. *Analyse des procédures d'attribution de terrains et de permis de construire* Ouagadougou: IFC.

World Bank. 2005. *Doing Business 2006: Creating Jobs*. Washington, DC: World Bank.

———. 2008. *Doing Business 2009*. Washington, DC: World Bank.

———. 2009. *Doing Business 2010: Reforming through Difficult Times.* Washington, DC: World Bank.

CHAPTER 2

Mozambique: Engaging Indigenous Groups to Develop Sustainable Business

Christopher Tanner

There is no formally recognized customary land in Mozambique, in the sense of large areas managed by traditional structures that are distinct from areas with "modern" forms of land tenure. Radical title to all land is vested in the state. And while land cannot be bought, sold, or mortgaged, the state attributes a single right to all land users, called the Land Use and Benefit Right, or its Portuguese acronym DUAT (Direito de Uso e Aproveitamento da Terra).

However, traditional structures with hierarchies of chiefs and sub-chiefs do have an important role to play in land and resource management. Although customary practices and leaders had been marginalized by Mozambique's governments since independence, field research after the 1992 Peace Accord revealed that customary systems were largely intact and were managing the access to land and use rights of most of the rural population by default. The public land administration was unprepared to handle the challenge of thousands of households returning to their old farms or looking for new land. The land reform of the mid-1990s, therefore, had to take customary land management into account in some way.[1]

The resulting 1997 Land Law gave customary land managers a formal role in the administration of land. While the new law restated the principles of state ownership, it also recognized customary norms and practices as one way of acquiring a state DUAT, with these local DUATs managed by customary land systems within local communities.

Land for settlers and colonial plantations had been removed from customary control through a system of formal survey and registration since colonial times. The 1997 law continues this approach. Investors looking for land must, therefore, find an area that has already been taken out of customary jurisdiction or find community-managed land that can be transferred to them through a legally defined process. Unlike in colonial times, however, the new law obliges investors to obtain the approval of the local people in *both* situations. The underlying objectives are to secure the DUAT for the investor on a consensual basis that prevents future conflict and to promote local development through agreed benefits accruing to the community as a result of the new investment.

Acquiring Land Rights

The state-allocated DUAT can be acquired in three ways,[2] with each resulting in a right that is identical to the others in terms of its legal weight and validity:

- Occupation by individuals or local communities according to customary norms and practices (historically or culturally acquired rights)
- Occupation in good faith (occupation that is unchallenged for 10 years)
- Formal request to the state for a new DUAT.

Rights Acquired by Occupation

Rights acquired by customary norms and practices are managed by the local land management system within a circumscribed space—a local community.[3] The local community is the titleholder of the DUAT, and all local community members have equal rights under a co-titling arrangement. As such, they should be consulted when any major changes are proposed that affect the community DUAT.

Inside this area, family plots and the shared use of common resources are managed by the prevailing customary system, resulting in de facto individual DUATs over land used by individual community members. However, in recognition of the fact that most local people do not have the resources or knowledge to register their land and that the public services could not survey and register thousands of customarily held plots anyway, DUATs acquired by occupation do not have to be surveyed and registered.

The absence of registration in no way weakens these rights. If local land rights do need stronger protection, a Technical Annex to the Land Law prescribes a participatory process—delimitation—to identify and map the collective DUAT of the overall community. Focusing on community boundaries and features such as rights of way, the process results in a map of the community showing its physical limits, private DUATs existing within the community area, and rights of way for public use (such as utilities) or customary use (such as access to water and sacred sites and traditional routes for moving cattle). The map is recorded in the cadastral atlas at the provincial level, and a certificate is issued. The neighboring communities are involved in the process to confirm that the delimited borders do not impinge on their rights.

Delimitation is not mandatory when requesting a new DUAT. However, it is deemed to be a priority in areas where there is a lot of conflict, when a new investment project is planned in local community areas, or at the request of the local community itself.[4]

Delimitation thus proves the existence of the community-held DUAT and defines its physical extent and location. It also confirms the legal personality of the community in a concrete and tangible form, including formally registering the name of the community. A local community can subsequently enter into contracts with third parties (such as investors) and open its own bank account.

In addition, a well-implemented delimitation identifies and consolidates a local representative structure that must include from three to nine people nominated by the community. These do not necessarily have to be local chiefs or leaders, but traditional leaders are often present or represented by family members such as sons who may be literate and more attuned to the ways of the outside world.

The process also empowers the community itself, by making it more aware of its rights and helping it to appreciate its resource base and what can be done with it. This might include activities such as those proposed by the investor that the community itself is unable or unwilling to undertake.

Good-faith occupation is subject to similar conditions and exemptions regarding registration. It is often linked with customary systems, as the great majority of such occupants are small farmers who have moved onto their land with some form of local consent.

New Rights Requested from the State

The third form of acquiring a DUAT is through a formal request to the state for a new DUAT. This is the road that all new investors must follow if they cannot claim land through a link to a local community. It is the *only* method open to foreigners, who must either be incorporated within a Mozambican registered firm if they are a business or have resided in Mozambique for five years if they are an individual.[5]

This process depends far more on surveyors (government or licensed) and public land administration services. All projects must be approved by the relevant line ministry (for example, agriculture, mines, tourism), and foreign investors must be cleared by the Investment Promotion Center of the Ministry of Planning and Finance. To speed up and attract investment, the Ministry of Agriculture passed a directive in late 2001 that requires the whole process to be completed in 90 days or less.

From the perspective of gaining access to community land, the most important requirement is that the application for a new DUAT be accompanied by a statement from the district administration declaring either that the land is free from occupation or that the occupying community will cede its rights in exchange for an agreed package of benefits. This statement indicates that the investor has carried out a community consultation and is essential for the rest of the process to go ahead. A provisional DUAT is then issued, and the investor has five years (in the case of a citizen) or two years (in the case of a foreigner) to implement the proposed project. When this is done, they receive a definitive DUAT.

Duration, Extinction, and Transmission of Land Rights

A new and definitive DUAT for an investor is valid for 50 years, renewable for another 50 years, and inheritable. Rights acquired by occupation are for residential or livelihood purposes and not subject to any time limit. The holders can pass on their right to heirs, and the right is not subject to any provisional clauses that require some form of real use before it is made permanent.

All DUATs can be extinguished on the grounds of public interest, where new projects are planned (such as the new gas pipelines in the south) or where the state determines that a new investment project has overriding importance. Examples of this are the Mozal aluminum plant in Maputo Province and the accelerated development zones set up to attract private investment. The law requires that appropriate compensation be paid to titleholders, and such cases lead to what is, in effect, a state-community consultation to determine what the local communities will receive or whether they will be moved to another area. In the case of Mozal, for example, a generous community development fund was set up, and local people were relocated to land near the new plant.

Private investments on land are private property and can be sold or used as bank collateral. In rural areas, however, the land that underpins the investment does not pass automatically to the new owner, who must ask that the DUAT for the land be transferred into his or her name. This introduces an element of uncertainty, which can undermine the willingness of banks and others to advance credit for rural projects. In urban areas, where the building or other infrastructure, not the land per se, is considered to be the main source of economic activity deriving from the DUAT, this transfer is automatic.

Protected Areas

DUATs cannot be acquired within the public domain. As such, no DUAT is allowed in either total protection areas, such as national parks, or partial protection areas, such as *coutadas*, the official hunting reserves created in the 1930s with specific conservation objectives. Licenses for approved economic activities are, however, allowed and are issued by the Ministry of Tourism, which has been responsible for these areas since 2000.[6]

Communities are living inside nearly all protected areas in Mozambique. Most communities say they existed before the *coutadas* or parks were created, thus having prior rights under the 1997 Land Law. Others claim rights acquired by good-faith occupation. Since there is no Mozambican equivalent of the South African Restitution Act with a specific cutoff date set for assessing whether historical claims are valid, the arguments hinge on interpretations of the law and its underlying principles.

The official position is that no DUAT is allowed inside national parks and *coutadas*, although the Ministry of Tourism has tried in recent years to accommodate local needs and negotiate with local people. Investors believe that they have a contract over an area that is nominally free of resident population and, in return, are required to deliver on agreed conservation and resource management objectives as well as to pay tax on income from hunting activities. The presence of communities is, therefore, a considerable practical as well as legal problem.

Similar issues arise on old colonial properties that, although not protected areas, are considered by the public land administration as having been alienated from local community jurisdiction. In the mid-1980s, the government began giving these areas to private sector interests, and the presence of local people living inside these properties quickly became a difficult problem to resolve.[7] What is really at stake is the underlying issue of how resident populations are treated when the state or investors want to take over land they perceive to be unoccupied or at least underused by a local population that lacks the necessary skills and resources.[8] Investors who are given licenses to exploit *coutadas* or DUATs over old colonial properties, but fail to achieve a satisfactory agreement with the local communities, soon find themselves embroiled in complex and entrenched conflicts.[9]

A Case Study: *Coutada* 9 in Macossa District

Macossa is in the northern part of Manica Province. More than 70 percent of the district is dominated by two large, forested hunting reserves, which border the Gorongosa National Park to the east. There are extensive areas of relatively undisturbed wildlife habitat and areas with low densities of human population, offering great potential for conservation and wildlife management. Inventories carried out in 2003 identified a wide variety of wild animal species, but the numbers are low after years of heavy illegal hunting, and restocking is essential if game hunting is to be commercially and ecologically viable.

Coutada 9 occupies 3,763 square kilometers and, as an official hunting reserve, comes under the jurisdiction of the Ministry of Tourism.[10] In 2003 the ministry issued a management contract to Rio Save Safaris, a Mozambican-Zimbabwean sports hunting business. The contract includes resource management and conservation obligations, with the ministry believing at the time that there were few, if any, local people living inside the *coutada* area.

Rio Save Safaris quickly found that, in fact, there was significant occupation and use of the area, especially in the west, where deforestation and subsistence agriculture made any kind of conservation activity all but impossible. There were also small but significant villages in the forested area to the east, where local subsistence strategies depended on the hunting of animals in the reserves, the gathering of medicines and honey in the forest, and agriculture in areas where seasonal rivers allow some form of cultivation.

While the population was, and still is, small, numbering several hundred families, it effectively occupied the land with a production system and livelihoods strategy that extended over many thousands of hectares.

The villages had been there for a very long time, with established traditional leadership and resource management structures. From their point of view, they had legitimate acquired rights, although these did not translate into DUATs according to the 1997 Land Law.

From the beginning, Rio Save Safaris accepted that the communities were there and that simply moving them out was not an option—this would effectively be a forced relocation and, in any case, it was not clear where they could go. Meanwhile, they had to stop the illegal hunting, which was rife across the whole area. Guards and rangers could be trained from the local community, but the costs of policing would be high without real community buy-in to the need to conserve the animal population. Without this, it would not be economically feasible to buy and bring in the new animals from Zimbabwe and South Africa that were essential for turning the *coutada* into a commercially viable safari venture. Besides, they needed good relations with local people if their business was to succeed in what was already a difficult operational environment.

Rio Save Safaris came up with a pragmatic proposal for co-managing the area with the communities, which was structured around the access to and use of different areas within the *coutada*. Most important, they proposed a way for the communities to participate in the income generated by the safari business, in return for their cooperation and in particular for giving up or at least significantly controlling their hunting. What emerged was a participatory land use plan that would support local livelihoods and allow the conservation and sports hunting enterprise to proceed. This involved a de facto zoning of the *coutada*, with different levels of community participation and land use in each zone:

- A core and partially fenced area in which the investor manages all of the resources and from which the communities will eventually leave of their own free will; the community will stop all hunting and in return will receive 25 percent of trophy fees generated in this area.
- A buffer zone that is managed for two years jointly by the investor and the community and thereafter by the community alone; the community will also stop hunting there, but in return for their greater role in management, they will receive 75 percent of trophy fees generated in this area.
- A third area, away from the hunting and conservation areas, where local agriculture is allowed; this recognizes the reality on the ground—giving up the pretence of preventing agriculture and restoring the forest habitat—and effectively reduces the area of the *coutada* that can be used as a hunting reserve.

Rio Save Safaris was keen to help local people to acquire greater knowledge of conservation issues and the skills needed to manage the *coutada* resources. They proposed to train and employ young community members, hire all their guards and rangers from the communities, and take local schoolchildren into the core area to teach them about wildlife and conservation. They also did their own research into the sociopolitical organization of the communities. Six distinct communities were identified, each with several villages and its own chief (*regulo*) and management structure. A map was produced of community occupation in the *coutada* and neighboring areas. It was then possible to sit down and discuss the proposal with the right leaders and with a reasonable idea of how each community could fit into and benefit from the proposed scheme.

The zoning and income-sharing ideas were fully discussed with the local communities as the basis for a constructive relationship between Rio Save Safaris and the local communities. The challenge facing everyone was to find an appropriate legal framework within which to formalize the agreements and conditions that would regulate the investor-community relationship in the longer term. Several questions were crucial in this context:

- Who are the communities?
- Who represents them?
- What are their rights within the *coutada*?
- Do they have a legal personality that allows them to enter into a contract with the operator?

These questions were discussed in early 2004 in meetings between local community leaders, Rio Save Safaris, and district administration and provincial service staff (tourism, land, forests, and wildlife). A Food and Agriculture Organization (FAO) food security project in the district was also involved and used FAO experience in community-based natural resource management and an Inter-ministerial Land Commission program to help find acceptable solutions. Among the options discussed was the possibility of doing a community delimitation exercise.

Rio Save Safaris, however, was particularly concerned *not* to bring the 1997 Land Law into the picture. They feared that if the issue of local land rights was introduced, all chances of their venture taking off would be lost in a wrangle over rights, both between the locals and the investor and between the communities themselves. They saw a formal delimitation exercise as fraught with problems and did not think it was necessary anyway, as they already knew who the communities were and had good relations with them.

The Tourism Ministry maintained its position that a community DUAT was not legally possible in a *coutada*. Government was also reluctant to accept the idea of zoning and downsizing the *coutada*.

Meanwhile, with support from the FAO team, Rio Save Safaris went ahead with its agreement with the communities. In the end, a new contract was negotiated and signed between the ministry and Rio Save Safaris, which included all of the elements above. The Provincial Cadastral and Geographic Service, after initial resistance, carried out a formal zoning of the *coutada*, along the lines of the community–Rio Save Safaris division, into core, buffer, and agricultural areas.

While these administrative issues were slowly being resolved, implementation of the agreement was producing significant results on the ground. In its first year of operation, the community received US$11,000 as its share of the trophy fees. The communities have continued to receive similar amounts every year since then and have become used to the idea that working with Rio Save Safaris is ultimately to their benefit. There has been a notable impact on the communities, as they have built health posts and improved other social infrastructure. Rio Save Safaris has trained a core of community men as rangers and workers at their bush camp, and the communities have become more organized and able to decide how to use the new income they are receiving. Meanwhile, to compensate for the loss due to the hunting ban, various income diversification and agricultural production activities were initiated via the FAO food security project, but later supported with income from payments by Rio Save Safaris.

Although the community-investor relationship is working well, there are the inevitable difficulties. Illegal hunting remains a problem. The district administration has been overseeing distribution of the hunting income and divides it equally among all of the communities. Some adhere to the agreement more than others, and a lot of the illegal hunting is by outsiders and controlled by powerful urban interests. Rio Save Safaris is now considering ways to allocate income in relation to the effort made by each community to control and end the illegal activities. They hope to do this by creating an association of the natural resources management committees that the FAO project helped to set up in each community. This will reduce the role of the district and allow the communities to assume greater control over how everyone performs.

As the program becomes more widely known, other people are moving into the area, looking for ways to share in the benefits. The communities are concerned because they see the income as "theirs," while Rio Save Safaris worries that migration into the area will increase pressure on an already threatened habitat and ecosystem. The good base established so far is, however, allowing them to work together with the communities to establish an effective registration system that ensures that benefits only go to the communities.

Meanwhile, Rio Save Safaris has been awarded the contract to manage the neighboring *Coutada* 13, where they are following the same model, which now enjoys the full support of the government, including the internal zoning of the new *coutada* area.

Conclusions and Lessons Learned

Accessing communal land for commercial development is not an easy matter. Several objectives—local development, nature conservation, and commercial profit—have to be harmonized and pursued at the same time. In particular, the limited choice of livelihood and the limited capacities of the local communities to understand and safeguard long-term conservation and business interests dictate that more time and effort will be necessary whenever commercial investment is sought on community land. There is no shortcut to multiple-partner consultations and negotiations in the development process.

In this context, land policy and land law are important instruments with transformational potential for development. The Mozambican policy and legal framework provides an opportunity to integrate customary and more formal forms of land management. Local rights are secured without falling into the dualist trap of separating the landscape, and the people who live in it, into distinct areas, which then often follow quite different and unequal development paths. At the same time, the needs of investors are taken into account with a long, renewable state leasehold.

The 2007 Rural Development Strategy calls for implementing the 1997 Land Law and using the DUAT as tools in a wider strategy to achieve economic and social objectives. The National Directorate for Promoting Rural Development is also adopting the progressive principles and mechanisms of the 1997 Land Law for a set of measures aimed at providing roads, extension support, and access to credit for the rural population. The same approach will, in turn, feed into the development of local development plans that serve local needs and support new community-investor partnerships.

Nevertheless, the practical application of this framework remains a challenge, as there are important legal, institutional, and capacity lacunas in the current land management system that continue to render investor access to community land a complex and uncertain process. To begin with, although DUATs acquired by customary occupation do not need to be surveyed or registered, the absence of registration does pose a problem for investors wishing to access community land. Without any documentation to prove that the community is the legitimate occupier of the area in question, a secure base on which to begin any negotiation is lacking. This means that delimitation and official registration, which cost from US$3,000 to US$7,000 per community[11] and take considerable time to complete, are inevitable first steps for most investors seeking to access community land.

Moreover, the current land legislation does not have provisions for renting DUATs to third parties, and this can be very problematic when communities try to form partnerships with outside investors. As prescribed by law, DUATs are delivered either for residential and livelihood purposes (in the case of rights acquired by occupation) or for investment purposes (in the case of new rights acquired from the state), and the titleholders are expected to pursue these activities themselves. Most local communities, however, do not yet have the necessary capital or skills to exploit their resources in a commercially viable fashion. This means that they will have to cede their rights partially or temporarily, under predefined conditions, to a commercial investor so that the latter can exploit the resources on their behalf. There has been considerable debate surrounding this issue, and the current legal thinking in Mozambique is that the rental of DUATs themselves is not allowable, but that it is possible to cede exploitation rights through a commercial contract that then leaves the DUAT with the original titleholder.

Similarly, while there is clear rationale for not granting DUATs under any circumstances within protected areas, including *coutadas*, the total ignorance of the local communities' presence inside these areas and the subsequent absence of any legal provisions regarding their rights are facilitating neither nature conservation nor sustainable exploitation of the natural resources. Both the constitution of Mozambique and the 1995 National Land Policy state the social and policy principles that "ensure the rights of the Mozambican people over land and other natural resources" and guarantee existing rights when new ones are given out. Without an enforceable legal and regulatory framework governing land and resource uses inside the protected areas, the investor who has a contract with the state has to improvise solutions, and whatever agreement is reached with the local people does not have any legal weight. This is a very precarious situation for all parties involved, especially the investor, who not only has to put in considerable time and money, but also has contractual obligations to deliver conservation and economic results.

Adding to the complexity is the limited capacity of public land administration services to facilitate the investor-community partnership. In essence, securing good, workable agreements for providing investors with access to community land is not only an administrative issue; it is also about finding solutions based on a common understanding of the needs of each side. Such a process requires a range of skills and services that are not widely available at present, either inside or outside the government. There is an urgent need to reform and upgrade land administration and management (as well as other public services), to adopt a real participatory approach, and to treat community land issues as an opportunity to produce a development model that meets the wide, disparate needs of all those who depend on land and natural resources.

Much remains to be done in order to bridge the conceptual and technical gaps that separate the stakeholders. Driven by overarching national development and economic growth imperatives, some in the government and administrative hierarchy advocate measures to fast-track or even bypass the community consultation procedures. At the same time, few communities or programs supported by donors or nongovernmental organizations understand the rationale for or the needs of commercial investment. Many donor-supported projects have focused on local community rights, which are clearly needed. But in order to build a successful community-investor partnership, both the community and the investor have to be active partners in efforts from the beginning. Failing a genuine interest on both sides in meeting the needs of the other, the community consultation process will remain a legal procedure to be fulfilled rather than a means to build successful long-lasting partnerships that can produce results for both parties, as well as for the general population, in the areas of conservation and sustainable development.

Notes

1. See Tanner (2002), which provides a detailed account of the genesis and development of the 1997 law.

2. Law 19/97, Article 12. The 1997 Land Law is now officially translated into English (as well as four local languages). See the land administration website, www.dinageca.co.mz.

3. See Law 19/97, Article 1, Number 1, for a complete definition.

4. Technical Annex, Article 7.

5. Law 19/97, Article 11.

6. In 2000 responsibility for national parks and conservation areas was transferred from the National Directorate for Forests and Wildlife in the Ministry of Agriculture and Rural Development and given to the Ministry of Tourism, including all land management decisions within these areas.

7. This process was studied by University of Wisconsin Land Tenure Center and Mozambican researchers in the early 1990s, producing important information on the local legitimacy of customary land structures and the strong feelings of local people regarding their inherent long-standing rights. See, for example, Myers and West (1993) as well as Tanner (1993).

8. See Durang and Tanner (2004), which includes an account of a large forestry plantation where this issue is particularly acute.

9. See Afonso and others (2004), which shows several conflicts of this kind in recent research.

10. See note 6.

11. See CTC Consulting (2003), which includes detailed accounts of delimitation and other land surveying costs.

References

Afonso, Angelo, João Paolo Azevedo, Sergio Baleira, Joao Bila, Elenio Cavoessa, Constantino Chichava, Eduardo Chiziane, Altino Moises, Carlos Pedro, Jose Santos, Carlos Serra, and Christopher Tanner. 2004. *Seminario para discutir os resultados da pesquisa sobre conflitos na area de terra meio ambiente e florestas e eauna bravia: 30–31 de agosto de 2004; Apresentações 'Powerpoint' da equipa de campo.* Maputo: Centro de Formação Jurídica e Judiciaria.

CTC Consulting. 2003. *Appraisal of the Potential for a Community Land Registration, Negotiation, and Planning Support Programme in Mozambique.* Maputo: Department for International Development.

Durang, Tom, and Christopher Tanner. 2004. "Access to Land and Other Natural Resources for Local Communities in Mozambique: Current Examples from Manica Province." Paper presented to the Green Agri Net "Conference on Land Administration in Practice," Denmark, April 1–2.

Myers, Gregory, and Harry West. 1993. "Land Tenure Security and State Farm Divestiture in Mozambique: Case Studies in Nhamatanda, Manica, and

Montepuez Districts." LTC Research Paper 110, Nelson Institute for Environmental Studies, University of Wisconsin, Madison.

Tanner, Christopher. 1993. "Land Disputes and Ecological Degradation in an Irrigation Scheme: A Case Study of State Farm Divestiture in Chokwe, Mozambique." LTC Research Paper 111, Nelson Institute for Environmental Studies, University of Wisconsin, Madison.

———. 2002. "Law Making in an African Context: The 1997 Mozambican Land Law." Legal Papers Online 26, Food and Agriculture Organization, Rome.

CHAPTER 3

Namibia: Developing Communal Conservancies to Redress Inequalities in Income and Wealth

Uda Nakamhela

Namibia is an arid Southern African country that did not gain independence until 1990. A century of colonization and South African apartheid rule has left profound marks on the country. A decade after independence Namibia still has one of the most unequal distributions of wealth in the world, with 10 percent of the richest residents owning 65 percent of the total wealth. This is also reflected in inequalities between communal areas (old indigenous reserves that hosted black populations) and commercial areas (mostly white-owned large-scale farms). Since independence, the government has been trying to redress these inequalities by reforming the laws relating to, among others, land, natural resources, and water management.

Under the constitution, all land, water, and natural resources belong to the state, unless lawfully owned by individuals. There are three main kinds of land according to tenure:

- Commercial land can be bought by private individuals, who then become owners of the land.

- Communal land, by contrast, remains vested in the state, which administers the land in trust for the benefit of the traditional communities residing on it. Communal land cannot be bought or sold.
- State land consists mostly of game parks and nature reserves, which are not inhabited by local communities at all (usually as a result of relocations during the colonial era).[1]

Communal Area Conservancies

The Nature Conservation Ordinance no. 4 of 1975 bestowed certain use rights over wildlife on the owners of private farmland. For farmlands of a certain minimum size and surrounded by a game-proof fence, the owners may apply to declare the area a private game park or private nature reserve. This allowed them to realize the commercial value of wildlife on the land through tourism development. All communal land was excluded from the possibility of becoming a game park or nature reserve.

In 1996 the government introduced the Nature Conservation Amendment Act no. 5, which amended the Nature Conservation Ordinance of 1975. The 1996 amendment removed the discriminatory measure by allowing certain areas of communal land to be registered as nature reserves. On communal land, conservancy is the term used for a nature reserve. Any group of persons residing on communal land can apply to the minister of environment and tourism to have the area they inhabit declared a conservancy.[2] Once registered, a conservancy enjoys the same use rights over the wildlife that hitherto only the owners of private land enjoyed. Conservancies form part of a growing community-based natural resource management (CBNRM) sector (Davis 2007).

Namibia's CBNRM program is a joint venture between government and nongovernmental institutions, communities, community-based organizations, and development partners. The program seeks to provide a facilitating framework and incentives for rural communities to care for their natural resources and to derive benefits from them.[3] In particular, it aims to allow the population to benefit from tourism development in communal lands through wildlife management and land management units—conservancies.

Conservancies are self-selecting social units or communities of people who choose to work together and gain rights to use, manage, and benefit from the consumptive and nonconsumptive use of wildlife within defined boundaries. In order to register a conservancy, the following requirements must be met:

- The conservancy must be legally constituted with clearly defined boundaries that are not in dispute with neighboring communities.
- It must also have defined membership and a committee representative of members.
- It is also required to draw up a clear plan for the equitable distribution of conservancy benefits to members.

Once these conditions have been met and approved by the minister, conservancies are registered and published in the government gazette. Once registered, a conservancy acquires new rights and responsibilities with regard to the use and management of wildlife. Consumptive rights include the conditional ownership and use of game that can be hunted as trophies or used for local consumption by conservancy members, cropped for commercial sale of meat, or captured and sold as live game. Nonconsumptive rights create opportunities for tourism, enabling conservancies to establish their own community-based tourism enterprises or to create joint-venture agreements with private sector entrepreneurs.

Communal area conservancies, and the income from them, have grown rapidly since being permitted by law. In 1998 there were four communal area conservancies covering 16,821 square kilometers and with about 14,500 residents. In 2007, almost 10 years later, there were 50 conservancies managing more than 118,704 square kilometers of communal land and with about 220,600 residents (Davis 2007, 10). A substantial number of these conservancies contain spectacular scenery, rich cultures, and burgeoning wildlife populations, all of which make them highly attractive to the tourism and hunting sectors.

Income from these conservancies rose from nothing in the mid-1990s to approximately US$3.8 million in 2007. Half of this income came from joint-venture tourism projects, and another quarter from trophy hunting. Of the US$3.8 million earned by the conservancies in 2007, just under US$1 million went to conservancy members as direct cash income from wages, and another US$600,000 went to conservancy committees as cash to cover their operational costs.

These numbers attest to the success of the strategy of bringing conservancies with tourism potential together with private investors who recognize the opportunities in developing tourism and helping conservancies to unlock this potential. Both partners contribute to the venture.

Conservancies provide rights to develop tourism, commitments to manage the natural resources (especially wildlife) actively, and a desire and willingness to learn and become involved in the tourism industry. Investors bring capital, expertise in tourism, and access to the market.

These joint ventures can be structured in various ways in order to maximize the benefits for both parties; the details need to be negotiated carefully and clearly before joint ventures can be formally embarked upon. The following are some of the options:

- Direct revenue sharing, including a lease fee calculated as a percentage of net turnover or a flat concession fee paid annually
- Levy for every bed-night sold
- Payment for game hunting
- Provision of training and employment for local inhabitants
- Secondary business opportunities.

Many agreements include a combination of options. Noncash benefits may also be included in the form of direct employee "perks" or contributions to social infrastructure, such as the development of schools and clinics. All agreements should include clauses for minimum performance to protect conservancies and operators against nonperforming partners as well as strict clauses regarding environmental impacts. Most important, conservancies may ensure that contracts provide jobs and build skills among members. The structure of agreements is under constant review.

By the end of 2007, 19 formal joint-venture agreements were operational and generating benefits, while eight conservancies were also receiving payment from partners, even though agreements had yet to be finalized. A further six conservancies were receiving income from operators for rights to traverse or use resources in them. The number of joint-venture agreements has increased 90 percent since 2005 alone, and the rate at which new opportunities are being taken up indicates that the private sector sees communal area conservancies as having substantial potential for tourism.

As an alternative to these joint-venture options, some lodges have recently been developed in closer partnership with conservancies. These involve conservancies as full or partial shareholders in the fixed assets of the businesses themselves. This is known as "community equity," in which a conservancy's funds are contributed to a tourism enterprise that is developed in partnership with a private investor. As with any equity investment, such a structure entails greater risk for the community, along with the possibility of larger returns from the investment and, if they so choose, the chance to be more involved in the management and growth of the business.

The concept of community equity arose from the realization that the funds could unlock potential tourism opportunities in places where it would be difficult for either the community or the investor to obtain capital, often because of the risk of investing in remote areas. In addition to increasing local benefits, the equity helps to promote the involvement of communities in the tourism sector. The concept can also be applied widely on communal or freehold land, and conservancies could gain equity in planned or existing businesses through concessions in national parks.[4]

Tourism and Wildlife Concessions on State Land

On state land that is uninhabited or on which no conservancies have been registered even though there is a resident local community, commercial operations can be pursued only through concessions granted by the Ministry of Environment and Tourism. Such concessions aim to create opportunities for business development and the economic empowerment of formerly disadvantaged Namibians through tourism, hunting, and forestry industries.

The Nature Conservation Ordinance no. 4 of 1975, as amended by the Nature Conservation Amendment Act no. 5 of 1996, vests wide-ranging powers in the minister of environment and tourism to authorize other parties to provide services, including tourism services, within protected areas on behalf of the state.[5] These concessions can also be granted on state land outside protected areas, including communal land, but the regional councils and traditional authorities have special roles to play and must be consulted in the process. This is to ensure that such concessions complement regional and local community development objectives and comply with the Communal Land Reform Act no. 5 of 2002.

Right of Leasehold on Communal Land

The Communal Land Reform Act no. 11 of 2005, administered by the Ministry of Lands and Resettlement, governs the allocation of rights in respect of communal land. Two types of rights may be granted to individuals, or individual households, in communal areas:

- A *customary land right* is allocated by the chief of the traditional community where the land in question is situated. It gives the exclusive right to use a certain area for grazing purposes and establishing a home.
- A *right of leasehold* is granted by a communal land board,[6] which governs the allocation of commercial land rights in communal areas. It is a form of land tenure under which a leaseholder can pursue agricultural or other economic interests (Mathieu and Méline 2005, 94). Most rights of leasehold are used to develop lodges.

A conservancy may be formed that includes areas under customary land rights. Usually the registration of a conservancy does not conflict with preallocated customary rights. Because conservancies are voluntary membership-based organizations, their zoning and management plans take into account the uses that are already taking place on certain portions of land within them. Therefore, an exclusive wildlife zone would not be created in an area that is already an important grazing area for one or more members of the conservancy.

However, disputes can arise when private sector investors and individuals who hold land rights inside a conservancy decide to enter directly into a lease agreement, thus capturing between them all of the benefits from the commercial development. Such private agreements are generally not supported by the concession policy or other government policies and legislation that seek to bring about broad-based development on communal land. The Communal Land Reform Act, for example, clearly stipulates that the right of leasehold may not be granted if the purpose for which the land in question is proposed to be used would defeat the objectives of the management and utilization plan of a conservancy.[7] Nevertheless, there are cases where the individual holders of customary land rights have used their influence to obtain support from within the conservancy committee for the investors' leasehold application, leading to legal disputes.

Other kinds of controversies erupted in 2009 when the Ministry of Lands and Resettlement, through the land boards, started to collect leasehold fees from the lodges on communal land. The lease amounts demanded were determined by the land boards and the valuations committee of the Ministry of Lands on the basis of the estimated turnover or profit of each lodge. The new demand for lease fees was prompted by a ministerial directive from the Ministry of Lands, which required that the land boards finance their functions from the fees they collect from the leaseholders. This is, however, in contradiction to the Communal Land Reform Act, which stipulates, "All expenditure in connection with the performance of the functions of a board must be defrayed from funds appropriated by Parliament for the purpose."[8]

In addition, the Communal Land Reform Act also states, "The amount payable … must be determined in a manner prescribed," and "moneys paid … must be deposited in the fund established by or under any law for the purpose of regional development." However, no regulations have ever been promulgated to prescribe how the fees should be determined, nor have any funds for regional development ever been established. The money that was paid by the few lodges ended up going to central government coffers (Ministry of Finance) without being ring-fenced as land board funds.

Insufficient funding is a serious problem for most communal land boards and is a major reason for their imperfect functioning. Nevertheless, trying to address the financing difficulties of the communal land boards through leasehold fees will prove to be counterproductive to the government's communal area development objectives. Directly or indirectly, the new fees will erode the benefits accruing to the relevant rural communities and create disincentives for private investors to invest in communal land. This difficult problem needs to be resolved.

Conclusions and Lessons Learned

A major concern facing the government of newly independent Namibia was the great inequality of wealth, income, and economic opportunity among its citizens. One dimension of this inequality was between the owners of land classified as commercial and the holders of less concrete use rights to communal land. An important step taken in this context was to allow residents of communal land the same opportunities that owners of commercial land had during the colonial period: the right to create conservancies on their land and to earn income by developing tourism (and other economic activities) on that land.

This initiative has had considerable success. Private investment, mostly in the tourism sector, was attracted to form joint ventures with organizations of residents of communal land. This not only created job opportunities for the occupants of communal land, but also increased the value of wildlife, which had the positive effect of increasing the number of wild-life in communal areas. In particular, the establishment of conservancies generated and continues to generate significant cash and noncash benefits to residents of communal land through the development of lodges and other tourism opportunities.

However, Namibia still has a long way to go. The existing system, covering only use rights related to wildlife, exists alongside a more recent system governing use rights related to other natural resources such as forest products.[9] These regimes need to be better aligned. More impor-tant, Namibia has yet to address sufficiently the issue of tenure over communal land.

The Commercial Land Reform Act no. 6 of 1995 and the Communal Land Reform Act no. 11 of 2005 form the basic legal framework pertain-ing to land matters in Namibia. One of the problems is that, with two separate pieces of legislation, the government cannot use the money from the commercial land fund (via the collection of land tax) for develop-ments on communal land. To address this issue, plans are at an advanced stage to combine the two acts. It is expected that the new act, which would address the question of tenure on communal land through land parcels and long-term leases (up to 99 years), will promote development in the long term.

Without stronger tenure over allocated portions of communal land,[10] the occupants have no way of protecting themselves from land grab prac-tices by more wealthy city dwellers who introduce large herds of live-stock onto communal land. Better land tenure rights for communal area residents would improve their chances of becoming investors on their own land and of protecting themselves against economically stronger city dwellers who unsustainably and unfairly exploit the communal (water and grazing) resources.

Another issue with weak tenure on communal land is that it limits the capacity of occupants to meet the collateral requirement for accessing bank loans. Indeed, although it has generally been agreed among stake-holders that the development objectives of rural communities would be better met if all leasehold and concession rights were granted only to organized groups such as conservancies or community trusts, the com-mercial reality of bank collateral demands a different arrangement if the communities wish to attract private investors. As a result, the prevalent joint-venture structure transfers the leasehold rights from the conservan-cies to the investors for the duration of the joint-venture agreement, with the stipulation that the right of leasehold will revert to, or be renewed in the name of, the conservancies at the end of the joint-venture agreement period.

It is to be expected that ameliorating these and other problems, including inadequate funding for administering these laws, would lead to additional investment and increase the productivity of communal land and its residents.

Notes

1. The Parks and Wildlife Management Bill, which is expected to be promulgated in 2010 as the Parks and Wildlife Management Act, makes provision for contractual parks, which are areas where local communities already reside, but which will nevertheless be proclaimed as parks so as to enable a co-management regime of tourism resources and tourism development.

2. Section 24A.

3. http://www.met.gov.na/programmes/cbnrm/cbnrmHome.htm.

4. Text and tables from Davis (2007, 46ff); the data are up to date for the end of 2007. The latest "State of Conservancy Report," as it is colloquially known among CBNRM practitioners in Namibia, was launched in late 2009, and is available online on the websites of the Namibia Association of CBNRM Support Organisations (http://www.nacso.org.na) and the Namibia Nature Foundation (http://www.nnf.org.na).

5. Policy on Tourism and Wildlife Concessions on State Land, 2007, Ministry of Environment and Tourism.

6. The composition and responsibilities of communal land boards are defined in the Communal Land Reform Act.

7. Section 31 of the Communal Land Reform Act.

8. Section 11.

9. Forest Act 12 of 2001, administered by the Ministry of Agriculture, Water, and Forestry.

10. The chief or traditional authority allocates certain portions of the communal land to households for the purposes of establishing a homestead or using fields as crop or grazing areas. These areas are not fenced off because they must remain open so that other people can access other parts of the communal land.

References

Davis, Anna, ed. 2007. *Namibia's Communal Conservancies: A Review of Progress and Challenges in 2007*. Windhoek: Namibia Nature Foundation.

Mathieu, Gwladys, and Vanessa Méline. 2005. *Natural Resource Management Rules and Practices in a Context of Legislative Changes in North Central, Namibia.* French version released in 2004. Windhoek: Namibia National Farmers Union, with financial support by the French Embassy, Service for Co-operation and Cultural Affairs.

CHAPTER 4

Rwanda: Reforming Land Administration to Enhance the Investment Environment

Didier G. Sagashya

Rwanda is one of the poorest countries in the world. A landlocked country in East Africa, it is the most densely populated country in Sub-Saharan Africa. Most of the population is engaged in subsistence or semi-subsistence agriculture. Genocide and war in 1994 impoverished the country and left the economy in shambles. To rebuild the economy, create jobs, and modernize the economic framework after the chaos of 1994, the government embarked on multiple reforms, including reform of the land tenure system.

Great progress has been made since 1994, with per capita income nearly tripling. Among many other indicators of success are good rankings on Transparency International's anticorruption index and the World Bank's Doing Business index. Tourism has been a fast-growing industry.

Land Reform

Land in Rwanda was governed by customary law until the Belgians, who took over control of the country from the Germans after World War I, introduced written laws to guarantee secure land tenure for settlers and other foreigners who wished to invest in Rwanda. This system remained in place after independence in 1962. After 1994, the government started to prepare for land reforms to ensure security of tenure for all land claimants.

Until the Organic Land Law was introduced in 2005, less than 1 percent of the land in Rwanda was registered under freehold or leasehold titles; the rest of the land belonged to the state by law. In reality, people continued to follow the customary rules in land use. There was a rudimentary cadastral system in the country, coupled with a weak and incomplete land administration. Urban land (inside Kigali City) and rural land (outside Kigali City) were managed by different institutions under outdated laws, and there was no clear policy direction. Further, there were no land use plans or proper zoning regulations for urban areas, including the capital city, Kigali.

As a result, the country faced widespread problems involving security of tenure, including numerous property disputes, land use conflicts, and discrimination against women. In the prevailing informal land market, land was not recognized as capital and could not be used as collateral to obtain credit. In urban areas, where new investment demand was high, there was no mechanism for allocating well-secured, well-zoned sites to potential investors, resulting in complexities for obtaining building permits. In rural areas, the lack of secure tenure led to resource misuse and land degradation. Across the country, ad hoc attempts to meet development needs led to some rent-seeking behavior.

All of these obstacles contributed to the difficulties of doing business in Rwanda. Among the 145 countries covered by the *World Bank Doing Business 2005*, for example, land access in Rwanda, as measured by registering a property in the capital city, was one of the most difficult in the world (World Bank 2004). It took 354 days to get a property registered—shorter than only 3 countries among the 145 surveyed. This outcome was hardly surprising, considering that there were only two registrars of land titles in the country at the time—the mayor of Kigali City for property within Kigali City and the director of lands in the ministry in charge of lands for property in the rest of the country.

The reform of the land management system was, therefore, a prerequisite for economic recovery and sustainable economic growth, especially given the pressure arising from the combination of a growing population and increasing land scarcity. The need for land reforms was clearly set in Rwanda's Vision 2020 and its Economic Development and Poverty Reduction Strategy—such reforms were part of the proposed foundation

supporting the reconstruction of social capital, development of infrastructure, development of the private sector, and modernization of agriculture, four of the six pillars of Vision 2020.

Establishing the Policy, Legal, and Institutional Framework for Land Reforms

Land reforms are a politically charged process in all countries, and
Rwanda is no exception. To ensure the broadest support for its vision, the
government started by developing a clear national land policy through
stakeholder consultation and consensus building. The preparation for the
national policy started in 1999, and the process picked up speed after
2001, when the then Ministry of Environment, Forestry, Lands, Mines,
and Water came in place to champion the process with the president's
support. Extensive exchanges between government officials, civil society
organizations, experts, and the general public continued until 2004, when
a new national land policy was adopted based on the broad agreement of
all stakeholders.

In the 2004 policy, social equity, economic efficiency, and land use
sustainability were set out as the guiding principles for subsequent land
reforms. Within this policy framework, the government has been pursuing land policy reforms since 2005.

The most important step in legislative land reforms was enactment of
the Organic Law Determining the Use and Management of Land in
Rwanda on September 15, 2005. This law, for the first time in Rwanda,
stipulated that all citizens had the legal right to acquire and use land
through a long-term lease (between 3 and 99 years). Whether acquired
through customary use, obtained from the competent authorities, or purchased, the right holders have the legal right to use the land for residential,
industrial, commercial, social or cultural, and scientific purposes. The
occupants of customary land are eligible for 99-year leases.

The law classified the land in Rwanda into two categories: state land
and individual land. State land has two subcategories: state land in the
public domain (land for exclusive public use purposes and national
reserves) and state land in the private domain (land that can be allocated
to private users, such as vacant land; land acquired by the state through
custom, written law, purchase, gift, exchange, or some other means;
swamps; and land occupied by state-owned forests). The law specified the
management, organization, rights, and obligations related to each category
of land, including land under state control. It created land commissions

from the national to the cell levels,[1] called for a national land use plan, and introduced procedures for allocating and leasing state land.

Implementation of the 2005 Organic Land Law required secondary laws to define the rules, procedures, and institutional details. For this purpose, the government established a task force in 2006 to prepare a set of implementation regulations, to prepare for establishing a land center, and to work out the details for implementing the national land policy. The then Ministry of Environment, Forestry, Lands, Mines, and Water[2] led the task force effort, with support from other ministries, including the Ministry of Local Governments, the Ministry of Justice, and the Ministry of Agriculture.

The task force had a mandate for one year only. In 2007 the Office of the Registrar of Land Titles was created and took over the responsibilities of the task force. Its main objective was to lead the legislative efforts. The government kept the legislative land reforms among its top priorities. Deadlines for drafting secondary legislation were set, civil society organizations were involved at all stages, and international nongovernmental organizations (NGOs) contributed to the drafting process. Consistent top-level support ensured full collaboration from all of the relevant government institutions as well as quick endorsement and adoption by Parliament of the secondary laws and orders. By 2010, a comprehensive set of secondary land laws and orders had been put in place, providing the legal, regulatory, and institutional framework for government operation at all levels.

The institutional framework for the implementation of land reforms has evolved over the past few years to include the following institutions in charge of land administration:

- *The Ministry of Environment and Lands* is responsible for addressing issues of policy, in particular through ministerial orders that set out procedures for the administration, planning, and allocation of land.

- *The land commissions* are monitoring bodies established by a presidential order in 2006. The land commissions operate at the national, Kigali City, and district levels, while land committees operate at the sector and cell levels. These commissions approve and monitor implementation of land administration and land use management procedures and guidelines.

- *The National Land Center* was established in 2008 (its law was enacted in 2009) and combined with the Office of the Registrar of Land Titles.

Its establishment was an important milestone in Rwanda's institution building with regard to land. Subordinated to the Ministry of Lands under a director general, the National Land Center is the main executive body responsible for managing and maintaining the land registry and for overseeing the leasing of state- and district-controlled land. In addition, it is responsible for systematic land titling, development of the national land information system, and development of the national spatial plan.

- *Office of the Registrar of Land Titles* was prescribed in the Organic Land Law and established by a presidential order in 2006. It has responsibility for signing certificates of land titles and long-term leases. It is headed by the registrar, who is supported by five deputy zonal registrars covering each of the four provinces of Rwanda and Kigali City.

- *District land bureaus* are found at the district level, with responsibilities for land use planning and land administration at the district, town, and municipality levels. Administratively answerable to the local authority, they are the public notary for land matters, including the certification of applications for land acquisition, maintenance of the cadastral index maps, and recording of all land to be registered by sporadic or systematic means on behalf of the Office of the Registrar. They are authorized to issue short-term leases and prepare records for issuing certificates of registration and title.

Some laws and orders needed explicit procedures and operations manuals to facilitate their implementation at the grassroots level. Two good examples of this effort are the Operations Manual for Land Tenure Regularization and the Procedures Manual for Expropriation in the Public Interest. Both of these were prepared for the purpose of assuring consistent, transparent government performance at the operational level.

The operations manual was needed because of the recognition that regularization efforts would involve extensive participation of grassroots officials with no previous experience. To guide such efforts, the government created a team to develop a set of operational procedures and standards. An initial draft manual was produced in 2007 with the assistance of a consortium of consultants (HTSPE/Matrix Development Consultant and Premier Consulting Group) in 2007. The government then pilot tested them in four cells, making adjustment as needed through field operations. By 2009, after two years of pilot tests, the operational manual matured into a systematic process, as shown in figure 4.1.

Figure 4.1   Land Regularization Process in Rwanda

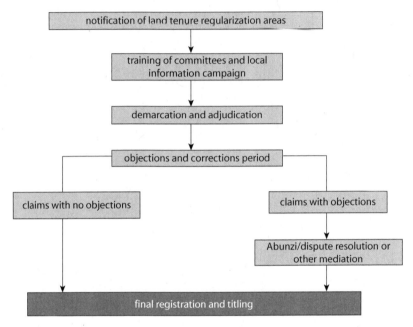

Source: Author.

The manual further sets detailed procedures clarifying who should be involved in what, the activities to be carried out, the specific steps to be taken, and their sequence. All operational officials must follow the nine procedures provided in the manual (see box 4.1).

The procedures manual clarifies areas of ambiguity in the Expropriation Law and offers practical steps to guide implementation of it. It also provides information to people whose land is subject to expropriation in the public interest as to their rights and obligations during the process. The first draft of the manual was prepared in May 2009 and subject to consultation with high-level authorities. The manual clarifies gray areas in the Expropriation Law, especially in Article 5, which lists acts considered as in the public interest. The most important improvement, however, is that the manual provides for monitoring the treatment of displaced persons and ensuring their proper rehousing or relocation, which is a crucial factor that was left out of the law.

By June 2010, up to 90 percent of the legal instruments required by the 2005 Organic Land Law had been enacted, with the remaining secondary legislation in the pipeline for approval and consultation. The biggest remaining challenge is to build the human and physical capacity of the

Box 4.1

Procedures for the Land Regularization Process in Rwanda

1. Notification of areas for a land tenure regularization program
2. Local information-dissemination public meetings and sensitization
3. Appointment and training of land committees and para-surveyors
4. Demarcation of land and marking of boundaries on an image or photograph
5. Adjudication, recording of personal details, issuance of a claims receipt, and recording of objections and corrections simultaneous with demarcation
6. Publication of adjudication record and compilation of a parcel index map
7. Objections and corrections period finalizing the record and disputant lists
8. Mediation period for disputes
9. Registration and titling and preparation and issuance of documents.

Source: Operations Manual for Land Tenure Regularization.

land-related institutions. As the administration and management of land constitute a new discipline in Rwanda, higher learning institutions, together with the National Land Center, are developing programs and research to produce qualified professionals.

Implementing Land Reforms: A Two-Pronged Approach

Designing the legal and institutional framework was a critical process, but the real test of the reforms came at the stage of implementation. Facing the magnitude of the reforms and the lack of resources and experience at the outset, the government adopted a pragmatic, two-pronged approach: introducing secure property rights to all citizens through pilots, on the one hand, and providing focused "one-stop shop" facilitation to fast-track investment projects, on the other. This approach sought to keep the momentum for reform, generate concrete results in a relatively short period of time, and rally public support for more reforms.

Piloting the Land Tenure Regularization Program

The Land Tenure Regularization Program, aimed at providing secure tenure to individual citizens, forms the backbone of land tenure reforms in Rwanda. As mentioned earlier, most land in the country has never been demarcated or registered. The country's high population density and hilly topography have resulted in widely scattered small plots—reportedly some 8 million parcels, of which some face disputes in the postconflict era. The goal of regularization, therefore, would have to be realized through painstaking efforts involving demarcation, adjudication, registration, and many other steps at the grassroots level. The success of such a process would depend on the cooperation among various local partners, including government agencies, civil society organizations, the private sector, and NGOs.

The Land Tenure Regularization Program is under the responsibility of the National Land Center and the Office of the Registrar of Land Titles, with the Department for International Development as the main donor supporter. For the first two years (2007–08), the program focused on the following four pilots, selected for their widely differing land use patterns, tenure situations, and geographic locations:

- *Mwoga Cell*, Mahama Sector of Kirehe District in Eastern Province, a less densely populated part with a high mix of agriculture and livestock farming activities
- *Nyamugari Cell*, Gatsata Sector of Gasabo District in Kigali City, a very densely populated, unplanned semiurban residential area
- *Biguhu Cell*, Ruganda Sector of Karongi District in Western Province, a very hilly agricultural area with high population density and a high rate of polygamy
- *Kabushinge Cell*, Rwaza Sector of Musanze District in Northern Province, a mostly agricultural area with very high population density and strong market orientation.

Using satellite imagery, the pilot project demarcated and adjudicated a total of 14,908 parcels of land in the four cells. The pilot projects built on strong community participation and relied on local capacity, which proved to be a key factor in their success.

The results of the pilot projects were used to design the Strategic Road Map for Land Tenure Reform in Rwanda. This detailed strategic plan, adopted by the government in March 2008, set out an implementation strategy for land tenure reforms in Rwanda. It included a timetable for the full implementation of titling, starting from the resources to be mobilized and the estimated number of parcels to be registered during a four-year program.

The pilot efforts produced immediate success. By June 2010, 1.5 million parcels had been demarcated and adjudicated (Kigali City, 146,294 parcels; Eastern Province, 289,421 parcels; Western Province, 359,654 parcels;

Northern Province, 347,925 parcels; and Southern Province, 384,332 parcels). The Land Tenure Regularization Program has started in all 30 districts, and activities are ongoing in 422 cells that fall within 112 sectors. In each cell, five members of the cell land committee and five leaders of each village have been trained. Disputes have occurred in less than 1 percent of the cases. Formal titles to be issued are being prepared, and the process for issuing these titles has started in Southern Province.

In parallel with the regularization effort, the government has also moved aggressively on improving the registration of property, a function that is under the overall responsibility of the National Land Center. Since 2008, as part of the effort to improve the Doing Business indicators, the government reviewed property registration procedures with a view to removing unnecessary steps and combining others. As a result, procedures for property registration were significantly streamlined. It now takes less than 60 days to register a transaction, compared with 354 days in 2009. This placed the country 38 among 184 countries covered in the World Bank's 2010 Doing Business report for property registration (World Bank 2009). Further, in April 2010, district land officers took oaths as notaries in charge of all land-related matters in land registration, transfer, and ownership; in May 2010, through the prime minister's instructions relating to implementation of the Client Charter on Land Administration and Land Acquisition, the delay for property registration was limited to 30 days.

Beyond the results that have already been achieved through land tenure regularization and land registration reforms, the government is developing a land administration information system. This will contribute enormously to improvement of the land market via digital land registry and transactions, thereby reducing the time required to register and transfer property. Since 2008, Dutch Kadaster has been hired through the Investment Climate Facility to help the National Land Center to develop simple, quick, cost-efficient, and responsive procedures to support the rapid development of Rwanda's land market.

One-Stop Shop Facilitation for Investment Projects

Improving the ease of doing business in Rwanda has been another priority for the government. While the general land tenure reforms continue to move forward, the government has found it necessary to facilitate investment projects within the existing land procedures in order to attract the investment urgently needed for economic development. The Rwanda

Development Board (RDB) was established in 2009 and mandated to assist investors in locating and acquiring land. This is done through a special unit, known as the investors' one-stop shop (OSS). Collaborating closely with the National Land Center and the Kigali Municipality (and its districts), the RDB has adjusted the form and location of the OSS over time in response to business needs.

Initially, the OSS was located in the RDB. Three senior land officers, each representing one Kigali District prioritized for investment promotion, were posted to the OSS. Their responsibilities included receiving and responding to all initial inquiries, hand-holding facilitation for all land-related application procedures, and providing site-related after-care services to investors as needed. However, the land officers had not been delegated power for decision making. All of the land procedures had to be processed by the district land offices and the National Land Center, entailing many signatures, as required by the law.

This initial arrangement provided some useful services to investors, who could now go to one place, the RDB, to obtain all of the information and submit all of the applications needed. However, the time required for processing site and construction approvals took as long as it did before because, after being submitted at the OSS, the processing of the applications continued to move through the normal channel of approvals. This disappointed many investors, who had been promised fast-track results, and frustrated the RDB, which took the satisfaction of investors as a top priority. In the meantime, the district land offices found it wasteful to post three senior land officers in the RDB, where the workflow did not seem to justify their full-time engagement.

In early 2010, the RDB, the National Land Center, Kigali Municipality, and Kigali districts decided to review and readjust the OSS structure for further improvement. An intensive consultation, including consultation with the clients, led to the decision to replace the existing land OSS within the RDB, which essentially served land information and facilitation purposes, with a new land OSS, with power to approve land applications under the coordination of Kigali City. In May 2010, the Prime Minister's Office issued an administrative order mandating the Kigali City land one-stop shop to speed up the process for projects under the following categories:

- Buildings with the capacity to receive at least 100 people a day
- Projects covering an area equivalent to or more than 4,000 square meters

- Business-oriented construction projects (factories, industries)
- Buildings with more than two stories
- Entertainment centers (recreational facilities).

The new OSS was given the mandate to issue deed plans, building permits, occupancy permits, renovation permits, and land titles, with a maximum delay of 30 days. The prime minister's order further required all government officials to implement the client charter in good faith. Failure to meet the deadline would lead to punishments as per the government statute on public service employees.

On May 15, 2010, the Kigali City Construction One-Stop Center was officially launched, with offices in the central district (Nyarugenge). Since its inception, the OSS has issued several working tools:

- Checklists for the investment sector (detailed study, site plan, project brief social and public, commercial and hotels, apartments and real estate, industrial)
- Site visit report forms
- Acknowledging receipt forms.

In line with the commitment to customer care services, the OSS has stepped up the communication effort, creating an online website that posts all of the dossiers required in the construction industry.[3] In addition, the OSS has institutionalized a monthly press conference with associated parties and stakeholders in the construction industry. A weekly meeting is also set up with the objectives of updating, monitoring, and evaluating the ongoing process of issuing permits.

Although it is still in its early implementation, the OSS has shown some promising results. During the first month of its operation, the OSS received 67 project applications, including 23 project proposals, 34 requests for construction permits, and 10 other land- or site-related applications. All of these applications were assessed in a timely fashion. Among these assessed applications, 39 percent of project proposals were approved and 23 percent of construction permits were issued. The OSS held its first monthly press conference in June 2010 and received positive feedback from the clients.

The new OSS is prepared to meet the challenges ahead. As a new establishment, it is acutely aware of the insufficient capacity, especially the technical skills both of the core OSS team and the various district land offices and municipal land use planning agencies whose technical support is required to help the OSS to work better. There is also a short-age of experience and accredited architects and civil engineers in the profession, as well as insufficient public awareness of land use planning and management. To fill these gaps, the government has set specific plans to recruit international experts in the short term, while focusing on aggressive local capacity building with a view to availing a list of accred-ited architects and engineers in the near future. These plans have been backed by secured funds.

Conclusions and Lessons Learned

Rwanda has come a long way since 1994. In November 2009, at a work-shop in Kigali entitled "Africa Land Policy Framework and Guidelines," which was attended by the civil society organizations assembled under International Land Coalition Africa, Rwanda was described as a prime example for all African countries in the implementation of the set guidelines.

To achieve all of the land reforms within a relatively short period of time, many elements have to be united. From the outset, the Rwandan government has held a clear goal for its land reforms: to develop a viable land market based on secure property rights for all citizens. However, at the start of the twenty-first century, the government was aware that, to achieve this goal, it had to begin the reforms almost from scratch, politi-cally, legally, and institutionally.

The strategy undertaken by the government combined the top-down and bottom-up approaches, featuring unwavering political will at the top and extensive engagement of all stakeholders at the various levels of implementation, including the grassroots. The government also followed a disciplined reform path, making steady steps, starting by building a broad policy consensus, followed by swift and comprehensive legislative reforms, which, in turn, were supported by determined implementation through initial pilots and aggressive follow-up. Institutional capacity building was at the core of the reforms at every stage. A dedicated, inno-vative, and pragmatic reform team played a pivotal role in steering the reforms, learning by doing throughout the course.

Institutional collaboration has been very important in all reform areas because the proposed reforms have social impacts that touch on the well-being of the population. The involvement of stakeholders was a key con-sideration right from the beginning, and a bottom-up approach to land reform planning has been adopted as much as possible. In addition,

NGOs, civil society organizations, and donors have been key players in Rwanda's land reform program.

As with all reforms that are of significant social magnitude, the land reform in Rwanda has required a comprehensive communication strategy and sensitization to ensure ownership of the reforms by local government and the population. In this context, starting with a few pilots has helped the government to concentrate limited resources in a few priority areas and to develop an implementation model with demonstration effects.

Through its land reforms, Rwanda has learned that, although it can borrow best practices from other countries, it is a unique country with unique issues. It cannot simply copy the practices of other countries. Instead, it has to find tailor-made solutions that are suitable for its context, while also reflecting international best practices.

Notes

1. A cell is the smallest administrative entity in Rwanda. Rwanda is subdivided into four provinces plus the city of Kigali; it has 30 districts, 416 sectors, and 2,148 cells.
2. The Ministry of Environment, Forestry, Lands, Mines, and Water was created in 2001. In 2008 it was renamed the Ministry of Natural Resources, which was split into two ministries in 2009: the Ministry of Environment and Lands and the Ministry of Forestry and Mines.
3. http://www.kigalicityconstructionosc.gov.rw.

References

Rwanda. 2009. Operations Manual for Land Tenure Regularization. Kigali.

World Bank. 2004. *Doing Business 2005: Removing Obstacles.* Washington, DC: World Bank.

———. 2009. *Doing Business 2010: Reforming through Difficult Times.* Washington, DC: World Bank.

CHAPTER 5

South Africa: Creating Win-Win Solutions for Business, Local Community Development, and Conservation

Lala Steyn

South Africa's history of colonial occupation, dispossession, and racial discrimination is well known. Two and a half centuries of conquest and settlement by European colonists deprived Africans of most of their original territory. Economic and legal instruments excluded African farmers from increasingly lucrative urban markets. Over many decades, the authorities made it impossible for Africans to use land outside the reserves—13 percent of the nation's area—that were set aside for them in the more remote areas. These reserves were consolidated into "homelands," and it was only with the ending of apartheid rule in 1994 that a process of land reform was put in place to address the racially skewed distribution of land.

South Africa's current land reform program involves restitution, redistribution, and tenure reform:

- *Land restitution* aims to restore land or provide alternative compensation to those dispossessed as a result of racially discriminatory laws and practices since 1914.

- *Land redistribution* aims to broaden access to land among the country's black majority, mainly for agricultural purposes.
- *Land tenure reform* aims to secure the rights of people living under insecure arrangements on land owned by others, either the state (that is, communal areas) or private owners.

The origins of many of South Africa's conservation policies can be traced to Western values and ethics as imported by colonists. For example, the Kruger National Park was established in 1926 when the Singwitsi reserve was combined with the Sabi game reserve, which was proclaimed in 1898. The Kruger National Park was managed according to exclusionist principles: the area was fenced off, residents were forcibly removed, and the area was restricted to white visitors. The first game warden earned the nickname Skukuza (which derives from Shangaan to mean the Sweeper) for the way he forced the indigenous inhabitants out of the park in the early 1900s. This was common to conservation throughout South Africa and resulted in a relationship of hatred and suspicion between black communities and white conservation authorities (Reid 2001).

The Makuleke Land Claim and Settlement Agreement

The Makuleke people were forcibly removed from their ancestral lands in the Pafuri reserve in 1969, when the Kruger National Park was extended northward. They were forced by soldiers at gunpoint to set fire to their huts and livestock kraals. The majority Tsonga-speaking portion of the community was relocated to Ntlhaveni in the former Gazankulu homeland, and Venda-speaking members went to the former Venda homeland (Bosch 1999).

In December 1995, the community lodged a land claim to the northernmost section of Kruger National Park. The claim was gazetted in August 1996 by the Land Claims Commission in terms of the Restitution of Land Rights Act. The claimed Pafuri area of the Kruger National Park is an environmental hotspot from a biodiversity viewpoint. During the initial stages of the claim, opposition was forthcoming from conservation circles. Some said, "If the Makuleke claim is upheld in respect of the land within the park, all conservation areas will be under threat" (Makuleke and Steenkamp 1998). These fears have since proved to be unfounded.

After two years of intensive and complex negotiations involving a total of 13 parties and facilitated by land mediators, a settlement agreement was reached in 1999 (see table 5.1). The Land Claims Court ordered restoration of the Makuleke community's ancestral land to the Makuleke Communal Property Association (CPA), representing the 15,000-household community. The restoration of the land was made subject to various conditions aimed at ensuring the protection of both the land's conservation status and the community's rights. The following are key features of the settlement agreement between the state and the Makuleke community:[1]

- The Makuleke community took *legal ownership* of the 22,734 hectares of pristine conservation land through a CPA, representing the community.[2] This section of the Kruger National Park was removed from Schedule 1 of the National Parks Act, because the act does not allow a contractual park on private land in a national park. It was reproclaimed under another section of the act.

- The land is to be used and maintained solely for the purpose of conservation and associated commercial activities in perpetuity, with title deed conditions registered in favor of the state, meaning that the state has the legal power to enforce this condition. The Makuleke have group freehold title and thus have the right to sell, alienate, or encumber the land, subject to it being used for conservation purposes.

- The land was reproclaimed part of the Kruger National Park as a contractual park between the community and South African National Parks (SANParks) for a period of 50 years.[3] After 50 years the parties will decide how to proceed, but the land will have to remain in conservation use.

- A joint management board, consisting of members of SANParks and the community, is responsible for managing the land. SANParks is contracted as an agent by the joint management board to conduct operational conservation management for the first five years. When the five years passed, it was agreed that SANParks would continue for the time being. The joint management board has a management plan that provides the framework for management and development of the area.

- The Makuleke have full conservation-related commercial rights to develop the land with financial revenue accruing to them, subject to the following conditions: (a) no mining or prospecting may occur, (b) no agricultural activities may occur, and (c) no large-scale settlement may occur. Settlement is limited to what is required for conservation-related commercial activities, such as lodges.

Table 5.1 Summary of Rights, Benefits, and Costs of the Settlement Agreement

Rights	Who owns and controls	Restrictions to right
Landownership	Makuleke CPA	Conservation use and associated commercial activities
Land use: agriculture, mining, residential		Not allowed, except for residential when consistent with conservation
Commercial rights	Makuleke CPA	Must be related to conservation
Use of natural resources	Makuleke CPA may use sand, stone, and so forth for building and other approved activities	Joint management board to set policy
Subsurface rights	State retains mineral resources, but mining and prospecting are forbidden	If state policy changes, rights must be offered to CPA at a fair and reasonable price
Land management	Joint management board	Management and development plan; SANParks regulatory provisions governing the park; state environmental regulations
Revenues and costs	Who receives	Who pays
Gate fees	SANParks, may be reconsidered	Visitors
Direct operational conservation management cost for Pafuri area		SANParks for the first five years; thereafter CPA pays up to 50% of costs, not to exceed 50% of net profit
Infrastructure used jointly for conservation management and commercial development		SANParks and Makuleke CPA, at a ratio determined by the joint management board
Commercial revenue, such as from hunting and lodges	Makuleke CPA	
Commercial development costs (for example, infrastructure solely for commercial activities, lodges)		Private sector concessionaire, as determined in contract with Makuleke CPA, subject to various development plans, building plans, and so forth
Development costs of Makuleke community where they live (that is, outside the park)	Makuleke CPA	Commercial revenue and funding from state departments, parastatals, and donors for various projects

Sources: From information in Bosch 1999; Turner 2004.

- No development may occur on the land until an environmental impact assessment has been undertaken and approval of the competent authority has been obtained.

- The CPA is committed to good governance, including using an open tender process to exploit the commercial opportunities.

Throughout the negotiations process, support was provided to the Makuleke by a group of committed social entrepreneurs who formed the organization Friends of the Makuleke. The Legal Resource Centre, a human rights public interest legal firm in South Africa, provided free, high-quality legal services. There was little direct cost to the state because the land was state land already used for conservation purposes. However, the state was willing to relinquish ownership to the CPA in line with its land reform program.

Conservation-Friendly Economic Development: Hunting and Lodges

Since regaining legal ownership of their land, the Makuleke have pursued two main economic activities—hunting tourism and photographic tourism[4]—through which they have generated revenue and benefits for the community since 2000.

The first hunt took place in 2000, with the hunting of two elephants and two buffaloes. An outfitter, who applied to the CPA through an open tender process, organized and managed the hunt. By 2003 the CPA was generating US$231,000 a year from hunting, which was used for school improvements, scholarships for top students, water supply, and food for the poorest families. Once the hunter has taken his trophy, the meat of the animal is distributed in the community.

However, hunting has been controversial because hunting for profit is not allowed in any of South Africa's other national parks. At one stage, SANParks stopped the hunts from proceeding and, driven by animal-rights groups both at home and abroad, public sentiment turned against the Makuleke. When the joint management board could not reach agreement on the types and numbers of animals to be included in the 2002 hunt, the dispute resolution mechanisms in the settlement agreement had to be used, and the dispute was resolved only after an expert had been called in to conduct an investigation, which ruled in favor of the Makuleke CPA (Collins 2003). Nevertheless, hunting did stop eventually and was replaced by other nature-based tourism facilities and activities.

The strategy of partnering with private sector operators was continued, and the Makuleke CPA has entered into two concession contracts with different private sector tourism operators who were identified through an open competitive bidding process observed by SANParks. In each case, the requests for proposals were advertised in the national media, the interested bidders were short-listed against criteria that promoted local economic development, and then negotiations were held with the preferred companies. Throughout the process, the Makuleke were supported at no cost by a well-known legal firm, Webber Wentzel Bowens, and by the Friends of the Makuleke.

To date, some R 60 million has been mobilized in terms of private investment by the two companies, the Outpost Safaris and Wilderness Safaris (Koch 2003). These concessions are build-operate-transfer agreements, as the private operator builds, operates, and then transfers ownership of the lodge to the CPA. At this stage, the CPA can decide whether to operate the lodge themselves or to ask the original operator or a new partner to operate it for them.

The first contract was signed with Matswani Safaris, which built and operated the luxury Outpost Safari Lodge, consisting of 12 stand-alone en-suite rooms overlooking the Luvuvbu River. The 24-bed luxury lodge, which cost nearly US$2 million to build, has a unique design that appeals to a niche market (Koch 2003). Matswani Safaris says that it entered the contract fully as a business and not as a charity. It obtained financing from the Industrial Development Corporation to undertake the necessary development, although the charges were high because of the perceived risk of the venture. It found that the involvement with the community was positive and provided a good marketing angle. Among the 30 people trained to work at the lodge, 1 had the necessary ability to become assistant manager and another, head housekeeper.[5]

The second contract was with Wilderness Safaris, a well-respected lodge operator in many African countries. The planned investment amounted to US$7 million for constructing four lodges with a total of 82 beds. The construction was to proceed in three stages. To date, two lodges and one tented camp for the wilderness trails have been built.

The two concession contracts have the following key features.

The lodge operators (concessionaires) get exclusive rights to build and operate a certain number of lodges of a certain size for a period of 15 years. The concessionaire has sole discretion to extend this, within predetermined limits, for two more periods of 15 years, as long as it is not in breach of a material term of the agreement. Lodges are built in exclusive-use areas, with limited access for specific purposes by others.

In exchange for these use rights, the concessionaire pays the CPA a percentage of gross annual revenue in quarterly installments. In the case of Wilderness Safaris, this is 8 percent, while for Outpost Safaris it is 10 percent. This mechanism was favored above a flat-rate approach because it holds out the potential for more revenue to flow to the community as the business becomes successful and ties the community to the project, thus providing security to the investor. Two safeguards are provided to mitigate the higher risk for the community.

First, the concessionaire immediately paid an up-front guarantee of US$23,077. If the concessionaire does not meet at least 50 percent of the project's annual payment targets for years four and five, this amount is forfeited. If the targets are met, then the CPA has to repay this amount. Second, if the targets are not met, the concessionaire and the CPA must meet and discuss the issue to find solutions, with the concessionaire having to consider topping up its payment to at least 50 percent of the target.[6] A lesson learned from the first contractual community park in South Africa, the Richtersveld National Park, was that using a fixed lease fee not linked to tourism revenue or management cost, while retaining access for community livestock, did not result in either proper conservation of the land or substantial revenues for the community. Furthermore, tying the CPA's share to gross revenues rather than net profits avoids the possible pitfalls related to, or at least arguments about, the accounting methods of the concessionaire. This has been a problem in many such concessions, especially hotels, all over Africa and indeed the world.

The concessionaire must employ Makuleke residents or train them if they do not have the necessary skills, unless they can demonstrate to the reasonable satisfaction of the CPA that no community member has the skill required or can be trained within a reasonable period of time. This guarantees a high proportion of permanent and temporary jobs, including the development of necessary skills for the Makuleke.

The Makuleke agreed to stop hunting in the exclusive-use area allocated to the concessionaires, which is the bulk of the area. It can hunt only in the small adjacent Mabilingwe area for three weeks out of a year at a time agreed to with the concessionaires. This restriction caused concern among some Makuleke, but the hunting concession was very successful in bringing in revenue that was then used for community projects. With the passage of time, however, the nature-based tourism facilities and ventures proved to be a better source of income and employment in the long run. The Makuleke leadership has expressed a desire to diversify business opportunities for their community and is considering other off-park options, such as investing in property or retail franchises.

The lodge development has to be consistent with the management and development plan approved by the joint management board. Environmental impact assessment approval must be obtained. The concessionaires also have to submit the architect's site development plan (including roads, staff accommodation, and other infrastructure) and an artist's impression of the lodge to the CPA for approval before construction can begin.

There is provision for the Makulele to have access to the concessionaires' income and audited financial statements, a performance guarantee in the amount of nearly US$80,000 provided by a commercial bank to mitigate financial loss in the case of breach by the concessionaire, mechanisms for dispute resolution, and various legal arrangements, such as warranties, insurance, and liability.

Institutional Arrangements, Good Governance, and Benefit Sharing

Although the Makuleke are now legal owners of the land from which they had been removed, the legacy of the past means that certain realities have to be taken into account. First, the Makuleke are poor, with 78 percent of households earning less than US$200 a month and a large number dependent on low-wage employment in the Kruger National Park and elsewhere (Reid 2001). Second, tensions between discredited and respected traditional forms of governance, a lack of technical skills and experience, and the inherent difficulties of collective forms of governance make engagement as equal partners difficult. In various other cases of restitution on conservation land, internal conflicts among the customary users, lack of group coherence, and inadequate facilitation and other state support have made development impossible. This has not been the case with the Makuleke.

Since the land claims agreement in 1999, the following benefits have flowed to the Makuleke community:

- About 400 people have received work, of which 80 percent is of a short-term nature.
- 80 permanent jobs have been created in the tourism facilities built and run by private operators.
- Two villages that had no electricity have been electrified, and plans to electrify newly established residential areas for the growing population are at an advanced stage.

- All five schools in the community have received US$7,692 each for improvements.
- Scholarships have been given to deserving students.
- Food has been provided to the very poor.
- The acquisition of skills and knowledge has included (a) conservation training of youth resulting in at least six of them acquiring full-time jobs in nature reserves; (b) leadership training in establishing private sector partnerships and commercial tenders, management, and finances; (c) hospitality and field guide training; and (d) training as cyber tracker rangers to address poaching.
- Small business has been stimulated within the villages—for the construction of guest houses, museums, and lodges.

Deciding on what, where, and how the money acquired through commercial activities should be spent is an ongoing challenge. The development forum, which is made up of representatives from all villages, advises the CPA on how benefits should be made available to the community. This form of consensus building with all sectors of the community ensures that the poorest sections of the community benefit from the new flow of funds and the jobs that are being created. For example, it was decided at one of the forum meetings that money from a trophy-hunting program would be used to feed the 10 poorest families in each village (Koch 2003).

The bulk of money is spent on social development that can benefit as many community members as possible—for example, electrification. Jobs that do not require specific skills, such as manual labor, are allocated through public advertising calling for community members to come forward for a job appointment. A lottery system is then used to select who gets the work. If a person has been given a work opportunity for two years, he or she has to stand aside and give others a chance.[7]

One of the key strengths of the Makuleke case is that a range of strong institutions were formed to perform different functions that have ensured that power is not concentrated in the hands of a few. These institutions have provided leadership, transparency, and accountability and enabled effective decision making. This new system of governance is shown in figure 5.1.

The landholding entity is the Makuleke CPA, which includes elected representatives as well as the chief and has an executive council. It has various subcommittees to address different issues. The joint management board, composed of representatives of the CPA and SANParks, oversees management of the land. There have been tensions between the CPA and

Figure 5.1 Makuleke Institutional Arrangements

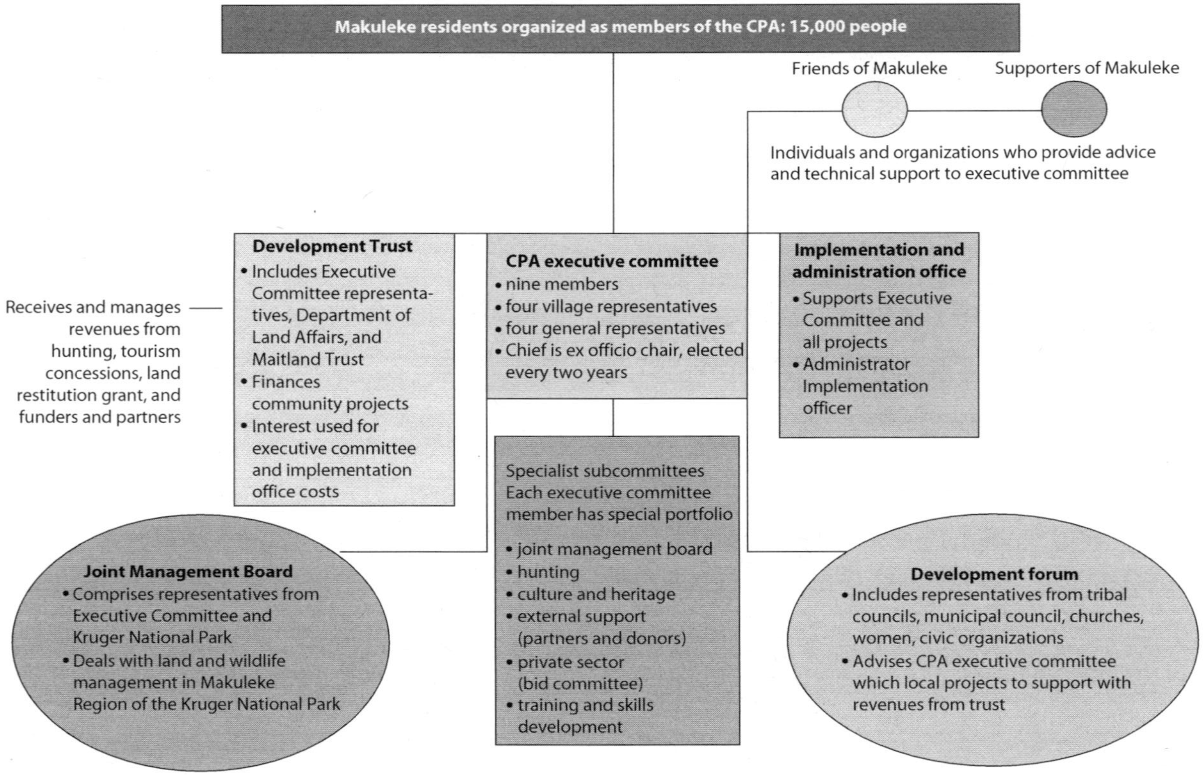

Makuleke residents organized as members of the CPA: 15,000 people

Friends of Makuleke   Supporters of Makuleke

Individuals and organizations who provide advice and technical support to executive committee

CPA executive committee
- nine members
- four village representatives
- four general representatives
- Chief is ex officio chair, elected every two years

Specialist subcommittees
Each executive committee member has special portfolio
- joint management board
- hunting
- culture and heritage
- external support (partners and donors)
- private sector (bid committee)
- training and skills development

Implementation and administration office
- Supports Executive Committee and all projects
- Administrator
- Implementation officer

Development forum
- Includes representatives from tribal councils, municipal council, churches, women, civic organizations
- Advises CPA executive committee which local projects to support with revenues from trust

Development Trust
- Includes Executive Committee representatives, Department of Land Affairs, and Maitland Trust
- Finances community projects
- Interest used for executive committee and implementation office costs

Receives and manages revenues from hunting, tourism concessions, land restitution grant, and funders and partners

Joint Management Board
- Comprises representatives from Executive Committee and Kruger National Park
- Deals with land and wildlife management in Makuleke Region of the Kruger National Park

Source: Koch 2003.

SANParks, which, according to advisers to the community, arose mainly because the change in mind-set on the part of conservation authorities to acknowledge and treat black community landowners with the same respect accorded to other private partners has not gone very deep. Also, views on hunting are very different. But these tensions appear to have eased, as time has passed and experience has been gained on all sides.

A development trust was established to manage the bank account into which the bulk of the money that accrues to the Makuleke is held and from which funds are released for community development. The Trust Act under which this trust exists has long-established safeguards to guard against financial impropriety and to regulate the services of professional trust administrators.

Makuleke community leaders have identified the following key elements in their success:[8]

- Community leadership that has integrity and is committed to the community interest and not motivated by personal gain
- The need for different groups and individuals within the community to work together, which is particularly important when there is success because, if this is not managed properly, fighting over resources can occur
- Transparency and continual consultation with the community
- Understanding of the development process and ability to follow all of the necessary steps
- Recognition that outsiders can play a critical role in facilitating processes where a neutral person or expert advice is needed
- The ability to cooperate despite tensions
- The continual strengthening of leadership through training and skills development
- Acceptance that community expectations of benefits will always be higher than what is delivered and that the leadership has to manage this discrepancy on an ongoing basis.

Conclusions and Lessons Learned

The Makuleke settlement agreement has been hailed as a win-win solution for conservation, land rights, and economic empowerment. The South African government highlighted the Makuleke model at the 2003 World Parks Congress as one of its most successful community conservation and development projects.

Since the settlement, the Makuleke community has undertaken various commercial activities that have generated revenue that has been used to develop and benefit the community. Although it is still early days, the Makuleke have made significant strides toward their conservation and development objectives. Government, nongovernment, and the private sector view this as one of the most successful initiatives of this nature in South Africa. Key factors in this success include a clear legal framework, strong democratic institutions, substantial technical support and skills development, favorable conditions for the chosen commercial activities, and partnership agreements with private sector operators that embody appropriate incentives to produce win-win outcomes.

- The legal framework governing the settlement agreement and the concession contracts is clear, perceived as fair and balanced, and enforceable. The Makuleke CPA has group freehold title to the land and the right to enter into commercial deals, which gives them the legal power to participate on an equal basis with the parks authority and private investors. Land use is restricted to conservation and related tourism use, which provides private investors and parks authorities with the security they need. The legally enforceable concession contracts provide the necessary commercial incentives and community revenues for a private sector–community partnership to work.

- The institutional arrangements include a range of strong institutions, which were formed to perform different functions and where power is balanced. The Makuleke CPA has proven to be cohesive, with committed leadership, avoiding the failure of many other CPAs that have been captured by a small elite group that skews the distribution of benefits. The CPA has managed to balance traditional and democratic institutional forms. The development trust is the key institution that holds and disburses funds. The joint management board brings together the parks authority and the community to deal with conservation management. Although this has been a conflicted relationship at times, it is good to have a joint decision-making body.

- The technical assistance and funding provided by various donors and nongovernmental organizations as well as the development of skills within the community have been essential to the success of the Makuleke development. A range of organizations and individuals, including the Friends of Makuleke, the Legal Resource Centre, and GTZ Transform, have been involved in supporting the Makuleke at no cost to the community. The work of these experts has been funded by various donor organizations. Over many years, technical expertise has been provided to strengthen community institutions so that they can engage with the state and the private sector on an equal footing and not be hijacked by individual vested interests. Skills development programs in the areas of leadership, conservation management, hospitality and tourism, and commercial skills are bearing fruit.

- The Makuleke have adopted a private sector partnership approach to generating revenue and have not attempted to fulfill a private sector role by, for example, establishing a development company. The open commercial bidding process was successful in drawing potential private sector partners. The hunting concessions have brought substantial short-term revenues, and the concession contracts hold the promise of long-term benefits.

Despite its success, the Makuleke case presents some imperfections and challenges that also offer important lessons. To begin with, there needs to be the correct mix between activities that generate short-term revenues and activities that generate long-term revenues. The concession contracts forbid hunting (which used to bring in short-term revenue) in the exclusive zone (the bulk of the land). However, until tourism generates similar revenue, the community is not receiving sufficient revenue. The problem is complex because continued hunting is likely to scare away game, and lack of game viewing will lead to low numbers of tourists and low revenue from tourism. In the Makuleke case, the solution may not lie in trying to balance irreconcilable land uses. With hindsight, other options could be considered, such as having the Makuleke exchange some of their land for an appropriately located game farm where hunting could occur. This could be located close to the Kruger, but not where it would chase away game from the areas where the lodges are located. To ensure buy-in, SANParks should have been a co-signatory to the concession contracts. This would have facilitated them undertaking the necessary conservation management, such as restocking of game.

It should be expected that conflict will arise when benefits start to flow. Powerful elites could take advantage to accrue benefits for themselves. It is essential that the right safeguards be put in place. To this end, a tradition of social democracy has to be nurtured continually, and the strengths of traditional and Western systems need to be matched to the functions required. For example, the African traditional system of collective decision making ensures participatory processes, while the Western system of trusts with outside trustees who exercise financial oversight is critical when distributing benefits. The issue of where revenues are paid and how benefits are fairly distributed should be dealt with in both the settlement agreement and the CPA constitution. It is best to have all moneys flow into the trust and then out for spending on approved development projects. The international experience is that balancing the power of interest groups and individuals within the community and having stringent safeguards in place are essential for good governance. Oversight and support by government and outside agencies should be ongoing to help to ensure that decisions are made in a collective, consultative, transparent, and accountable manner.

The extent of support provided to the Makuleke is unusual in South Africa and has relied on commitment and ad hoc access to donor funding. For the Makuleke model to be used elsewhere, access to resources over the long term to support such expertise is essential. One option would be to establish a facility where similar community initiatives can draw on technical expertise and assistance to facilitate access finance. Such a facility should not involve the staffing of another "development" institution, but rather the creation of an easily accessed source of funds that community groups can use to acquire the expertise they need.

South Africa has strengthened the conditions favorable to tourism development that it inherited and has reaped the reward through increased access to the global tourism market. It has successfully balanced conservation, fairness to and involvement of the communal users of the land, and the economic imperative to make development profitable. It is important to attract private sector partners with an experienced track record and a strong profit motivation—operating under rules and other arrangements that assure attainment of the conservation and fairness goals as well. In the conservation sector there is an element of trophy or philanthropic capital that may be invested for conservation reasons, in the absence of or with disregard for a sound commercial basis. In such cases, tourism uptake could be low, and the ratio of revenue to concession fees could lead to difficulties. Success requires design for the triple-win approach and laws and processes to promote all three objectives. This is not easy, but it can be done.

Notes

1. As some of the claimed land fell outside the Kruger boundaries, some 3,600 hectares were added to this national park.

2. The CPA is a legal entity established by a Land Reform Act passed to create group landholding entities that are able to enter into agreements that will benefit the community without jeopardizing ownership of the land.

3. Most claims for restitution to established conservation land in South Africa are presently resolved on the basis that (a) landownership is given to the claimant community on condition that it remains for conservation use; (b) the land use is determined to be related to conservation and tourism; and (c) some form of management agreement or lease is entered into with the responsible parks authority. The expectation is that benefits will accrue to the community primarily through nature-based tourism.

4. In South Africa an estimated US$77 million a year is earned directly through hunting sales. In 2001 US$5.2 billion was earned from foreign tourism in the category of photographic tourism. See Collins (2003).

5. Personal communication, Matswani Safaris.

6. Personal communication, Webber Wentzel Bowens legal firm.

7. Personal communication, Makuleke community leaders.

8. Personal communication, Makuleke community leaders.

References

Bosch, D. 1999. *The Makuleke Land Claim Settlement Agreement.* Johannesburg: Deneys Reitz Attorneys.

Collins, Steve. 2003. *Optimising Community Benefits from Conservation: Visual Tourism Versus Hunting in the Makuleke Contractual Park in South Africa's Kruger National Park.* Eschborn, South Africa: GTZ Transform.

Koch, E. 2003. "The Makuleke Region of the Kruger National Park: Community-Led Partnerships for Conservation and Development." Unpublished paper used as the basis of a booklet entitled, "Removals, Restitution, and Development in the Our Hearts Are Healing Makuleke Region of the Kruger National Park."

Makuleke, L., and C. Steenkamp. 1998. "The Makuleke Experience." Paper prepared for the workshop on "Land Claims on Conservation Land," International Union for Conservation of Nature, South Africa Country Office.

Reid, Hannah. 2001. "Contractual National Parks and the Makuleke Community." *Human Ecology* 29 (2): 135–55.

Turner, Robin. 2004. *Communities, Conservation, and Tourism-Based Development: Can Community-Based Nature Tourism Live Up to Its Promise?* University of California, Center for African Studies.

CHAPTER 6

China: Shenzhen Special Economic Zone as a Policy Reform Incubator for Urban Land Market Development

Xiaofang Shen and Songming Xu

Shenzhen has been a pioneer of China's significant economic opening and market transformation since 1979. However, one of its most extraordinary experiences has not been fully understood and, at times, has been buffeted by controversies. This is the role Shenzhen has played in China's land policy reforms and urban land market development. Revisiting the zigzags of the particular journey reveals that land policy reforms are politically challenging and that the vision, determination, and pragmatism of the leadership are critical to the success.

The Beginning of the Journey

In 1980, when Shenzhen was designated as one of China's first special economic zones (SEZs), it was an obscure border town in Guangdong Province, with a population of 20,000, mostly peasants and fishermen,

The authors are grateful to many individuals who generously shared their experiences and insights with the authors during the field research trip in 2004.

and a per capita GDP of a miniscule Y 600 (US$150) per year. There were about 20 small manufacturing facilities, and the only major infrastructure was the Kowloon-Canton railway that passed through it. Nevertheless, its designation as a special economic zone was strategic. Shenzhen offered a potentially attractive site for industrial relocation for the export-processing industries of Hong Kong,[1] where a severe shortage of space was causing land values and labor costs to escalate.

To take advantage of this opportunity, however, Shenzhen had to make secured and well-serviced land available to investors. This was a formidable challenge at the time. As with the rest of China, land was constitutionally defined as a resource "solely owned by the public, which cannot be possessed, bought or sold, rented or leased, or transferred in any other forms, by any individuals or organizations."[2] In urban areas, all land belonged to the state; in rural areas, land was "collectively" owned. The government allocated land to state-owned enterprises, organizations, and other social and economic entities following the "three no's" principle—no use fee charged, no time limit set, and no transfer allowed.

Shenzhen also faced a significant challenge in raising the initial capital necessary for infrastructure development. From the very beginning, the Shenzhen SEZ authorities recognized that, to attract export-processing industries, Shenzhen would need to develop, from scratch, adequate industrial and trade infrastructure, including roads, ports, power, and other public utilities. Being a new SEZ, Shenzhen received ample policy support from the central government, but insufficient budgetary allocation.

The urgent need to develop its infrastructure, coupled with a severe shortage of capital, forced Shenzhen reformers to think outside the box, which led them to look at the financial potential embedded in land value. For the first time, land was considered a valuable asset. Shenzhen has 327.5 square kilometers of land, of which 98 square kilometers were suitable for construction purposes. Shenzhen reformers started to ask themselves, Why not offer this valuable asset to investors, who were eager to pay for it, and then use the financial gains for the initial development of infrastructure?

Moving toward State Land Transferability

The proposal by Shenzhen reformers gained the consent of the central government, which decided to treat this idea as an experiment within the confines of the SEZ. The first step was passage of the Provisional Regulations of Land Control in the Shenzhen SEZ (hereafter, the provisional regulations) by Guangdong Provincial People's Congress in November 1981. This was the first legal document that enabled foreign investors to gain long-term land use rights in China. It allowed inves— tors to apply to the SEZ authorities for a land use certificate, which was good for between 20 and 50 years, depending on the sector and activity. It also provided standard land use fees within the SEZ, ranging from Y 10–Y 30 (US$2–US$6) per square meter per year for industrial land to Y 70–Y 200 (US$15–US$42) per square meter per year for commercial land.

The provisional regulations set certain limits on the right to use land. For example, they stated explicitly that the land use certificate provides the right only to use the land, not to own it, and that "it is forbidden to buy and sell land, or to do so in a disguised way, and to let or transfer land without prior permission." The provisional regulations also set time limits for development to take place, as a way to prevent land speculation and to make sure that development would take place as planned. Investors who, absent justifiable reasons, failed to meet these requirements would have their land use certificates revoked.

Although there was now a legal basis for allowing investors to have access to land, the very concept of offering land to foreign investors was groundbreaking in China. Many across the country were highly critical of the idea. As the conservatives in Beijing tried to reign in Shenzhen, Shenzhen officials sought to rebut the criticisms, arguing that, while landownership rights should remain with the state, as the constitution stipulated, usage rights could be made transferrable to private investors (do Rosario 1985).

While this political and ideological tug-of-war continued, there was growing recognition that the challenge Shenzhen faced was a rising problem for the whole country. The new economic opening called for accelerated construction of infrastructure and urban expansion, which meant an increasing need for capital. Many started to question the rationale for maintaining the "three no's" principle for land use, and some even pushed for charging a land use fee. However, the efforts to make domestic enterprises pay for land uses failed miserably because these were state-owned enterprises that were either unwilling or unable to pay for land costs.[3] Meanwhile, foreign investors were looking for construction land, and many were willing to pay.

Steadfastly pursuing market reforms, the Chinese government designated another 14 coastal cities and districts as SEZs in 1984, including important metropolises like Shanghai, Dalian, and Qingdao, as well as the entire island of Hainan. By 1987, all coastal SEZs were allowing foreign investors to lease land from the government, both to accommodate investors' need to access land and to raise capital for infrastructure and real estate development.

Opening the Possibility for Market Competition

Allowing state land to be legally transferred to private investors was a breakthrough toward the creation of a land market in China, but determining how the transfer should take place remained a critical issue to be resolved. From the very beginning, the Shenzhen reformers recognized that land had a market value and that the only way for this value to be fully realized was through market mechanisms. Free land allocation was abolished in 1982 with the Implementation Regulations for Land Management in Shenzhen, but in the early 1980s, China lacked a good understanding of, even less the experience in, market-oriented allocation such as public tendering and auctions. Consequently, all state land transfers to private users were done administratively, based on government approvals and case-by-case negotiations. A minimum land use fee was required, but it was usually much lower than the market value. Frequently, even this small fee was waived, as local officials were anxious to attract new investment projects.

There were several problems with this approach. First, ad hoc project approvals were time-consuming, and decisions were often discretionary because the criteria and procedures were complicated and lacked uniformity. Second, by allowing arbitrary judgments and negotiated deals, the process opened the door for rent-seeking behaviors. Even though Shenzhen made remarkable efforts to simplify administrative procedures in the 1980s and managed to create a government facilitation window to help investors to navigate the process (Wong and Chu 1985), the problem of abuse of power remained and would continue as long as the system continued to make such behavior lucrative.

Finally, the original expectation for raising revenues from land use fees to cover large parts of the costs of capital construction failed to materialize. To develop the initial industrial and export zones, Shenzhen had to invest huge amounts of capital to level the ground; build roads; establish telecommunications, power, and other public utility infrastructure; and construct trade and logistics facilities, including seaports and airports. By the end of 1986, the annual collection of land use fees was only 1.5 percent of the annual government revenue, or 6 percent of the capital investment for infrastructure. These fees did not even cover the interest payment on the money the government had borrowed from the banks. Conservatives, especially SEZ opponents, used this financial imbalance to criticize the Shenzhen reforms.

In October 1986, the Shenzhen government created a task force to push for improvements in the land allocation system, with a view to moving from a purely administrative process to one based on market competition. The group conducted a market study in Shenzhen and invited real estate experts from Hong Kong to share their insights and provide advice. At a seminar organized by the Shenzhen government, Professor Wu-Chang Zhang, dean of the Economics Department at Hong Kong University, pointed out that land leasing fees made up about one-quarter of the annual revenue of the government of Hong Kong, and in some years it was over 40 percent. He used a simple calculation to illustrate his points: if Shenzhen released 400,000 square meters of construction land per year and charged HK$50 (US$6.4) per square meter, it would produce HK$20 million (US$2.6 million) of revenue a year. He then noted that the market price for 1 square meter of construction land in Hong Kong at the time was about HK$10,000. Professor Chang's words silenced the room.

In mid-November, a small group led by the deputy mayor of Shenzhen went to Hong Kong for a 10-day study tour. They visited the government agencies responsible for public land management and urban development, attended seminars and workshops organized by professionals and private sector organizations, and observed public land auctions. By the end of December, the group presented a special report to Shenzhen municipality leaders.

The report argued that, for state land allocation to meet market needs, a system allowing for "open competition" was superior to one based on administrative approval. It further stated that a competition-based system was an effective way to help the government to generate income and recover its capital investment as well as to attract serious investors and shift land to more productive uses. The report also pointed out that market competition would help to enhance the transparency of the system and give foreign investors more confidence in Shenzhen's investment climate. The report concluded by recommending that the Shenzhen government step up the effort to implement competitive mechanisms, starting with pilot programs.

This recommendation was adopted immediately by the Shenzhen government. Preparations for the first public land auction experiment in China, scheduled for late 1987, got under way quickly. Two brainstorming seminars were organized, and central government officials and professionals from other parts of the country were invited to discuss land systems around the world and international best practices in public land management.

On December 1, 1987, China's first state land auction took place in Shenzhen Municipal Hall. A member of the Politburo of the central government, the deputy governor of the central bank, and mayors and senior officials representing 17 Chinese cities attended the event. More than 60 foreign and domestic journalists were also invited to record the historic moment. The land to be auctioned was 8,588 square meters located in the popular Luo Hu (罗湖) residential area and designated for commercial housing development. The use right for the land was assigned for 50 years (later extended to 70 years). The auction was advertised in the newspaper ahead of time and attracted 44 developers, 9 of which were foreign. The gavel used for the auction was a present from the government of Hong Kong, specially ordered from Great Britain.

The auction lasted 17 minutes. The winner was a Shenzhen–Hong Kong joint-venture company, which won the land for Y 5.25 million (US$1.1 million), 2.6 times the starting price. Within a year, the company had completed the construction of a residential complex of 154 units, all of which were sold within one hour of being put on the market, leaving behind a long line of potential buyers.

Introducing market competition to state land allocation has undoubtedly produced greater land revenue for the government. In the 22 months between November 2000 and September 2002, for example, Shenzhen organized 17 competitive primary land allocation events and completed 31 land use right transfers involving 1.68 million square meters of construction land. These transfers resulted in total land fees of Y 5.3 billion (US$641 million). The land fees were, on average, 27 percent higher than the asking prices (Shenzhen Bureau of State Land Resource and Land Use Planning 2002).

According to the Shenzhen State Land Bureau, the benefits extended far beyond revenue gains. Open competition played a critical role in bringing efficiency and transparency to the land management system. In the past, when land transfers depended on negotiation, the process was time-consuming and unpredictable. With no reliable market data, land valuation was extremely difficult. Indeed, many Shenzhen land officials were pleased with the competition-based system because they could finally pass on the valuation risks to the market. The most problematic aspect of negotiated allocation of land, however, was that land often ended up in the hands of those who were well connected, but did not have sufficient capital to develop it. This deprived those who needed land for true investment purposes from getting it to implement their projects.

The private sector clearly benefited the most from the shift to market competition. Business representatives and local media praised the new system, pointing out that serious developers were more concerned about being treated unfairly when a competitor got land at a below-market price than about paying the high price of land on the market. Fair competition was the foundation for market development and the only way to curb "shady" transactions and encourage others to come out into "sunlight," as one local paper characterized it. Thus began what became a popular saying as such reforms later proceeded throughout China: "Don't go to the *shizhang* [the mayor], go to the *shichang* [the market]" (Yan 2001).

Deepening Land Market Reforms

The success of land market reforms in Shenzhen sent a strong message to reformers across the country that land use rights should not only be transferable, but also be transferred through market competition. The initial successes boosted the confidence of legislative reformers at the national level.

In April 1988 the Chinese constitution was amended by the removal of the language prohibiting the leasing of state land and the addition of the statement that "land use rights can be transferred according to relevant provisions of the law."[4] This was followed by a revision of Article 2 of the national Land Administration Law in December the same year, specifying that "the use rights of state and collectively owned land can be legally transferred" and that "the state allows paid use rights to land [by individuals including investors]." In May 1990, the State Council issued No. 55 Order, known as the "Interim Regulations of the People's Republic of China concerning the Assignment and Transfer of the Use Right of the State-owned Land in Cities and Towns" which specified the duration of the use rights based on the type of uses—40, 50, and 70 years for commercial, industrial, and residential development, respectively (Article 12). It also provided that the use rights were renewable, subject to government approval, and could be transferred to third parties and be pledged for bank loans according to the relevant regulatory procedures (Article 4).[5]

Investors considered the duration and transferability of use rights under the Land Administration Law sufficient to meet their basic needs. The new land regime thus laid an important foundation for investment growth in China.

Regarding market-based systems for land allocation, however, despite the success of the first land auction in Shenzhen, it took 14 years for market competition to be legally required as the sole venue for allocating state land. Establishing a market value for land through market competition was still a revolutionary concept for China in the 1980s, and it threatened the interests of many who benefited from the less transparent screening and approval process. Auctions and public tendering also required new market knowledge and professional skills that had to be built up over time.

The milestone was finally reached in March 2001 by Administrative Order no. 100 of the Shenzhen Municipality. The order formally abolished negotiation-based state land transfer for all land allocated to "commercial users," which included commercial housing, office buildings, tourism, trade, and other commercial activities. This order was soon followed by national Administrative Order no. 11, issued by the Ministry of State Land and Resources in May 2002, which required all transfers of state land to commercial users to be conducted through public tender and auction, the so-called "*zhao pai gua*" (招拍挂) principle.[6]

To further promote market-based land transactions, Shenzhen's Administrative Order no. 100 allowed, for the first time in China, "free secondary transactions" of state land use rights as long as the seller paid the full "market price"—that is, the unsubsidized price—to the state. Until this order, although state land use rights were in principle transferable, transferring the rights to a third party required government approval. This change not only eased the procedures for land transactions in the market, but also helped the government to collect more payments for land while encouraging more efficient use.[7]

The next step was to extend the new land allocation principles to industrial land. Up to then, many local governments had offered industrial land to investors free of charge or at much lower-than-market values as an incentive for investment. Research conducted in 2004–06 at both national and local government levels looked into the benefits and costs of such practices, and Shenzhen once again served as a test ground for competitive allocation of industrial land.

In November 2005, the Shenzhen Land and Real Estate Trade Center organized the first public industrial land tendering. The company Xin Ji De (新基德公司) won the land with a bid at 3.6 times the original asking price (Liu and Zhu 2005). In March 2006 the second public industrial land tendering was also a smashing success, with the winning bid nearly four times the originally proposed price (Shenzhen Bureau of

State Land Resource and Land Use Planning 2006). By September 2006, Shenzhen Municipal Government issued regulations on the use of industrial land for bid, proposing that Shenzhen would publicly remise industrial lands (AsiaInfo Services 2006).

By June 30, 2007, the State Council prohibited all state land for any private uses (including industrial) from being transferred through administrative decision or negotiation. This marked completion of the shift from administrative negotiation to market competition.

Implementing Market-Oriented Land Use Planning and Zoning Regulations

In parallel with the land transfer reforms, Shenzhen SEZ also led China in adapting to the Western concept and practice of land use planning and zoning systems that meet market needs. From the very beginning, Shenzhen reformers recognized that the development of an adequate land use planning and zoning framework, coupled with appropriate infrastructure, was critical to attracting investors. Export-oriented investors from Hong Kong were demanding with respect to the clarity and consistency of the relevant laws, regulations, and procedures governing zoning, construction, and environmental compliance. They would invest only if they were assured that the physical environment was secure, predictable, and supported by the infrastructure services they needed (Yeh 1985).

In 1980 Shenzhen, like the rest of China, had an urban planning system designed to support a command economy. The model typically allocated land to various *dan wei* (单位), or production units, such as large state-owned enterprises, government organizations, or other state-owned institutions, which were responsible for providing housing, health care, child care, and other basic services to their own employees. Consequently, each city had a two-tier urban planning structure. First, at the municipal level, urban technicians prepared a broad master plan based on the planned economic needs; then, the *dan wei* provided the details of the plan and implemented it. In theory, *dan wei* plans should conform with the city master plan. In practice, since there was no mandate or legal sanction for failing to follow the master plan, the *dan wei* tended to focus on their own needs and ignore the interests of the surrounding areas in planning and executing detailed land use and construction schemes.

Such a system had a detrimental impact on urban development in China. It led to inefficient land use and disconnected urban patterns typical of many cities. Moreover, the master plans were often prepared in an ivory tower, with beautiful drawings but little connection to realistic needs. Authorities responsible for roads and public utilities often failed to cooperate with each other in planning and maintaining their networks. Most problematic, plans were treated with no respect by politicians, who could order ad hoc changes as they saw fit. A popular rhyme among planners at the time went as follows:

> Planning, planning (*guihua, guihua*, 规划，规划)
> Draw it at the table (*zhuoshang huahua*, 桌上画画)
> Hang it on the wall (*qiangshang guagua*, 墙上挂挂)
> One word from the superior changes it all (*buru zhangguan yiju hua*, 不如长官一句话。).

This kind of land use planning was clearly unable to serve the needs of private investors. Real estate developers from Hong Kong, who were Shenzhen's main initial targets, expressed strong concern about the lack of a regulatory framework and the overriding political influence over land use and urban planning. This was because the values retained in the invested properties could quickly be endangered by ad hoc changes in the surrounding areas.

To give foreign investors confidence, the Shenzhen authorities tried to introduce the Western concept of urban planning and zoning regulations as early as 1981. The SEZ's Provisional Regulations on Land Control, for example, contained clauses introducing the legal concept of land use planning and development control. According to the regulations, the Shenzhen government was mandated to develop a land use master plan, which the People's Congress would pass into law. The plan would be legally enforceable, and politicians would be prohibited from altering it. The regulations further established a land development control system, which required all proposed land development projects to be submitted to the municipal planning authority for approval. Land development and construction without the approval, whether by a public entity or a private investor, would be deemed illegal. Finally, the regulations set specific rules and monetary punishments to prevent environmental pollution by the rapidly growing industries.

These new planning concepts and principles sent the right signal to private investors. However, to implement a comprehensive, market-oriented land use planning system required substantial legal, financial, institutional, and technical support, none of which was in place at the outset. To overcome the difficulties, Shenzhen followed a more pragmatic, phased development planning strategy. The master plan prepared in the early 1980s was never passed into law. It was never more than a policy statement recommending a broad distribution of land uses. The master plan maps were drawn to a scale of 1:25,000 or 1:10,000 and accompanied by a series of special-subject plans developed for infrastructure development, such as power and gas supply plans, communication and transportation plans, and water supply and drainage plans. For the early industrial and residential district development projects, the Shenzhen authorities required the developers (mostly joint ventures) to prepare detailed plans, using the master plan as a general guide, and then to submit them for approval.

Thus, on the surface, the first 10 years of Shenzhen's urban development process were not markedly different from the process being undertaken throughout the rest of the country. Under the surface, however, Shenzhen was undergoing a rapid transformation. Wherever possible, the Shenzhen reformers sought to test and demonstrate the advantages of the new urban development model. One of the most notable examples was construction of the Shenzhen airport. During the planning process, a high-level official attempted to force a shift in the airport's location to Shenzhen Bay, close to the areas reserved for future downtown development. The Shenzhen urban planners resisted this political influence and held true to their original master plan. Their efforts helped to avoid a possible disaster for the city. The Shenzhen reformers also refused to allow the private sector to lure them away from their plan. For example, the Shenzhen authorities rejected a proposal by a well-known investor from Hong Kong to develop a 20-square-kilometer, high-end residential district in Futian (福田) because, based on the master plan, Futian was expected to be part of the commercial center of Shenzhen (Wang 2000).

As the SEZ entered its second decade, it was imperative that land use planning and zoning regulations be regularized. Shenzhen's population had now expanded to several million, and competition for land had intensified significantly. Massive land development by private developers put increasing pressure on the government to have a longer-term urban development vision in order to maintain development momentum. The lack of legal status for the master plan and zoning regulations created vulnerabilities that could be and were exploited; from time to time, influential high-ranking politicians and private developers put pressure on the SEZ to alter its plans to allow for special treatment. Finally, there was rising pressure to coordinate the urban development plans of

Shenzhen and Hong Kong, as their economic development was increasingly interlocked.

In the 1990s, the Shenzhen government accelerated its efforts to reform the land use management system, with a goal of moving toward the zoning regulatory system common in Western countries. The Shenzhen reformers learned quickly, sometimes from their own mistakes. For instance, one of the initial efforts to copy the planning process of Hong Kong did not prove productive, as too much emphasis was put on techniques that were beyond Shenzhen's level of development and could not be supported by its existing legal framework. In the interim, there were heated debates over the appropriate level of detail and degree of flexibility in the master plan, as well as over how to balance rapid yet orderly development. In the mid-1990s, the Shenzhen government sent professional groups to Hong Kong and to Singapore to study how those economies combined planning tools and market forces to support both efficient and sustainable development.

After two years of intensive preparation, the Provisions for Shenzhen Urban Planning were adopted in November 1998 (Schenzhen Municipal Government 1998). This local legislation was the first in China to establish a formal three-tier process for land use planning and development control, with central emphasis on the middle tier, the zoning regulations (*fa ding tu ze*, 法定图则). The document set an ambitious goal of covering the whole city with detailed zoning plans by the end of 2010 by following important principles and procedures:

- At the top, the *master plan*, which contains planning at the city and district levels, reflected essentially a policy and strategic process based on forward-thinking research and development. These plans were meant to provide a framework and general guidance for future zoning regulations and urban designs.
- In the middle, the *zoning regulations* were part of a legal process. They contained not only the technical but also the legal details for urban design. The zoning regulations must be based on both a long-term development vision and short-term market needs, developed through intensive consultation between the public and private sectors. The Planning Commission responsible for preparing zoning regulations was composed of 29 professional members, including no more than 14 government officials. Drafts of the zoning regulations had to be displayed openly to invite public comments and suggestions. Once passed by the People's Congress, the zoning regulations became law and had to be

implemented and respected accordingly. Past legal documents had to be publicly accessible, and there had to be public supervision of their implementation.

- At the bottom, developers were responsible for *project construction blueprints* and detailed implementation designs. All developers were required to comply with zoning regulations when designing the construction blueprints and to submit them to the authorities for approval before construction could start.

The recognition of zoning regulations was significant for China's next stage of urban development. Until then, urban planning was a tool to serve the command economy; moving forward, it became a means to bridge government and market functions. Most important, zoning regulations now had legal status and were no longer subject to ad hoc political interference. As a leading expert summed it up, strictly speaking, zoning regulations developed through the legal procedures and passed by the People's Congress were no longer technical products, but legal products. They should be considered as "the contracts" between the regulators and citizens based on mutual respect and should be publicly supervised to ensure enforcement (Wang 2000).

To support implementation of the provision, the Shenzhen government established a one-stop shop (OSS) to process all land transaction and development procedures in one place. The OSS also provided legal and technical consultation services for its users. With the help of information and communications technology, the government rapidly upgraded its land information system to allow for faster and more accurate sharing of information. The technical and institutional improvement of the city's urban planning system contributed to the efficiency and quality of overall government services and the attractiveness of the investment environment. In 2003 a World Bank study found that Shenzhen had the best investment environment in China (World Bank 2006).

Results: Benefits and Costs

The Shenzhen SEZ may go down in history as the most important and most successful pilot project in China's economic transition and development. Leasing land to domestic and foreign investors played an indispensable role in creating this economic miracle. Shenzhen went from a stagnant, dirt-poor rural area with only 3 square kilometers of land set aside for construction to a city spanning 1,988 square kilometers, about

46 percent of which is construction land. From 20,000, Shenzhen's population has grown to 13 million and enjoys the highest GDP per capita in China (more than US$13,000), thanks to three decades of continuous growth of 15 percent a year. The city is well connected with the rest of China and the world by air, train, sea, and road. The direct trains that run at 10-minute intervals between Hong Kong SAR, China, and Shenzhen are frequently packed with residents of Hong Kong SAR, China, taking shopping trips to Shenzhen.

This transformation has come at a cost. Green space has shrunk dramatically, and urban areas are becoming very congested. At 46 percent, Shenzhen's ratio of construction to total land is significantly higher than anywhere else in China today, including Beijing (20 percent), Shanghai (30 percent), and neighboring Hong Kong SAR, China (25 percent). Land use efficiency also fails to balance out the increasing scarcity of land. One recent study by the municipal government points out that, while Shenzhen's GDP output per square kilometer (Y 0.4 billion, or US$58.4 million) is among the highest in China, it falls considerably short of output in either Hong Kong SAR, China (Y 1.43 billion, or US$208.8 million) or Singapore (Y 1.84 billion, or US$268.6 million).[8]

Even more problematic, the fact that new policies had to be implemented in a fluid and unclear legal and institutional transition resulted in some adverse consequences, including favoritism and hoarding of subsidized land. Based on a survey conducted in the early 1990s, one scholar further argues that, while developers and property investors benefited significantly from land subsidies, local tenants and the local government have not benefited as much as they should have (Zhu 1994).

Despite the early success of testing the market competition models in disposing of state land in Shenzhen, replicating the practice nationwide has been painstaking and slow. It took the national government more than 15 years since the first land auction experiment in Shenzhen to stipulate the *"zhao pai gua"* (招拍挂) principle[9] in law; even then, implementation has been poor. According to national statistics, negotiated land transfers continued to prevail between 2002 and 2005, counting for more than 65 percent of the total state land transferred to private use compared with less than 20 percent using competitive methods (Man 2010). This indicates that reform of China's land market is a long-term process, requiring continuing efforts based on both central government and local government support.

The overall economic impact of Shenzhen's land policy will require more sophisticated cost-benefit analysis that should include not only the immediate impact on the local economy, but also the profound impact on the national economic transformation. From the very beginning, as seen in this chapter, Shenzhen was meant to be a reform incubator for testing difficult policy changes, such as embracing the concepts of private land use rights, land transactions based on market value, and regularized land use planning. As such, some mistakes and even failures over the course were part of the risks that the early reformers had to take. In this context, the significance of Shenzhen's land reform experience goes beyond the immediate economic gains for the city and should include the political benefits for China in its overall economic transition. In other words, the investment was worthwhile.

Shenzhen's government is fully aware of the need to improve its land management system even further. In setting a new strategic direction in 2010, the government called on officials at all levels to think of land in terms of "resources, assets, and capital," or the "three Zi's" (ziyuan, 资源; zichan, 资产; ziben, 资本), and to treat it accordingly. Priority measures are being developed to conserve land, on the one hand, and to maximize its efficient use, on the other. As many in Shenzhen remind themselves today, "The 'miracle' of the past 30 years would not have been possible if not for the adherence to the principle of continuous reforms towards market development" (Shenzhen Commission of Resources and Urban Planning 2010). Shenzhen can sustain its success and continue to lead the nation in meeting the challenges of the upcoming decades as long as it continues to build on these strengths.

Notes

1. This book uses "Hong Kong" when a time period prior to the colony's 1997 return to China is being specified, and "Hong Kong SAR, China," for any time period following the return to China.

2. China Constitution, Provision 10, Chapter I, 1982.

3. Some experiments with the collection of land use fees were carried out in Fushun in 1984–85, but the total amount collected in one year was only Y 20 million to Y 30 million, barely enough to build one overpass for a highway.

4. Amendment One (2) of the Constitution of the People's Republic of China, April 12, 1988. http://english.peopledaily.com.cn/constitution/constitution .html.

5. http://www.fdi.gov.cn/pub/FDI-EN/Laws/law_en_info.jsp?docid=51011.

6. Article 4, Provisions of State Land Divestiture through Tendering and Auction [招标拍卖挂牌出让国有土地使用权规定], Administrative Order no. 11, May 2002, by Ministry of State Land and Resources, Beijing.

7. "Establish Stable, Fair, and Regular Land Market—Interview with Chen Yu Tang (陈玉堂), director of Shenzhen Bureau of State Land and Natural Resource," internal circular, 2004.

8. Shenzhen Bureau of Resources and Urban Planning Bureau.

9. Article 4, Administrative Order no. 11.

References

AsiaInfo Services. 2006. "Shenzhen Makes Progress in Industrial Land Reform." AsiaInfo Services, October 2. http://business.highbeam.com/74/article-1P1-129552300/shenzhen-makes-progress-industrial-land-reform.

do Rosario, Louise. 1985. "Into the Red Zone." *Far Eastern Economic Review* 129 (September 19): 61–63.

Liu, Xiaoyun, and Lei Zhu. 2005. "First Industrial Land Auction Succeeded in Shenzhen, a Landmark of China's Industrial Land Reform." *China Land and Real Estate Journal*, December 26.

Man, Yanyun. 2010. "An Overview of China's Local Government Land-Based Fiscal Situation." *Newsletter of Peking University–Lincoln Institute, Center for Urban Development and Land Policy* (March): 9–18; in Chinese.

Shenzhen Bureau of State Land Resource and Land Use Planning. 2002. "An Update on Shenzhen Land Market Development." Shenzhen Bureau of State Land Resource and Land Use Planning (August 13).

———. 2006. "Review of the Twenty Years of Land Management Reform in Shenzhen." *Journal of State Land and Resources* (国土资源通讯) 19. http://cqvip.com.

Shenzhen Commission of Resources and Urban Planning. 2010. "Further Strengthen the Land Management under the New Situation: Thoughts and Suggestions." Shenzhen Commission of Resources and Urban Planning, Shenzhen.

Shenzhen Municipal Government. 1998. "Provisions of Shenzhen Municipal Urban Planning," *Shen zhen cheng shi qui hua tiao li* (深圳市城市规划条例). Shenzhen Municipal Government, Shenzhen.

Wang, Fu Hai (王富海). 2000. "From Planning to Planning Regulations: The Evolution of Shenzhen Urban Planning." *City Planning Review* 24 (1, January): 28–33. http://www.cqvip.com.

Wong, Kwan-Yiu, and David Chu. 1985. "The Investment Environment." In *Modernization in China: The Case of the Shenzhen Special Economic Zone*, ed. K. Y. Wong and D. K. Y. Chu, 176–89. Hong Kong SAR, China: Oxford University Press.

World Bank. 2006. "China: Governance, Investment Climate, and Harmonious Society; Competitiveness Enhancement for 120 Cities in China." World Bank, Washington, DC, September.

Yan, Mei Rong. 2001. "The 'Two Revolutions' of Land Use System: Bring Shenzhen Land Market into Sunshine Era." *China and International Real Estate Market Journal* [中外房地产导报] 12 (June): 6–9.

Yeh, Anthony. 1985. "Physical Planning." In *Modernization in China: The Case of the Shenzhen Special Economic Zone,* ed. K. Y. Wong and D. K. Y. Chu, 108–30. Hong Kong SAR, China: Oxford University Press.

Zhu, Jieming. 1994. "Changing Land Policy and Its Impact on Local Growth: The Experience of the Shenzhen Special Economic Zone, China, in the 1980s." *Urban Studies* 31 (10): 1611–23.

CHAPTER 7

Arab Republic of Egypt: Simplifying Procedures for Tourism Development in the Red Sea Area

Ahmed M. G. Abou Ali

Organized tourism in the Arab Republic of Egypt dates back to at least 1860 when the British Thomas Cook Company organized tours of the Nile and the pyramids. However, while evidence can be found of the Egyptian state's explicit or implicit promotion of tourism in the 1960s, only in recent decades has the Egyptian government recognized tourism as a pillar of development and a significant source of national income. Since 1988, tourism has become a principal source of Egypt's foreign exchange earnings, accounting for 1 in 10 jobs directly or indirectly (Berkeley Research 1998).

In the mid-1980s, after the appointment of Fuad Sultan as the minister of tourism, liberalization and expansion of the tourism sector were aggressively pursued. Amid serious budget limitations, the need for foreign currency earnings, problems of foreign debt, and a balance of payments deficit, Sultan was asked to provide infrastructure services that would be comparable to those of the tourists' home countries. Under these circumstances, the focus on attracting more foreign direct investment to the sector was a must.

Traditionally, tourism in Egypt was concentrated inside the cultural heritage and archeological sites along the Nile valley, which were administered by the Ministry of Culture's Supreme Council of Antiquities. To expand and upgrade its tourism offering and prolong tourist stays in the country, the Ministry of Tourism (MOT) decided to focus on tourism development in coastal zones. At the same time, studies commissioned by the MOT concluded that the country's northern coast did not have a competitive advantage with respect to areas already developed around the Mediterranean Sea. The Red Sea area, with its rare aquatic life, naturally became a priority development zone.

The Initial Problems

Acquiring a piece of land for a tourism project was not a simple matter back then. It required the potential investor to obtain approvals or secure clearance from several ministries and local governments. These bodies had very different concerns, and there was no mechanism for effective coordination among them. They included the following entities:

- Ministry of Tourism for a preliminary approval for the project
- Ministry of Defense for clearance that the specified plot is not a prohibited military base
- Ministry of Petroleum for clearance that the specified plot is not in an exploration area
- Supreme Council for Antiquities for clearance that the specified plot does not sit atop any monuments
- Ministry of Agriculture for clearance that the specified plot is not part of agricultural land
- The governorate within which the specified plot is located, as governorates generally have claimed the right to approve tourism projects and allocate lands.

Such administrative hurdles proved to be insurmountable for the majority of potential investors. Most went away after spending a considerable amount of time and money without being able to start their projects. As the General Authority for Investment concluded, tourism projects before the 1990s were rare.

The Ministry of Tourism commissioned studies on this problem and narrowed the myriad issues that it had to deal with down to two main constraints: (a) the lack of available land with infrastructure to meet tourism demands and (b) the plurality and conflicts of jurisdiction between the MOT and several other ministries and local governments with respect to project approvals and land allocation. The MOT also suffered from a lack of available funds, overstaffing, low staff motivation, and inadequate technical capability. In addition, rapid development in the Red Sea and South Sinai region quickly led to concerns over planning, zoning, and environmental control. Consequently, the reform measures aimed at developing tourism in the Red Sea area were introduced in light of the following concerns:

- Empowerment of the MOT as a regulatory authority
- Regulation of the use of state-owned land
- Coordination between the various authorities involved
- Observation of environmental standards.

Establishment of the Tourism Development Authority

A significant early step toward liberalizing the tourism sector was the introduction of Law no. 1 of 1973, which assigned overall management of the tourism sector to the Ministry of Tourism. The ministry was given considerable freedom in setting rules and regulations within the sector, as well as the discretion to provide tourism establishments (for example, hotels) with tax exemptions and duty exemptions on the import of essential products. Also in 1973, Law no. 2 gave the MOT the authority to designate areas for tourism development or expansion and to arrange for the provision of infrastructure.[1] For close to two decades, however, the organizational structure of the MOT was deficient. In the late 1980s, with recognition that the government's role in tourism should shift from that of an owner to that of a promoter—promoting Egypt as a place to visit and, more important, promoting Egypt as a place to invest because it is a place where people want to visit, the MOT went through a streamlining process in order to strengthen its technical expertise in support of a private sector–led tourism development strategy.

Although the early efforts to reorganize the MOT led to the establishment of the General Authority for Promotion of Tourism in 1981, the most important step toward institutional strengthening of the MOT was the creation, pursuant to Law no. 7 of 1991, of the Tourism Development Authority (TDA) in September 1991, affiliated with the MOT. As stipulated in Presidential Decree no. 374 of 1991, the TDA's broad mandate is to develop tourism areas within the framework of national policies and economic plans. To that end, it was empowered to make all necessary decisions and procedures, including the following:

- Executing national strategies for the development of tourism
- Determining the priorities of areas selected for development and projects
- Developing plans and detailed execution programs pursuant to fixed timetables
- Preparing, executing, and supervising infrastructure projects
- Promoting private sector investments
- Entering into foreign and local loan agreements
- Managing, exploiting, and disposing of land allocated by the state for the establishment of tourism development areas.

The chairman of its board is the minister of tourism, and board members include experts and representatives of several ministries. The resolutions of the board are mandated to be sent to the minister of tourism within a week from their date of issuance and are effective if no objection is received within 15 days of their delivery to the minister. If the minister objects to the resolutions, the matter is put to the board for a second time, and the board has the power to overrule the minister by a two-thirds majority.

Presidential Decree no. 445 of 1992 confirmed that the land plots allocated for tourism purposes by the Ministry of Tourism prior to 1991 would be considered tourism areas. These plots, which had previously been controlled by the governorates, the New Urban Communities Authority of the Ministry of Housing, Utilities, and Urban Development, or other government agencies, were mostly undeveloped public desert land along the Mediterranean Sea, the Red Sea, and the Gulf of Aqaba, extending 5 kilometers inland from the coast.[2] Their boundaries were determined by the various decrees from the MOT. As the tourism industry gained importance in Egypt's economy, the TDA was mandated to formulate an integrated tourism development strategy. To that end it was given broad responsibility over Egypt's coastal zones, in charge of managing and exploiting these lands with all the rights of the owner.

The establishment of the TDA provided investors with a centralized place to go for available land. Each plot has a specified price in U.S. currency. Investors submit feasibility studies and project plans to the TDA to obtain the approval of the MOT to establish the project. With assistance from donor programs (the World Bank Group and the United Nations

Development Programme), the TDA drew principally on private sector and academic expertise in planning for the development of Egypt's tourism resources and in guiding and promoting increased private sector investments in the sector. Its establishment provided the sector with a stronger institutional framework for coherent, private sector–oriented, and environmentally sound tourism development.

Establishment of Tourism Development Zones

As defined in the Civil Code, all uncultivated lands with no apparent owner are owned by the state. Law no. 143 of 1981 was issued to regulate the management, use, and disposal of such lands. In particular, it defined desert land to be land located outside the city zoning areas by 2 kilometers and owned by the state. However, there was no provision regarding land for tourism development.

The process of creating a coherent and transparent land allocation policy started in the mid-1980s, when foreign investors in the tourism industry started to target their projects at resort tourism outside the traditional Cairo-Luxor-Aswan areas. Acknowledging the near impossibility of achieving its tourism development targets under the existing system of land allocation, the prime minister constituted an interministerial committee to develop a detailed plan for lands in Egypt. The committee submitted its recommendations in May 1987, which set off a power struggle among the various ministries and agencies over control of "their" land.

A long negotiation process ensued over the next few years. First, a set of priorities was determined. Then lands required for military use and operations were set aside, as were areas for agricultural reclamation. One by one, each concerned ministry and agency had to map out the areas considered core to their activities. Based on these priorities, agreements were negotiated between the concerned ministries and agencies, resulting in signed memorandums of understanding. For example, the MOT and the Ministry of Petroleum were able to agree on the specific areas for petroleum exploration and tourism development. Sometimes, new rules had to be imposed by law when it became clear that less powerful instruments would not produce the required outcome. The end results of these persistent legislative and government efforts were a more clearly defined land use plan, including a plan for agriculture, urban development, and tourism purposes, as well as a more streamlined system of land allocation.

The Prime Minister Decree no. 2908 of 1995 (as amended in 2005) set the rules and conditions regulating the management, exploitation, and disposal of the land allocated for tourism development. Tourism lands allocated to the TDA can be exploited either directly by the TDA or indirectly by private investors pursuant to a sales contract or a lease or usage contract. The maximum duration of the usage contract or lease is 25 years, renewable with a new contract and conditions. The decree sets out the conditions for the establishment of such projects, as well as the procedures for the preliminary and final allocation and contracting of the land. Investors must execute the project in accordance with the schedule previously approved by the TDA.

To speed up the approval process for tourism projects, the Prime Minister Decree no. 4248 of 1998 further clarified the procedures by stipulating that the minister of state for administrative development would issue the forms of the required documents, set the fees for the relevant services, and set maximum times for performing these services. Other administrative authorities cannot request other documents or fees and are obliged to perform their services in the specified time period.

In 2001 the President Decrees nos. 152, 153, and 154 were issued, designating the strategic areas for tourism development. These presidential decrees also determined lands reserved for military use, created the National Council for Planning of State Land Use, and initiated the plan to determine the use of state lands through 2017. With these decrees, a system was put in place to resolve the conflicts that arise from time to time in public land management.

Coordination among the Various Authorities

Given the large number of ministries and agencies involved in the development of tourism projects, a key difficulty during the reform process was the coordination among the various supervisory authorities involved in the allocation of land, licensing and registration, and regulation of the establishment and operation of projects. Planning and zoning issues were also a concern.

Regarding land allocation, although there were clearly defined objectives, a common understanding of the issues faced, and a determination of the entities involved to find solutions, there was no defined approach or mechanism for managing the process. Several new legislative and governmental decrees were issued to clarify the roles and responsibilities of each entity, starting with the key Law no. 7 of 1991, which established the TDA and outlined the powers of each authority involved in the land allocation and exploitation process.

Ministry of Defense and Military Production

The location of the Red Sea region on the eastern borders of Egypt mandated a significant role for the Ministry of Defense and Military Production (MODMP) in any development of the region. Although nearly all of the Red Sea areas are designated as desert land owned by the state and controlled by the TDA for tourism development, the MODMP plays an indirect role in the process, as investors must obtain its clearance to proceed with the development. Since these lands had been cleared in advance by the MODMP when they were allocated to the TDA for planning, management, and disposition, there was clearly no legal basis for such a procedure. Indeed, it was the TDA's own board of directors, in the first board meeting, that self-imposed the additional procedure of requiring investors to acquire the MODMP's prior approval for all development projects out of "security concerns." Subsequently, the TDA has attempted to address the delays caused by this extra bureaucratic step through signing a protocol with the MODMP's Operations Unit (*Haiet El-Amaliat*).

The Governorates

Areas within cities, including those on the Red Sea, are outside the mandate of the TDA. They are managed by the local governments, which found themselves deprived of control over their prime coastal lands in favor of the TDA and thus of a potential and major source of local revenues. As a result, they are not enthusiastic about facilitating tourism development processes from which they derive no financial benefits and yet whose service delivery cost they participate in covering. This has been a source of friction between the investors and the local governments, as the latter have the power to impose additional taxes and charges on tourism projects within their localities. Frictions and delays have also arisen when the MODMP has delegated its authority for issuing security clearances for tourism projects to the local governments. A few investors reported that governorates were in reality slowing the development process. One quoted case was the Red Sea Governorate, which reportedly used the power delegated by the MODMP as an opportunity to negotiate with investors a payback deal for local development.

Several regulations were issued to deal with these frictions. One of the efforts aimed at resolving the remaining frictions was the creation of a ministerial investment dispute resolution committee at the cabinet level, with both the prime minister and the minister of local development as members. Despite significant improvement, the Egyptian Federation of Tourism Chambers (EFTC) has called for unification of the supervisory authority within the TDA.

Egyptian General Petroleum Corporation
The Egyptian General Petroleum Corporation (EGPC) is the government agency that is responsible for oil and gas exploration and controls the activities of international oil companies in Egypt.

The TDA and the EGPC have reached an agreement on allocating some areas of the Red Sea coast for the primary development of oil or tourism and some for mixed use. The agreement requires oil exploration companies to carry out environmental impact assessments and to respect the environment. Although not involved in the agreement, the Egyptian Environmental Affairs Authority (EEAA) supports the arrangements and has ultimate responsibility for ensuring that oil and gas exploration and exploitation have no adverse impacts on the marine environment. The EGPC has developed an oil spill response capability in Ras Ghareb on the Gulf of Suez, approximately 100 kilometers north of Hurgada, and is considering establishing another oil spill response station in Hurgada. Petroleum exploration and operation companies operating in the Gulf of Suez are required to have oil-combating capability. But contingency planning, decisional hierarchy, and communications networks are inadequate to provide a rapid and integrated response capability. The available equipment is suitable only for tackling small spills in relatively good weather.

Other Public Entities
Other entities that exercise a direct or indirect influence over the tourism development process include the Ministry of Irrigation and Water Resources, the General Authority of Coastal Protection, and the General Authority for Investment.

Egyptian Federation of Tourism Chambers
As the representative of Egyptian tourism professionals, the EFTC worked closely with the MOT and the TDA in developing a national strategy for the tourism industry. Through constant interaction with the concerned government bodies, including the Office of the Prime Minister, the MOT, and the Supreme Council of Tourism, the EFTC regularly

made recommendations to improve the tourism environment. Regarding land access for investors, the EFTC focused on two key issues:

- Clear determination of city boundaries so as to make land outside the city available for the TDA to develop freely
- Simplification of the procedures for registering land allocated for tourism investment and purchase by private investors. In this regard, the EFTC proposed establishing a registration office for tourism development projects within the TDA.

The proposals made by the EFTC and other private sector entities were rarely adopted immediately, but they influenced the negotiations among the various government bodies involved in the process.

Observation of Environmental Standards

Law no. 4 of 1994 for the Environment created the Egyptian Environmental Affairs Authority. The law aimed principally at (a) enhancing the functions and authority of the EEAA and (b) addressing in an updated manner the issues of land, air, and sea pollution. It introduced the notion of environmental impact assessment as a precondition for licensing new projects whose construction or activity might affect the safety of the environment. It also provided for the establishment of an environmental protection fund.

Before the establishment of the TDA in 1991 and the issuance of Law no. 4 of 1994, environmental standards were not an issue of concern. The environmental impact assessment then became a requirement that the TDA upheld and which the Red Sea Governorate imposed as part of its required clearance for tourism project development. In 1999, supported by the U.S. Agency for International Development and the TDA, the Red Sea Sustainable Tourism Initiative was set up to introduce improved systems and regulations for assessing and monitoring environmental impacts. This led to increased cooperation between the TDA and the EEAA. Between 2000 and 2003, the TDA organized more than 30 national and regional conferences, workshops, and training seminars focusing on sustainable tourism in Egypt. The TDA now plays an important role in guiding developers to adopt high-quality standards in design, construction, and operation. Environmental mitigation measures are legally binding for investors throughout project implementation, and a rigorous enforcement regime is in place.

Nevertheless, tensions exist between the TDA's development role and the EEAA's mandate of environmental and natural resources conservation. Several conflicts have pitted the two entities against one another in coastal areas characterized by rich natural flora and fauna and where development may pose significant risks to the coral reef ecosystem. From the viewpoint of the TDA and some investors, the EEAA's stringent environmental and development regulations at times go beyond what is deemed as technically and financially viable development. The TDA believes that the EEAA's rigid environmental standards need to be relaxed in order to promote further tourism development.

Impact of the Reforms

By increasing the transparency and predictability of the regulatory environment for land access and by reducing the time and cost required to obtain administrative approvals, the reforms that took place in the 1990s had a very positive impact on tourism investors in Egypt. In addition, in accordance with Investment Law no. 8 of 1997, Prime Ministerial Decree no. 1034 was issued in 2002 to encourage the development of integrated tourism projects and provide details of the incentives for such projects. The Red Sea and South Sinai region was a primary beneficiary of these reforms.

From a low starting point, private investment in tourism reached LE 67,535 million (US$15 billion) by 2004, with total employment of 381,995 in the tourism sector. Egypt's tourist capacity as of 2002 was 132,109 hotel rooms, with an additional 102,464 rooms under construction, of which 79 percent is located in the Red Sea and South Sinai area (Egyptian Tourism Federation 2002; Business Studies and Analysis Center 2005). The following are among the major projects that took off during these early years of reforms:

- Sheikh coast tourism complex near Sharm el-Sheikh was a US$100 million complex, fully owned by the Preatoni group of Italy. It consisted of a 300-bed five-star hotel, 150 apartments, and 60 villas. A planned golf course and yacht marina would bring the total investment to more than US$400 million. This resort area already had other established developments with a total of 4,000 rooms.
- Ras Abu Soma complex along the Red Sea coast would eventually be home to up to 13 hotels, private villas, a marina, a golf course, a cinema,

and a shopping area. Development was financed partly by a US$130 million World Bank loan for the tourism sector.

- Sahl Hashish Bay, south of Hurghada on 12 kilometers of the Red Sea coast, was a US$3 billion project that aimed to construct six hotels and 500 villas over the next 10–15 years.
- Orascom Hotels Company launched plans for a US$50 million expansion of the tourist center in Hurghada (along the Red Sea).
- Marsa Alam development, another key development area in the Red Sea, featured a US$1.2 billion project of "Port Ghalib," with a core phase including a marina, three five-star hotels with a capacity of 950 rooms, diving and fishing hotels with a capacity of 200 rooms, and 400 residential accommodations. The development would also feature an airport.

By 2003, a significant portion of Egyptian tourism flow was directed to the Red Sea region, including South Sinai, which captured 54 percent of incoming tourism (Business Studies and Analysis Center 2005). The number of visitors to Egypt continued to grow at the same pace as the country's receptive capacities (see table 7.1).

Table 7.1   Tourism Activities, 1982/83–2000/01

Year	Tourist arrivals (millions)	Tourist nights (millions)	Hotel capacity (rooms)
1982/83	1.4	9.1	21,413
1983/84	1.5	8.7	25,000
1984/85	1.6	9.0	27,023
1985/86	1.4	8.2	287,700
1986/87	1.4	11.8	27,578
1987/88	1.9	15.8	33,663
1988/89	2.1	18.4	36,002
1989/90	2.9	22.1	40,319
1990/91	2.0	16.5	45,385
1991/92	3.0	20.2	46,930
1992/93	2.9	19.0	51,226
1993/94	2.4	13.7	55,763
1994/95	2.8	17.7	58,780
1995/96	3.5	22.8	63,376
1996/97	4.1	26.0	68,000
1997/98	3.4	21.5	75,700
1998/99	4.3	25.7	87,500
1999/00	5.3	34.0	97,000
2000/01	5.5	33.0	105,000

Source: Ministry of Tourism, Al Ahram Center for Political and Strategic Studies.

Tourist receipts were US$3.4 billion in 2002/03, accounting for a quarter of the nation's total foreign currency income.[3] The sector also contributed US$1.6 billion in taxes to government revenue, representing 19 percent of total tax income.

Conclusions and Lessons Learned

Land use in Egypt faces one of the most difficult situations in the world: land and water resources are acutely scarce; archeological and petroleum explorations require any land development to be extra cautious; and there is an overriding concern for security of the national territory. Egypt also has a century-old tradition of bureaucracy that hinders cooperation among ministries and central-local government authorities. It is not surprising that, until the land impediments were effectively addressed, the risk was too high and incentives too low for investors to invest in the Red Sea area.

A strong futuristic vision of the MOT during the mid-1980s, the need to generate foreign currency, and the strength of competition in the region led the cabinet to intervene during the 1990s. The innovative decision to require the key ministries to, one by one, clear areas along the Red Sea coast not under their priority concern has proven instrumental to reaching a cross-ministry agreement on the areas to be used for tourism development. The various indicators of the growth of the tourism sector during the 1990s and following years suggest significant improvements starting in 1989/90 compared to previous years, which coincided with the changes that took place within the Ministry of Tourism and in the regulations regarding project approvals and land allocation. The Egyptian tourism sector has experienced major development, despite several unfortunate events that took place during the 1990s.

Coordination among the various supervisory authorities involved in the establishment and operation of tourism facilities and the reduction in the bureaucracy involved in licensing and registering a tourism facility are among the key factors in the success of tourism development in Egypt and the Red Sea region in particular. The leadership role of the private sector, being the key investor, contributed significantly to the success of the sector.

Despite these improvements, access to land remains difficult in Egypt. Many sensitive factors must be taken into account when new development projects are to be considered, and this requires a further reduction in the bureaucracy and streamlining of the multiple-entity involvement in the procedures and licensing of facilities, particularly at the level of local governments. Continued improvement in coordination between the ministries and local governments will both facilitate private investments and safeguard vital public interests.

Notes

1. The organization of the MOT to fulfill its mandate was set forth by Presidential Decree no. 1951 of 1974, later substituted by Presidential Decree no. 712 of 1981. Subsequently, Prime Ministerial Decree no. 933 of 1988 allocated lands for tourism projects, entrusted the supervision of these lands to the MOT, and mandated the collaboration between the MOT and the Ministry of Housing, Utilities, and Urban Communities within the comprehensive reconstruction and tourism exploitation plan.

2. Law no. 143 of 1981 was issued to regulate state-owned land, which was defined in the Civil Code as uncultivated lands with no apparent owner. Law no. 143 defined desert land as land owned by the state in private ownership that was located outside the city zoning areas by 2 kilometers.

3. Excluding the revenue generated from land sales, leasing fees, and land property tax in the tourism sector, for which no data were available.

References

Berkeley Research. 1998. "Tourism and Egyptian Economic Development." Berkeley Research, Berkeley, CA.

Business Studies and Analysis Center. 2005. *Tourism Sector Developments in Egypt 2005*. Dokki: American Chamber of Commerce in Egypt.

Egyptian Tourism Federation. 2002. *Annual Report 2002*. Dokki: Egyptian Tourism Federation.

CHAPTER 8

Mexico: Revitalizing Baja California via Stakeholder Collaboration

Ray Gordon

Baja California is a long, thin peninsula, very arid, with only two significant cities: Tijuana, along the United States–Mexico border in the north, and Ensenada, about 100 kilometers farther south. The remainder of the long peninsula is primarily rural, with small towns strung along the Trans-Baja highway, the primary north-south route from Tijuana to the southern tip of the peninsula at Cabo, mostly along the Pacific Ocean. The communities range from small fishing villages and resort enclaves of several hundred residents to towns of several thousand people. The main economic activities are fishing, seafood processing, fruit and vegetable farming, aquaculture, wine making, manufacture of construction materials, transport, shipping (Ensenada), and tourism.

In the area immediately south of the city of Ensenada are several small communities with local businesses focused primarily on local service delivery, food production, and construction. Most of the communities depend on Ensenada as the primary urban center.

There are several development constraints in this region:

- The area has an arid, semi-desert climate with limited and only seasonal rainfall. This makes many low-lying areas vulnerable to flash floods during rare heavy rains. Floods frequently damage vital infrastructure such as paved roadways and bridges.

- The central part of the peninsula is mountainous and has limited access on poorly constructed roadways.
- Government has limited funds to construct or maintain infrastructure throughout the region.
- There is a lack of freshwater resources, especially from underground aquifers. Limited precipitation prevents surface water resources from attaining sufficient size—in fact, most rivers exist only as dry riverbeds when there are no storms to feed them.
- Low population densities preclude intensive manufacturing or commercial projects that require a large local workforce.
- Local fish stocks have been overfished, and most indigenous species have been severely depleted.
- Soils are generally of poor quality, and in most locations topsoil is limited in depth and must be enhanced using expensive fertilizers.

Over the last 20 years, the demise of local fisheries and farming operations in Baja California led to significant underemployment in the region. More recently, the worldwide economic downturn has caused a sharp drop in tourism from the United States as well as in the construction of second homes for non-Mexican residents. Unemployment is high, and many agricultural and winery jobs are seasonal, with several months of no work in those industries. An additional problem has been the recent government crackdown on the illegal drug trade throughout Mexico, which has shifted organized crime activities to the sparsely populated Baja region. Local crime rates have skyrocketed, putting a severe burden on Baja government and law enforcement agencies.

The Beginning of an Aquaculture Project

Due to a significant drop in groundwater levels, a berry farm located in this area had to cease operations. The lack of freshwater prevented the continuance of economical farming on the parcels, especially since the location adjacent to the Pacific Ocean meant that saltwater infiltrated the underground aquifers. To find an alternative use of the land that was both economically viable and consistent with the agricultural designation of the property, in 1997 the owners of the property retained scientists and marine biologists to conduct research and studies of the best potential use of the land.

The research took several years and focused on several areas: (1) identifying the marine biology of local indigenous species; (2) determining what animals and plants had lived in the Pacific Ocean near the facility, when their populations declined, and most important, why the species declined or disappeared; (3) studying similar facilities around the world that farmed comparable animals; (4) determining the necessary staffing requirements, including scientists and researchers, and local sources for such specialized staff; (5) studying worldwide market trends for production and consumption of target species, including numerous overseas fact-finding missions as well as attendance at international seafood shows and exhibitions; and (6) drafting a comprehensive business plan.

Based on the findings of the research and discussions with local community leaders, the landowners determined that growing indigenous seafood species would best take advantage of the site's waterfront location and its ample supply of clean seawater. The development of an aquaculture farming facility would revitalize the areas occupied by the abandoned berry farm and provide increased employment and economic activity for the locality. It was also discovered that the local waters were once teeming with abalone, which were taken in numbers large enough to push the local stock to virtual extinction in a matter of decades. Therefore, abalone was selected as the first species to grow at the site.

As the design of the project advanced, it accumulated multiple goals. It started as a private sector business deal; however, it was decided from the beginning that the project would incorporate alternative energy systems, recycle all waste materials, use sustainable products, restore ocean kelp forests, and improve local ocean water quality. Community relations were also important from the beginning. In order to build goodwill toward the project, the owners and managers of the company established strong relationships with local civic leaders representing both local businesses and citizens, such as key business owners, town mayors, town council members, and other community organizations.

Initiated as a private project, the aquaculture development, in the process of obtaining the required permits, caught the attention of local government officials, and a dialogue was established. The government offered assistance at two levels: the central government of Mexico and the state government of North Baja. At the federal level, programs had already been established to stimulate private investment in targeted industries and to create jobs in certain regions, including the promotion of aquaculture farming operations in several viable locations along the Sea of Cortez (sometimes called the Gulf of California, it separates the Baja peninsula from the rest of Mexico), the Pacific Ocean, and the Gulf of Mexico on the country's eastern coast. The subject facility is thus eligible for loans and grants specifically aimed at generating employment in aquaculture projects in Baja California. The state programs, which included research assistance from local universities, were tailored to several locations within the state, both along the Pacific coast and on the western edge of the Sea of Cortez. Through ties of staff marine biologists with local university marine biology programs, the universities assisted in some of the research and provided interns to train at the facility, which led to several former students being hired on a permanent basis.

An additional assistance offered by the government was the ability to develop portions of the waterfront immediately in front of the facility that normally are restricted from permanent private use. This permission was contingent on the project providing local employment while adhering to strict environmental standards for water quality and minimal adverse impact on the marine environment.

Land Use Regulations

There are three primary classes of land control in Baja: private ownership, community property, and federal lands. Private ownership of land is legally protected and historically well established, with records available at local government offices. Several large agricultural and manufacturing parcels are owned by private individuals or companies. The community lands are not owned by any individual, but they are open for use by any Mexican national living in the area. These are usually traditional properties along the waterfront that are used for fishing or small plots of land farmed for food by local families. Federal property includes beachfront property that must remain accessible to everyone and areas reserved for military installations, communications, and ecological preservation.

The land use regulatory environment in Mexico is extensive, but in most cases these regulations can be complied with fairly easily and are not a serious barrier to the successful implementation of privately financed projects. Virtually all regulations are established by state and federal agencies, with their local representatives responsible for inspection and enforcement. Land use disputes, which are mostly the result of long-standing boundary ambiguities or ill-defined access rights of way, are resolved at the state or local level after formal application to the relevant agencies.

For the aquaculture project, the subject site comprises a collection of parcels totaling approximately 3 square kilometers located along a sparsely populated stretch of the Baja peninsula just west of San Quintín, the regional hub for commercial activity. It is south of Ensenada and about 200 miles south of the border with the United States at Tijuana. Immediately to the north and south of this town is a series of smaller communities stretching along the Trans-Baja highway.

The site boundaries for the project were determined based on the requirements set by the original research studies. In addition to the original berry farm, the site included several adjacent parcels that were owned by the berry farm owners, but not used to grow berries. An extensive review of local records showed that the boundaries along the waterfront were not clearly established on existing legal maps and had to be resolved after discussions with adjacent landowners and the local planning department. New land surveys were conducted to ensure that the properties were precisely defined and ownership was clarified with local government.

The project lands were zoned for agricultural use. The development of a commercial aquaculture farm was deemed to be within the allowable agricultural uses. The only special approvals needed were for access across the beach to install saltwater supply lines for the facility.

Project Planning, Design, and Construction

It took the project five years to complete the initial research and planning. The process included topographic surveys of the properties; hydrologic studies; mapping of coastal waters and subsurface conditions by boats and divers out to 2 kilometers offshore; design of staff housing, laboratories, grow-out facilities, reservoirs, water handling, and utility systems; development of procedures manuals for production staff; development of a strategic marketing plan; and development of a staging plan for construction.

The development plan was prepared by the landowners following a dynamic process, evolving as the research progressed. As it became clearer what species would be grown, the focus shifted to what types of grow-out technologies should be employed. When the best system was determined, the final overall master plan for the facility was completed to accommodate those systems.

In 2002, upon the completion of planning, the design and construction of the project facility began. The aquaculture development included some ancillary facilities in addition to the aquaculture farm itself. These facilities included laboratories for research and food supply development within the primary farm property; housing for supervisory and lab employees on an adjacent parcel; large algae ponds for use in naturally purifying wastewater; workers' housing on land closer to the existing town and the major highway; and a processing plant on land adjacent to the town commercial center. The scale of the project was significant, as the main site was a full square kilometer in area. When completed, the project was expected to be by far the largest abalone farm of its kind in the world.

According to the plan, the project was implemented in phases. The first phase of construction (lab, spawning, and initial grow-out) was completed by 2005, and the second phase of expansion (grow-out facilities, seawater reservoir, and manager housing) was completed by 2008. With these, the basic facility was in place. Further expansion is planned in additional phases as revenues increase and additional funding is secured. It is anticipated that all construction will be completed within another four years.

Challenges in Land Development

The local topography presented challenges in project development. Flash flooding during occasional heavy rains and steep slopes often caused difficulties in constructing roadbeds. The procurement of adequate supplies of construction materials and appropriate equipment was difficult, as these were in short supply from local sources. This was solved by identifying qualified suppliers and procuring materials from various sources, both in Mexico and in the United States.

One of the biggest hurdles facing development in Baja California is the lack of adequate utility services. Electricity is generated remotely and is transmitted over a long distance to coastal regions. This limited supply is further hampered by poor maintenance of transmission lines in the region.

To deal with frequent power outages, the facility installed emergency diesel generators on site as a short-term solution. Planning is under way for two types of alternative energy systems: windmills and solar-voltaic arrays.

The project has a significant waterfront composed of shallow tidal areas, gently sloping beaches, large dunes, and several species of fragile flora. The Mexican government's Environmental Protection Agency has jurisdiction over all coastal lands as well as the authority to review and approve adjacent development. On several occasions, environmental officials were invited to visit the site to inspect the work and discuss mitigation measures that were being considered for water intake, natural bio-filtering water treatment systems, and erosion protection. This proactive approach provided valuable feedback on what measures local officials would approve and streamlined the approval process.

Seawater supplies are designed to be recycled to reduce pumping demands and conserve water in the reservoirs. Because freshwater supplies are limited in the arid environment, desalination facilities are planned to provide freshwater for employee consumption and product processing. Waste is treated on site using primary treatment and algae holding ponds before discharge. This system minimizes the impacts on adjoining properties and avoids contamination of groundwater aquifers. Water quality is tested periodically to ensure that both incoming and outgoing seawater meets or exceeds all established standards.

Support from and Benefits for the Local Community

The local population is generally a well-knit community that supports its members even though public facilities and resources are limited. The aquaculture facility was designed to provide a range of employment, from highly skilled scientists to menial workers. Jobs have been generated for biologists, managers, and skilled workers, as well as construction and maintenance personnel. The projected construction program will provide permanent employment for skilled construction crews who will build new grow-out facilities, expanded laboratories, housing, and infrastructure. Facility managers will be responsible for training foremen, who will, in turn, be responsible for developing the skills of the specialized construction and operations crews.

At the same time, programs have been initiated to educate local youth in aquaculture, environmental protection, and the local culture. Parents have been encouraged to take part in the programs, which have been warmly received. A key to the success of these programs has been the active involvement of local residents along with the Mexican managers of the facility.

A housing complex is planned for a parcel immediately north of the main facility. The housing, which will be staged to accommodate the growing workforce over time, will be built in a series of clusters, each with a central area for communal activities. The houses were designed to be environmentally friendly and were built with easily obtained local building materials that local labor could build with no heavy equipment. Solar and wind power will be used along with careful orientation of the structures to take advantage of the cooling effect of prevailing winds.

Conclusions and Lessons Learned

The Baja aqua farm project piloted a new approach to sustainable economic development. After a considerable gestation period, during which extensive background research was conducted to identify viable alternative use of the land resources, an integrated aquaculture facility was established in a rural area of Mexico hard hit by economic downturn, promising to generate important benefits for the region. The Baja aquaculture project, with its strong emphasis on community participation and public-private partnership, provides a potential model for replication in other parts of Baja California. Its success rests on several factors.

Strong political will to revitalize the Baja economy was a prerequisite for the development of this project. Once the local economy began to slow, the government made a high-profile commitment to establishing programs to fund the expansion of select industries, including aquaculture farming. The state and local economic development and planning agencies worked closely with each other to facilitate and fast-track the approval process and program implementation.

The relevant business, land, environment, and other regulations and procedures are relatively transparent in Mexico, with decisions made public via publications and other media outlets. Through early engagement of community representatives along with government regulatory agencies, there was a very good flow of information among the partners. The local planning authority was very forthcoming in providing data for planning purposes and kept good records of property ownership, property surveys, and existing utility services. The general public was kept informed of and involved in project planning and development.

Both the private investor and the federal government made significant funds available for development of the aquaculture facility. To date, the bulk of the project is privately financed, with government loans and grants applied for and pending approval once the program legislation has been formally adopted. Cost management was essential in the early stages of development, as many similar development projects had failed because the initial capital outlay was too large and lagged well behind the starting point of revenue generation. In the case of the Baja aqua farm, costs were kept under control via the establishment of a department to source construction materials and equipment at discount rates through auctions and surplus sales. Incremental, staged development was also essential to managing the build-out of such a large-scale economic development project.

By reconciling public and private interests and by anchoring regional socioeconomic development in viable commercial success, this approach has shown its potential to bridge the various planning, resource, and other gaps. Active collaboration at all relevant stages of project development by local residents, local state and federal government institutions, and the private company investing in the project has permitted the attainment of various goals, including environmentally clean and sustainable development, job generation, education and training, and a better prospect for the future in what was economically a very depressed area. As Baja California and other local communities urbanize, it is expected that the concepts can be applied more widely.

CHAPTER 9

Turkey: Modernizing Land Information Systems through a Stepped Approach

Ali Beba

Turkey is a middle-income country with a population of more than 74 million. It covers a vast area of 800,000 square kilometers and has a well-established land market, with a tradition of private ownership since Ottoman times. Today, privately owned land covers about 45 percent of the country, including most residential and individual farming land. Residential properties in urban areas and farms in rural areas are, for the most part, privately owned. In general, private land and real estate properties can be freely bought and sold in a viable market. The country has a fairly well-developed system of land registration, with deeds registration dating back to the 1840s and cadastre registration dating back to the 1930s. Turkey has never been occupied by other nations, and the government has never nationalized land properties on a massive scale. Therefore, the country has well-kept land records with regard to both plots and owners.

The country also maintains a significant amount of state land (55 percent of the country), often referred to as "treasury land." Treasury land, which can be managed by central and local government agencies, is important to those who want to invest in industrial and tourism sectors.

Access to treasury land is problematic due to the public land management system, which requires dual approvals of both the central and local authorities; the process moves through a cascading structure of four administrative levels: district, municipality, governorate, and central government. Depending on how the land will be used, the approval process also involves multiple line ministries, planning authorities, and infrastructure, environment, and utility agencies. Thus, the red tape involved in accessing treasury land is both "vertical" and "horizontal."

As the country entered the twenty-first century, issues related to access to both categories of land became acute. Regarding private land transactions, the advantages of having a long-established system became disadvantages, as paper-based records had accumulated to such an extent that tracing and verifying information were extremely difficult and time-consuming. Updating the records for transactions, subdivisions, mortgages, and other transfers all depended on tedious manual work, which was slow, costly, and prone to human error. Regarding access to treasury land, available plots were difficult to identify and approvals were difficult to obtain because so many local and central authorities were involved and the paper-based files moved slowly up and down the bureaucratic structure. A business survey conducted by the Foreign Investment Advisory Service in 2001—the Administrative and Regulatory Cost Survey—revealed that land transactions took up to 24 months to complete.

Site development was also a problem, as investors complained about the slow and difficult process of obtaining the various approvals needed. More than 20 public agencies were typically involved in issuing zoning approvals, environment licenses, building permits, and the various utility approvals. All communication was done manually, and there was little sharing of information among the agencies. As a result, investors had to provide the same information multiple times and travel back and forth among the agencies in order to move the application ahead. The process, according to the 2001 business survey, took 15–30 months to complete.

The situation was frustrating not just to investors, but also to the government agencies running the system. Up to 2001, all land records were maintained manually, and agencies spent a significant amount of staff time on tedious extraction and updating of data. Manual labor also carried the risk of errors, loss of data, and discrepancies between the recorded data and the real condition of properties. Moreover, communication among the agencies involved was a major problem. In the Greater Istanbul area alone, a total of 77 land registrar and 21 cadastre offices were in operation, while in the Ankara region, 82 land registrar and 37 cadastre offices were in operation. Information sharing among such a large number of agencies was difficult as long as all information was paper based. Further, the cadastre database was not integrated with municipal physical planning information, meaning that valuable spatial information was not used for multiple purposes, while millions of dollars of government resources were wasted on maintaining duplicate data.

Finally, difficulties in updating and accessing land data meant that governments were unable to monitor and enforce the legal procedures for undertaking property transactions and development. Illegal construction and the sale of property at less than market value were widespread. This meant significant loss of revenue for the government because of failure to collect property-related taxes effectively.

TAKBİS and Its Objectives

In 2001 the government reacted to these problems with a program called Automation Project for the General Directorate of Land Register and Cadastre, known as TAKBİS. The ambitious program aimed at digitizing all land registry and cadastre records and developing a comprehensive land information system that integrated land records, land use planning, zoning, infrastructure, public utilities, and many other types of spatial information that were currently dispersed in different public agencies. Through such a system, the land registrar and cadastre offices would gain the ability to update the legal and geodetic data in a timely, consistent manner. The physical planning, infrastructure, and utility authorities could share the high-precision geographic information and gain a common basis for planning and conducting their work. The end result would be significantly enhanced efficiency and effectiveness of land administration and land use management, as investors, bankers, lawyers, and all citizens would gain easy, reliable access to the multilayered information they needed for business planning, transactions, and development.

Based on the objectives, the TAKBİS design included data for the following tasks:

- Transferring land ownership
- Managing the environment

- Supporting emergency services
- Planning new towns
- Facilitating new sector development, such as industrial zone, agricultural businesses, tourism, and minerals exploration
- Administering land taxes
- Planning and managing utility services.

First Pilot Implementation: Çankaya and Gölbaşı (Ankara)

The TAKBİS project faced serious financial constraints from the outset. According to the feasibility study, the total cost for developing and implementing the TAKBİS system for the whole country was an estimated US$100 million to US$120 million, reflecting the vast territorial coverage, procurement of hardware and software, training of staff, and installation and operation of the system. Although the program was expected to generate new income and become self-sufficient by 2015, the initial cost was beyond the capacity of the General Directorate of Land Register and Cadastre (GDLRC), which is the leading authority for TAKBİS.

Several other important hurdles had to be overcome to get the project off the ground. In 2001 the open sharing of information and comprehensive institutional cooperation were still novel concepts for most government ministries and agencies whose participation would be crucial to the success of TAKBİS. The sheer number of the potential participating institutions, including more than 600 land registrar and cadastre offices across the country and more than 50 specialized public agencies at the central and local government levels, indicated a daunting need for coordination and cooperation. Finally, the general level of computer literacy was low in most government offices, requiring a huge amount of training.

For all of these reasons, the GDLRC decided to take a stepwise strategy, focusing initially on a few pilots carried out in prioritized districts in Ankara, the capital of Turkey. Such pilots would allow the government to use its limited resources to create a showcase relatively quickly, to test an operational model, and to learn from the experience. Once proven successful, the model could then be improved and extended to other regions of the country.

The first pilot chosen was Çankaya District of Ankara, with US$7.25 million in funding support from the GDLRC. Çankaya District has seven operations offices—five land registrar and two cadastre offices—with 60 staff. These offices are responsible for land and cadastre registrations for a population of more than 1 million, covering 135,000 parcels and 20,000 buildings.

Çankaya was chosen as the first pilot because of its strategic locality. This is where the Presidential Palace, almost all ministries, and most administrative headquarters are located. Also, it is physically close to the GDLRC and to the Ankara Regional Directorate of Land Register and Cadastre (RDLRC). Moreover, the district has both urban and rural characteristics of a rather typical Turkish settlement, with mixed types and styles of construction and land use. By starting the national project in this district, the GDLRC hoped to gain experience and use it in evaluating other regions with similar characteristics.

By focusing on the pilot, the government was able to move relatively quickly. The GDLRC started the conceptual planning of TAKBİS in May 2001. By October of the same year, it had selected and reached an agreement with a state-owned, military-based software company, HAVELSAN, for development of the necessary software. It was agreed that the GDLRC would have the overall responsibility for financing and administering the TAKBİS project, while HAVELSAN would have full responsibility for developing, debugging, and implementing the TAKBİS software. HAVELSAN was also accountable for implementing the project on a national basis.

Between October and December 2001, a technically strong expert group consisting of computer specialists, mapping engineers, and land and cadastre office personnel was devoted to investigating and selecting the most appropriate software technology for implementing TAKBİS. Before the end of 2001, this process was completed, and the technology systems were selected. For the next six months, the expert group focused on developing specific software by making intensive use of modern technologies, including general packet radio service and three-dimensional mapping. This software included the Land Register Application, Cadastre Application (Annex 3), Project Follow-Up, and Resources Management programs, among others. By June 2002, the necessary software development was completed, and the available data were digitally integrated into the TAKBİS system. Between June and December 2002, existing raw (physical) data were digitized at Çankaya. In the meantime, a second pilot, targeting the Gölbaşı District of Ankara, was chosen, and its preparation following the TAKBİS model was actively under way, led by the Gölbaşı RDLRC.

One major task during this period was to convert the paper records into digital forms so that they would be ready to be loaded into the

TAKBİS system. All of the physical folders were bar coded for efficient and reliable digital scanning. The bar-coded archive data were loaded into the TAKBİS system between December 2002 and October 2004 at both the Çankaya and the Gölbaşı RDLRCs. During this process, two procedures were followed in order to ensure accuracy:

- *Integration of land register data with cadastral data.* Cadastral data were cross-checked against land register data. By this process, missing pieces of data such as sections of maps and plans of different scales were identified, and these gaps were filled with data from up-to-date maps.
- *Internal integration of cadastral data.* Hard copies of cadastral data were compared against digital registers at the directorates and also against TAKBİS data.

Hard copies of the maps were computerized using the software entitled RASTER. This computer program is widely used for digitizing maps through high-precision scanning.

Approximately 30 staff members in each directorate were trained to implement these operations. The training was delivered by the GDLRC and HAVELSAN. Data were screened and entered by at least two trained personnel. A special protocol was designed and implemented for data entry.

To ensure high quality and a smooth process during data entry, the GDLRC formed an expert team for the task under its supervision. All data entered were backed up daily, weekly, and monthly. These backups were sent to the GDLRC for safekeeping.

Initially, the efforts focused on harmonizing land registry and cadastre information. The five land and two cadastre offices were connected to each other through an online system. They all used the same database, which was also installed in the GDLRC. Thus, any changes made in any one of these offices were immediately recorded in all other offices as well as at the GDLRC. This allowed the GDLRC to have a very reliable record-keeping system that was updated regularly. The system tracked and checked out all of the transactions by the name and code (*chifre*) of the transacting expert, thus reducing to a minimum the level of human error.

Presently, TAKBİS is fully operational at both the Çankaya and the Gölbaşı RDLRC offices.

Expanding Implementation of TAKBİS to Istanbul and the Rest of Turkey

In 2002, following the launch of the first two pilots in Ankara, a third pilot began in the Kadıköy District of Istanbul. Like the other two pilots, Kadıköy was selected because of its social and economic significance. It is located in the center of the megalopolis of Istanbul, being one of the oldest and yet fastest-growing districts for the last 25 years. It thus faced the greatest growth challenge as well as the strongest commercial, social, and environmental pressure.

Again, the GDLRC provided overall supervision and support for implementation of this pilot, and HAVELSAN provided the technology and know-how in support of implementation. Making use of Çankaya's experience, Kadıköy was able to implement its program at a much faster pace, despite its size and economic complexity. Within one month, the computers and the necessary hardware were acquired; in the next four months, entry of physical data was completed. The project became fully operational in about six months.

Unlike the first pilot (Çankaya District of Ankara), which received significant funding support from the GDLRC, the Kadıköy pilot in Istanbul was required to cover its own costs from the outset. The initial software development and implementation for this pilot cost more than US$200,000, which was covered mainly by the local RDLRC offices drawing from their transactional revenues. There were significant additional costs due to training and other implementation needs. All in all, budgetary constraints imposed a constant challenge, and the implementing agency struggled to measure implementation of the pilot against its financial resources.

As of 2006, the pilot stage was completed and, due to financial constraints, the system was put in operation in only three RDLRC offices. Thus, the pilot project could not be extended fully online during its first year in all of the RDLRC offices in Kadıköy, as was originally planned. In the following year, the local administration intervened and allocated the necessary funds from its own resources, allowing the project to be fully implemented.

The initial success of the pilots in both Ankara and Istanbul gave the government of Turkey more confidence in the system model. In 2002 the government launched the Central Population Administration Information System (MERNİS), aimed at modernizing the public administration of land in the entire country. Since then, TAKBİS and MERNİS have become the two basic public projects that are used as the foundation for developing a comprehensive electronic government system.

In 2002 Parliament passed a decision launching national implementation of electronic government projects, including TAKBİS. With this political and legal commitment and support, TAKBİS has been implemented rapidly throughout Turkey. Today, the system is operational in all 81 provincial centers of Turkey, facilitating 30 cadastral register directorates, 437 land register directorates, and three cadastral land register offices. In the course of implementation, the government gradually eliminated the use of different software in different regions and directorates and standardized land application procedures across the country.

Stakeholders' Participation: The Key to TAKBİS Design

The participation of multiple institutions is the key to the successful implementation of any land information system around the world. TAKBİS is no exception. From the beginning, TAKBİS aimed to interconnect approximately 50 national and local authorities in different sectors:

- Municipalities and their agencies, responsible for urban planning, local tax collection and audits, infrastructure, and utilities
- Ministry of Economy, responsible for treasury land (publicly owned land)
- Ministry of Agriculture and Rural Affairs, responsible for agricultural planning
- Ministry of Public Works and Settlement, responsible for public works
- Department of Transport, responsible for roads and railways
- Ministry of Environment and Forestry, responsible for forests and environmental protection
- Ministry of Industry and Commerce, responsible for land expropriation for industry and commercial zones
- Ministry of Culture and Tourism, responsible for land for cultural and tourism activities
- Ministry of Energy and Natural Resources, responsible for decisions on building dams and energy activities, including transfer lines
- Mapping services institutions
- Ministry of Justice, responsible for land disputes settlement
- Banks, telecommunications services, corporations, small businesses, and other private citizens who need land-related information to locate

business sites; ensure property security; undertake land transactions, including loans and mortgages; pay proper taxes; and make payments on bills for a specific site.

Like other places where such an ambitious system has been implemented, initial resistance from the various agencies was inevitable. In the case of Turkey, the political commitment from the top (the parliamentary decision in 2002) played a critical role in pulling together the institutional buy-in essential to the system's implementation. In addition, the system was carefully designed to support this objective. Although implementation of TAKBİS was led by land registrar and cadastre authorities, the system's design from the beginning emphasized the flexibility needed to enable as many participants as possible to join the network.

Based on the design concept, the responsible agencies were asked to digitize maps and make them available for the system. The system then integrated all digitized information, creating a database containing full and detailed geographic, topographic, and hydraulic information important to development planning and investment site selection. Further, the system allowed the inputting of all information related to properties, including the history of ownership, mortgage, allotted portion, and type of permitted development, all of which used to be recorded in separate and often inconsistent manners but now were captured in the same network and could be retrieved quickly when needed.

The new harmonization of the various government functions has helped to remove many of the problems previously faced by investors, who, in the past, had to spend a significant amount of time and energy traveling from agency to agency collecting information and applying for the various approvals. Now those interested in land permits in Turkey are likely to obtain reliable, up-to-date land data fairly quickly from any of the cadastre offices where the TAKBİS system is fully operational. These offices act like a virtual "one-stop shop." Also, since these offices are integrated electronically with the permitting authorities at the municipal level, investors can download and complete permit procedures online without physically traveling to the various offices.

Initial Impact of TAKBİS on the Investment Climate

TAKBİS has brought significant benefits to the investment climate as well as the overall land management system in Turkey. It has improved the efficiency and transparency of land transactions and saved a tremendous amount of duplication for both clients (that is, investors and all citizens) and responsible agencies alike.

In Çankaya, for instance, the volume of work more than tripled from 2004 to 2007. The processing for a normal land transaction used to take two to four months; it now takes less than one week. Moreover, the system has improved the service quality, produced close to 100 percent reliable data, and reduced the costs for clients by about 50 percent.

In Kadıköy, likewise, land registration is significantly faster and costs are lower than a few years ago. Clients used to wait three days to one week for information verification, but now they can have the data on the same day. Investors and citizens also stressed that the legal process for settling land disputes is now much easier, since they can gather and cross-check data in a more reliable environment and within a shorter period of time. The system also contains security mechanisms that allow the disclosure of information only to real persons or their authorized representatives.

The benefits to the government agencies are as obvious. In most places where TAKBİS has been implemented, the time allocated for unit operation is considerably shorter. Under the manual system, an officer could handle 20–30 transactions a week; now an officer can handle around 100–120 transactions a week. Before TAKBİS, officers had to work overtime to deliver the paperwork; now all of the work is managed online during office hours, with no more need for backup work and overtime payments to the staff. Furthermore, the system has significantly reduced the room for human error.

Computerization of land information makes it possible for agencies to share information quickly. With the help of the information network, urban planners can access more accurate land data; infrastructure agencies can coordinate better with each other in planning and construction; tax authorities can better monitor revenue collections and track illegal transactions; disaster control agencies can quickly determine victims' needs and design rescue actions; and agencies responsible for environment, forestry, and tourism resources, among others, are in a better position to make informed decisions when carrying out their duties. The list of beneficiaries is almost endless.

Finally, the system has helped to improve the coordination between the central and local government authorities, including national, provincial, municipal, and district. Publicly owned and managed land—treasury land—has been registered with precision. Its allocation is much more streamlined, more transparent, and time-efficient. Land revenues for the government are better collected and tracked.

Despite these achievements, implementation of TAKBİS continues to encounter several difficulties:

- Staff training is a major problem because staff turnover is high. Each new staff member needs to be trained on how to use the TAKBİS system and the associated software before being given the authority to use it. In general, roles and responsibilities of staff change frequently in local and central governments in Turkey. Staff are frequently rotated from one duty to another, and there is always a need for training. In addition, those who become highly qualified are often attracted to the private sector, which offers higher compensation.
- The dependence on a computerized system means that errors in the information technology system can cause serious interruptions of the operation.
- Long waiting times are sometimes required in processing land applications when data need to be corrected, since this can no longer be done by individual actions but must follow much stricter procedures set by the regulatory requirements.

Conclusions and Lessons Learned

Piloting provided a pragmatic solution to initial financial resource constraints. It allowed the government to jump-start implementation with initially limited resources and experience. It reduced the costs and risks of initial learning. For example, Çankaya made subsequent implementation in other cities much easier, less costly, and, as seen in the case of Kadıköy, much faster.

The section of technology must be carefully investigated by a group of experts coming from different disciplines, including computer software specialists, three-dimensional mapping and global positioning system experts, and municipal and land register officers. Software design should be flexible, allowing additional information to be input as it becomes available and allowing the system to expand into large territories and to incorporate more participants.

Finally, and most important, political leadership and institutional buy-in are the keys to overcoming the institutional challenges in the system applications. In Turkey, during the inception phase of TAKBİS in 2002, the decision was made at the parliamentary level, which allowed the development of a legal framework for TAKBİS together with MERNİS. The decision to move toward electronic government was based on the realization of these projects in the whole country. Without the parliamentary decision, the implementation of TAKBİS would not have been possible.

CHAPTER 10

Vietnam: Improving Access to Land for Small and Medium Enterprises

Ivan Nimac, Stephen B. Butler, Huong Mai Huynh, and Lan Van Nguyen

The gradual liberalization of the economy in Vietnam, including access to land for the private sector, emanated from a major policy decision taken by the central authorities in 1986, which recognized, for the first time, the importance of the market in driving economic development. The enduring motivation was to develop Vietnam into an industrial country quickly. The policy to implement this objective, known as *Doi Moi*, or "renovation," was broad and transformed the Vietnamese economic space during the two subsequent decades.

Nevertheless, the reform of the processes associated with business access to land reflects an incremental approach. The sensitivity of land both as an ideological icon and as a valuable and relatively scarce resource warranted caution. The *Doi Moi* reforms in land policy were carried out through successive revisions of the Land Law in 1987, 1993, and 2003. Each revision represented further liberalization of the legal framework for land without altering the basic principle that the state, as representative of the people, owns the land.

The 1987 Law on Land placed agricultural land in the hands of households. By creating the conditions for permanent and stable use of land, it provided a legal basis for land use by smallholders. One of the sought-after policy consequences of the new land regime, which was observed in succeeding years, was that persons granted the new, secure land use rights had a much greater tendency to invest in their land, resulting in higher productivity.

Whereas under the 1987 law, the operation of the land market was under state management, the enactment of the 1993 law brought the private market further into the picture. It introduced, among other things, the ability to transfer land use rights legally, including by lease and mortgage.

The 2003 law, which remains the most comprehensive legislation to date on the allocation and use of land in Vietnam, formalized the property market further by providing a clear definition of the land regime and the authority of the state in land markets. It sought to achieve three main public policy objectives: encouraging investment and economic development, emulating the efficiency of a true land market within the restriction of state ownership, and maximizing the use and value of land.

Increased Focus on Small and Medium Enterprises

In 2006 the government was concerned that, despite more than 15 years of reforms, there was an ongoing lack of clarity in land use rights, an absence of market-oriented long-term leases, and continuing problems in the use of land as collateral by investors. A 2003 study on informality in Vietnam found that 80 percent of the small and medium enterprises (SMEs) surveyed would expand if land were more readily available (Tenev and others 2003). Very large swathes of land in the major cities were occupied by state-owned enterprises. In an environment of rapidly increasing numbers of SMEs, demand for land was not being matched by availability. Access to, affordability of, and security of land were inhibiting the overall development of the local private sector.

In response, the International Finance Corporation (IFC) initiated the Business Access to Land program with the objective of assisting the government in preparing for the next set of land policy reforms. Over a period of four years, the program progressed from diagnostics, to solution design, and, subsequently, to implementation of legal and administrative reforms in order to strengthen the regulatory environment concerning business access to land. As most previous work on land in Vietnam had concentrated on the primary market (government-held land) and had not given sufficient attention to the issues facing SMEs, the IFC program focused on the experiences of SMEs, the main drivers of employment and growth. The program aimed to produce measurable changes, including a reduction in time and costs for businesses to access land with secure rights and a shift from informal to formal land transactions and investment.

Land Access Problems Facing SMEs

At the request of the Ministry of Natural Resources and Environment (MoNRE) and with its active collaboration, the IFC conducted a survey in August 2006 in 12 provinces[1] in order to understand the constraints and to benchmark land access practices, covering three types of entities:

- SMEs (50 in each province for a total of 660 enterprises) that had recently acquired land
- Intermediaries (5 to 7 in each province for a total of 70 intermediary organizations) that provide brokerage or equivalent services to SMEs acquiring land
- Officials of the regional Departments of Natural Resources and Environment (DONREs; 3 to 5 in each province for a total of 40–50 officials).

The survey results presented a mixed picture regarding achievement of the objectives of the 2003 Land Law. Some of the objectives were being advanced, including development of an active secondary land market, a sense of secure land rights, useful forms of land tenure, and a generally good perception of land rights registration as a beneficial administrative practice. Moreover, land administration was considered to have improved since adoption of the law. It was also found that there was a great deal of investment in land improvement and construction across all forms of land tenure, but particularly in connection with the freehold-equivalent right of long-term and stable use frequently held by SMEs.

At the same time, the results suggested that the scarcity of land for the development and expansion of businesses was a serious constraint to further development, especially among the growing number of SMEs; the market mechanisms were underdeveloped; and certain land administration procedures—in particular, allocation of state land to businesses and registration of land rights—were considered to be administered inefficiently. It was furthered determined that, although more than 70 percent of the SMEs obtained their land rights in secondary market transactions, a significant number obtained land directly from provincial and local governments.[2]

The study concluded that the SMEs would be well served if (a) the development of the secondary market could be facilitated by improving land transfer and registration procedures and (b) the supply of land could be expanded by improving the process of land allocation and by making it more welcoming to SMEs.

Implementing Land Policy Reforms

A workshop for multiple stakeholders was co-organized by the MoNRE and the Vietnam Chamber of Commerce and Industry (VCCI), representing the private sector, to discuss the results of the study and their implications for reform of land policies. The findings led to the formulation of reform proposals in many areas related to the efficiency of land administration procedures. These included implementation of competitive procedures for land allocation, land use planning and zoning, land valuation and pricing, simpler administrative procedures and better interdepartmental coordination at the provincial level, and development of monitoring and evaluation systems.

After consultations with government officials and other stakeholders, it was ultimately decided that two areas of work—administrative simplification at the provincial level and further development of the Land Law at the national level—would be pursued. This decision was strongly influenced by the enthusiasm of the provinces, many of which were cognizant of their rankings under the provincial competitiveness index,[3] and encouraged by the early success of the ongoing efforts to simplify business entry. It had also become clear that there were limits on what could be achieved in subnational policy reforms so long as national laws needed further refinement. Continued work at the national level on land legislation, therefore, would ensure greater local success in adopting the proposed reforms.

Legal Reforms

The emphasis on legislative development was timely, as the government had put on its agenda a comprehensive review and modification of the Land Law by 2011. This would be done under the guidance of the MoNRE and the drafting committee that it chaired, which had representation of other public agencies and policy institutes. In 2008, however, the government decided to prepare a set of interim amendments to the Land Law for immediate adoption. This approach was not unusual, given that the government had consistently sought to make small improvements, while at the same time keeping an eye on the larger, long-term picture. The interim amendments would not be a substitute for the longer-term plan to undertake a comprehensive revision of the Land Law, which would still move forward on the original schedule; rather they would attempt to address pressing problems in the short term.

The amendments as prepared by the drafting committee led by the MoNRE took up many IFC recommendations:

- Simplify state land valuation procedures and the definition of market value
- Clarify the land use planning responsibilities of the four levels of government (national, provincial, district, and communal)
- Eliminate dual agencies for registering the rights to land and constructed property
- Expand grants of long-term, stable use rights by waiving land use fees and clarifying the rights of business firms to acquire land use rights
- Clarify the right of citizens to resolve land disputes in court once administrative remedies had been exhausted
- Eliminate the need to have the local people's committee sign off on issuance of each land use right certificate (LURC).

However, the draft amendments also contained provisions that caused concern among some stakeholders, including the IFC. For example, the proposed amendment sought to make the government land recovery operations easier by reducing the time needed to move people from the land and by establishing cash payment as sufficient compensation for the taking of land. The proposed amendments also established rules for creating local land development corporations with wide-ranging powers to recover and hold land for long-term economic development purposes.

While it was a well-intentioned rationale, the introduction of these provisions was controversial. Cash compensation at market value would in many cases be inadequate to provide replacement housing for the landholder, as the supply of housing was small and the replacement cost of housing could well be greater than the price that would be paid for the land. In most areas little or no government-owned housing would be available. Simply delivering a substitute residential land site to the land-owner would be very problematic, as temporary accommodations would be required while replacement housing was being constructed. None of these halfway measures could provide satisfactory solutions to the prob-lem of residential resettlement.

The use of land development agencies is also a complex issue. Simply delegating state powers to quasi-public corporations will not solve the problems encountered today with land recovery. There should be some concern that these land funds at the local level might take too much land and monopolize the market, squeezing out private sector investors in land development. They may waste public resources by speculating in land and land development. They will not necessarily improve the treat-ment of citizens in land recovery or advance social interests such as affordable housing, as they have few incentives to do so, and it is unre-alistic to think that, by turning over state functions to independent corporations, the state will be insulated from criticism for poorly con-ducted land operations. The unregulated proliferation of land funds could exacerbate, not solve, current problems.

At the consultative workshops organized by MoNRE and the National Assembly's economic committee, the IFC shared concerns about the risks associated with these provisions. It also raised the land use planning issues, which the current amendments failed to address.

In late September/early October 2008, the government decided to postpone the submission of amendments to the National Assembly until 2009. This decision came after concluding that the amendments failed to resolve several key issues regarding the planning system, pricing, and land funds and that the drafting team needed to analyze the issues further and study international experience and lessons. In June 2009 the National Assembly issued a resolution requesting the preparation of comprehen-sive amendments to the Land Law by 2011,[4] and the submission, there-fore, was once again deferred to allow for additional research on planning, resettlement, and compensation policies related to land recovery.

Administrative Reforms

Since 2005, the provincial competitiveness index produced jointly by the VCCI and Vietnam Competitiveness Initiative has attracted consid-erable attention from provincial governments. Despite the strong interest in reforms, however, many local authorities lack the tools or methodol-ogy to implement reforms. This prompted the more reform-minded officials in some provinces to seek assistance from development agencies on overhauling their existing business regulations and procedures. In this context, while work on the legal framework was taking place, some provincial governments requested IFC assistance with efforts to simplify and reengineer their land processes.

Based on the level of interest expressed by local leadership, pilot programs were launched in Thua Thien Hue Province, Bac Ninh Province, and later in Binh Dinh Province, focusing on improving interdepartmental coordination on land matters and simplifying administrative procedures for business access to and use of land. This effort was built on the prior diagnostics, which showed that interdepartmental coordination and administrative procedures were key constraints to business and a concern of local officials.

Due to the complexity of administrative procedures for accessing land and the number of authorities involved, many of which have a vested interest in maintaining the status quo, the first step in each locality was to create a task force of senior officials with decision-making powers to guide and drive the project. These task forces included the directors or deputy directors from all key authorities involved in land allocation. In each province, the task force worked on a reform proposal, with assistance from the IFC. The task force then submitted the reform proposal to the Provincial People's Committee (PPC) for approval. After approval, with technical support from the IFC, the task force developed the approved proposal into a legal document. This legal document was in the form of a local regulation or statute on the procedures for interagency coordination and was reviewed for legality by the Department of Justice. Finally, the legal document had to be submitted to the PPC for issuance.

The research and analyses involved in this process were detailed and painstaking. They began with in-depth interviews with stakeholders, that is, businesses and staff of relevant agencies. Taking account of the information gathered about how the procedures for access to land actually functioned, which often differed from official documents, the procedures for businesses to access land inside industrial zones, district-level industrial areas, and parcels outside of the formal zones were mapped. The mapping included the steps needed for identifying land and for obtaining investment certificates, land allocation decisions, LURCs, construction permits, and environmental clearances.

These assessments were far more detailed than those done in the earlier study, looking not only at the "external" steps and procedures that an investor would see, but also at the "internal" steps and procedures that were taken to process applications within the responsible provincial agencies. Information was gathered about the institutions overseeing the procedures, the local legal basis for the procedures, the detailed process of the procedures including assessment criteria and tools, and requirements of the application, including fees and charges. The resulting detailed process maps provided a basis for identifying unnecessary or even counterproductive administrative constraints that could be simplified or removed.

The detailed study showed that accessing, registering, and improving land was a complex, time-consuming process involving between 8 and 11 sequential umbrella procedures under which there were many subprocedures related to investment approval, site selection, environmental clearance, land grants, and construction permits. It took investors approximately 200 days to complete the administrative process as well as 40 visits to and 20–30 interfaces with different authorities. Investors had to prepare 60–70 types of documents due to overlapping requirements and appraisals.

In addition to duplicative documentation and review requirements, the low level of information provided to potential investors and the limited availability of written guidance, particularly at lower levels of government, also contributed to the long delay for completing the land application process. This meant that direct consultation and verbal instruction on the procedures were the rule, with investors frequently being required to revise applications after submission.

Reforms that were designed on the basis of these analyses at the provincial level were presented to the Office of the Government of Vietnam, the central body that is leading a national administrative reform initiative—locally known as Project 30 (named after Decision 30 by the prime minister). Given the IFC's strong engagement in the land regulatory review during the first phase of its program, as well as its efforts to reengineer and streamline the administrative process for obtaining approval to access land in the three pilot provinces, the IFC was selected to lead the Land-Construction Working Group of the Advisory Council of Administrative Procedures Reform, which was charged with recommending regulatory improvements and providing follow-up implementation assistance on procedures in the areas of land access and construction.[5]

Results and Next Steps

Between 2006 and 2010, the IFC Business Access to Land in Vietnam program adopted a systematic approach to analyzing and finding solutions to the problem of investor land access in Vietnam. Through this program, a large amount of information was gathered that the government could use as baseline data for its ongoing reform efforts. These data serve as important monitoring and evaluation benchmarks against which improvements made through new processes can be measured.

On the legal front, the government has made several important improvements to the land-related legal framework. The government enacted Decree no. 84 in 2007,[6] pursuant to the 2003 Land Law, which directly increased investor confidence in the land market. Among other things, the decree clarified the concept of "stable use," a highly desirable form of land tenure.[7] The decree also stipulated compensation and dispute resolution procedures related to government acquisition of land.

In 2009 the government adopted a unified real property registration system,[8] which includes rights to both land and structures. Previously, Vietnam operated a divided registration system in which land and objects attached to land were registered separately by different agencies. This is not uncommon in transitional countries, but it is inefficient and places an unnecessary burden on citizens. The adoption of the universal legal concept, which establishes that objects constructed on land are legally presumed to be the property of the holder of the land right, is a significant step that simplified the registration process and conforms to international best practice.

Working toward drafting the new comprehensive Land Code, the government is focusing its efforts on reviewing resettlement and compensation policies, including local and international best practices, and on implementing the unified registration system, among others. Further consultations will be undertaken to achieve optimum results with the new Land Code.

On the administrative front, concrete progress has been made at the provincial level. On the basis of considerable preparatory work over one and a half years, the PPC of Bac Ninh Province issued a decision on November 27, 2009, to implement simpler land approval procedures.[9] This regulation reduced the time required for investors to complete the entire land access procedure by 27 percent (from 151 to 110 days), the number of visits to government departments by 66 percent (from 36 to 12), and the number of documents required by 46 percent (from 62 to 33). Figure 10.1 provides a quick snapshot of the process before and after reforms in Bac Ninh.

Benefiting from the experience in Bac Ninh Province, the PPC of Binh Dinh Province replicated the reforms over a period of eight months

Figure 10.1 Land Approval Procedures in Bac Ninh before and after Reform

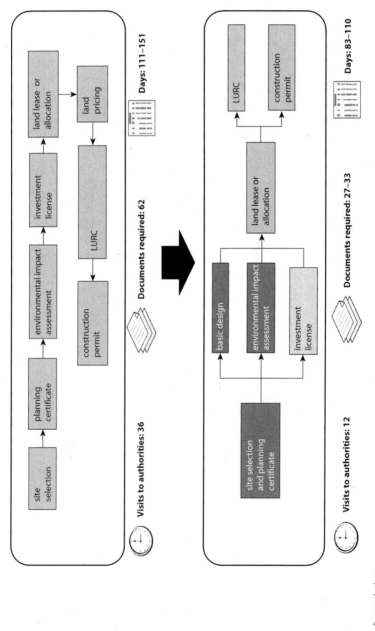

Visits to authorities: 36

Documents required: 62

Days: 111–151

Visits to authorities: 12

Documents required: 27–33

Days: 83–110

Source: Authors.
Note: LURC = land use rights certificate.

and issued a similar decision on April 8, 2010.[10] The procedures for obtaining access to land for investment were greatly simplified, with the days required reduced from 209 to 112 (46 percent), the visits to authorities dropped from 36 to 20 (44 percent), and the number of documents required halved from 57 to 26 (54 percent).

With the new regulatory framework in place, the task forces in these provinces are working closely with the IFC to ensure proper implementation of the new regulations. This includes the training of staff from related agencies and the distribution of informational material to investors.

The demonstration effect of these changes is likely to be large. As one effort to make this happen, the methodology for the work piloted in the three provinces is being developed by the IFC into a manual to facilitate replication of similar reforms in other provinces of Vietnam.

Conclusions and Lessons Learned

Several lessons were learned from Vietnam's experience with land reform. The most important lessons of a policy and operational nature include the following:

- Influencing policy and legislative development in a sensitive area such as land relations, with many vested interests and potential conflicts between economic best practice and strongly held views on social and intergenerational equity, is a long-term process that requires development of credibility, continuous engagement, and participation of all key players.
- Developing relevant data, accompanied by well-planned dissemination, consultation, and advocacy, is an effective way to gain credibility and get a seat at the table in policy development.
- Changes in administrative processes also affect vested interests and can take a long time. Practically every component of an administrative process appears rational and necessary to someone who benefits from it. At the same time, most processes can be made more efficient by meticulous analysis of the details. Small, focused changes in the short run may create the perception of progress, diminish opposition, and lead to greater change over time.
- Success of subnational reforms may depend on the scope of discretion of subnational governments under applicable laws. Long-term progress may require changes at the level of national legislation as well as efforts

of local governments to devise management solutions within the constraints of the law.

Land policy is one of the last major areas for ongoing legal and economic reforms in Vietnam. Constant reform efforts have been made to create efficient mechanisms within the constraints of state ownership of land. The market that exists still fails to satisfy all participants, but it appears to be developing at a reasonable pace, improving business access to land.

Notes

1. They included Bac Ninh, Binh Dinh, Binh Duong, Hoa Binh, Lam Dong, Lao Cai, Long An, Nghe An, and the cities of Ho Chi Minh, Ha Noi, Can Tho, and Da Nang.
2. Only a small portion of SMEs obtained land in state-sponsored industrial zones.
3. The provincial competitiveness index is the result of a major collaborative effort of the U.S. Agency for International Development–funded Vietnam Competitiveness Initiative and the Vietnam Chamber of Commerce and Industry. This index is computed annually to rank all Vietnamese provinces according to certain indicators of their business climate and receptivity to investment.
4. Resolution no. 31/2009/QH12 by the National Assembly, dated June 17, 2009, about the national agenda of legal and regulatory development for the period 2007–11.
5. The IFC is a key member of the Advisory Council of Administrative Procedures Reforms, which is headed by the head of the Office of the Government and started to operate in September 2009.
6. Decree no. 84/2007/ND-CP, dated May 25, 2007, offered additional regulations on granting LURCs, withdrawing land, determining the order of and procedures for compensation, supporting resettling residence, and settling complaints on land.
7. In Vietnam, all land is owned by the state, while individuals, households, enterprises, institutions, and registered legal organizations—foreign and domestic, private or state owned—have rights to use the land. All land users must obtain a current validation of their rights (formalization), including an LURC and entry of the right in the land register. Many preexisting land rights, particularly those of individuals and households and those for residential and agricultural land, are recognized. Enterprises that hold land rights under prior laws may also be legally entitled to some or all of the land they occupied

before adoption of the Law on Land. Many of these preexisting rights are characterized as long-term, stable rights of use.

8. Law no. 38/2009/QH12, dated June 19, 2009, of the National Assembly of Vietnam modified and supplemented several articles relating to basic investment and construction: Construction Law no. 16/2003/QH11, Bidding Law no. 61/2005/QH11, Enterprise Law no. 60/2005/QH11, Land Law no. 13/2003/QH11, and Housing Law no. 56/2005/QH11.

9. Decision no. 165/QD-UBND.

10. Decision no. 159/QD-UBND.

Reference

Tenev, Stoyan, Amanda Carlier, Omar Chaudry, and Quynh-Trang Nguyen. 2003. "Informality and the Playing Field in Vietnam's Business Sector." International Finance Corporation, World Bank, and Mekong Project Development Facility, Washington, DC.

CHAPTER 11

Hong Kong SAR, China: A Case of Developing a Land Market Based on Long-Term Leasing

Chung-min Pang

By any measure, Hong Kong SAR, China, is one of the most prosperous and efficient economies in the world. Its post–World War II development has made it one of the wealthiest and most important financial centers in Asia. It has had no problems in attracting foreign direct investment, and business confidence in the territory is high, as reflected in the many multinational corporations that have set up their Asian headquarters there.

This success could not have happened without a workable system to provide private businesses with the land they need for industrial, commercial, and residential uses. Given the shortage of naturally flat land and, recently, high population density, land is an extremely scarce resource. Therefore, a good system for accessing it is even more important than might be the case in larger, geographically more diverse places.

Even before the developments of the last 160 years made land such a scarce resource, the government was forced to pay attention to land policy. In the early days of the British Crown colony, the British government made it plain that the territory was expected to pay its own way. Looking for sources of revenue, the Crown colony authorities naturally saw the sale of rights to land as a prime source of revenue that could not be neglected. Unlike many nations, both developed and developing, land policies never took a back seat in government policy making. They were never neglected or permitted to evolve accidentally.

The system of land administration has gone through substantial changes and faced many challenges over the past 160 years. Since its initial establishment, the territory has expanded twice, first adding the Kowloon peninsula and then the New Territories. On each occasion land was acquired in a different form. This plus some early ad hoc tactics led, among other things, to a proliferation of leasehold periods, from 75 years to 999 years!

More recently, uncertainties arose as a result of political and economic turmoil: the chaotic years of the Cultural Revolution on the mainland; the economic crisis of the early 1980s, which led to the establishment of a currency board and the pegging of the Hong Kong dollar to the U.S. dollar; the initial negotiation for the return of Hong Kong to China; and finally the change of sovereignty in July 1997, which coincided with the Asian financial crisis. As we shall see, the ways in which the authorities dealt with all of these challenges were crucial to the success of the framework for accessing land in Hong Kong SAR, China, and provide valuable lessons for other places, even though their situations may be quite different.

Land Access under the Crown Colony Regime

The British seized Hong Kong Island by force in 1841. It was formally ceded to them under the Treaty of Nanjing in 1842, ratified in 1843. The British Crown then became the legal owner of the island. By this time, land had already been sold by the local British administration, land had been sold by Chinese residents to foreign merchants without a proper land registry, and British merchants had started building without official approval. To prevent the situation from getting out of hand, the occupying authorities announced in May 1841 that land was only to be rented out and not sold freehold. This was accomplished by public auction, with allocations going to those bidding the highest annual ground rent. Nonetheless, purchasers were led to believe that, subject to approval by the British government, the land they leased would eventually be sold to them.

Upon ratification of the Treaty of Nanjing in1843, land sales that had already taken place were declared null and void. However, full discretion was given to the island's first governor to handle those sales as he saw fit and, in particular, to take action as necessary to cure these sales so that the interests of those who had purchased land and built on it would be protected. The authorities also declared that no ground rent would be claimed for the period up to June 26, 1843. Thus began what would be a consistent policy of protecting the interests of private land rights, even if changes in the system needed to be made.

Eventually, the British government decided that land would not be sold outright but would only be leased, with the period of the leasehold fixed at 75 years where land was required for building and at 21 years where it was not. Lease renewals were at the discretion of the government. While the failure to offer freehold sales was a disappointment to the merchants, it did not appear to discourage them from purchasing leases, bidding high rents, or constructing buildings.

In 1848 the colony was hit by its first recession. This led to vigorous lobbying by local merchants for a reduction in their ground rent. In this, they were supported by the governor. However, British authorities in London held the view that a reduction in rents arrived at by auction would be unfair to the unsuccessful bidders and proposed instead that the term of the leases be extended. In December 1848, leaseholders were informed that their 75-year leases would be extended to 999 years!

Starting in 1851, some modifications to the system were introduced that continued to favor the lessees. Ground rents were no longer fixed at auction, but were set by the Crown Surveyor; bidders for a given parcel paid a one-time premium that was set at auction. Lessees were given the right to subdivide their lots and to sublease portions of their land. Given the very long life of the leases and the fact that purchasers were bidding a one-time premium, rather than the ground rent, the leasing of land was effectively transformed into freehold transactions. The right to subdivide and transfer a portion of one's leasehold land further consolidated the quasi-freehold nature of land transactions and gave leaseholders great flexibility and control.

When the British were granted a perpetual lease to Kowloon in 1860, the same principles were applied to that land and a number of 999-year leases were granted in the early years. However, a Land Commission appointed in 1886 found the 999-year leases to be "ill-advised." Future leases were to be limited to 75 years. In response to the protests that followed this recommendation, the British government made the concession of agreeing to the renewal of leases for one further term of 75 years on their expiry.

These changes in land administration coincided with negotiations for the lease on the New Territories. Since this overall lease had a life of only 99 years, it was obviously not possible to grant individual leases in the New Territories under the same terms as those prevailing in Hong Kong Island and the Kowloon peninsula. A new approach was required, not least because of the already resident and much larger population in the New Territories.

A survey of the area mapped every field and house. A Land Court was set up to confirm landownership and adjudicate disputes. The New Territories was divided into 477 demarcation districts, for each of which a Block Crown Lease was issued. If a resident established his title to the satisfaction of the Land Court, his particulars were entered into the schedule for the Block Crown Lease opposite the lot number allocated to his piece of land, and a lease was issued to him for 75 years commencing on July 1, 1898, with a right of renewal for a further 24 years less the last three days, on its expiry. Thus, after July 1, 1898, all granting or transfer of leases was for 75 years less the time already elapsed since that date.

For nearly a century thereafter, this standardized land use regime underpinned the rapid development of the economy.

The Transfer of Sovereignty

As 1997 approached, the question of the expiring lease on the New Territories loomed ever larger. Clearly, this issue had to be addressed properly if businesses were to have the political and legal certainty they required to continue conducting their business in the territory. Britain's concern for Hong Kong's long-term economic prosperity and the part that land played in ensuring such prosperity was one of the key motivations for Britain initiating negotiations with China over the future of Hong Kong. This is clearly illustrated in paragraph five of the introduction to the white paper published by the British government on September 26, 1984:[1]

> In the later 1970s, as the period before the termination of the New Territories lease continued to shorten, concern about the future of Hong Kong began to be expressed both in the territory itself and among foreign investors. In particular there was increasing realization of the problem posed by individual land leases granted in the New Territories, all of which are set to expire three days before the expiry of the New Territories lease in 1997. It was clear that the steadily shortening span of these leases and the inability of the Hong Kong Government to grant new ones extending beyond 1997 would be likely to deter investment and damage confidence.

The joint declaration issued by the Chinese and British governments on May 27, 1985, defined the basis for Hong Kong's return to China. It stated that property rights would continue to be protected by law and that all rights in relation to land leases granted previously in accordance with the relevant laws would be recognized. Specific rules were provided for granting new leases or renewing expiring leases during the transition period. It was further stipulated that all premium income obtained from land transactions would be used to finance land development and public works. A Land Commission with equal representation of British and Chinese officials was set up for the duration of the transition period to oversee implementation of these provisions. The establishment of the Land Commission in 1985, 12 years before the transfer, gave China a prolonged opportunity to get involved with and to understand land administration in Hong Kong.

With regard to the granting of new leases for land, a limit of 50 hectares was set, at China's insistence, on the amount of new land that could be granted in any one year, but flexibility was allowed to grant additional areas. As it happened, the 50-hectare quota was exceeded every year, especially during the three years before the transfer of sovereignty.[2]

These actions constituted substantial support for and assurance to lessees. By removing political and legal uncertainty about the future, the joint declaration achieved the objective of boosting business confidence. This can be seen by looking at the price index for private domestic dwellings during this period: home prices peaked in 1981, when they were about 50 percent higher than 1979 levels; they fell precipitously in 1982 at the announcement of negotiations between Great Britain and China. By 1984 they had dropped back to the same level as in 1979, but with the announcement of the joint declaration in May 1984, they began to rise again, surpassing the 1981 peak by the end of the decade.

Land Access and Land Rights since the Handover to China

Following the joint declaration, the Basic Law was passed on April 4, 1990, spelling out the new constitutional arrangements that would come into effect on July 1, 1997. Note the seven-year lead time. The topic of land rights and land access was an important component of the Basic Law (see the annex to this chapter), which offered protection to all existing landowners, converted all former Crown or government land into Chinese state-owned property, and gave the government of Hong Kong SAR, China, the authority to grant new leases and manage such land.

It reaffirmed the essential provisions in the joint declaration. In particular, it offered a significant concession to the holders of nonrenewable leases by extending them to June 30, 2047, without payment of an additional premium.

By incorporating elements agreed to in the joint declaration, the Basic Law gave the land administration process consistency and transparency and removed any political or legal uncertainty from it.

Until June 30, 1997, the governor had the power to grant and dispose of land in the territory. To ensure a seamless legal and administrative transfer, the Hong Kong Reunification Ordinance no. 110 of 1997 vested the power to lease and grant state land in the chief executive of Hong Kong SAR, China. The previous system of delegations relating to land remained unchanged. Within 15 days of coming into office, the Executive Council of the government of Hong Kong SAR, China, had endorsed all of the policies that had been applicable in the almost 13-year transition period. Beginning on July 1, 1997, new leases and renewed leases would be granted for 50 years from the date of grant or renewal. This meant that new and extended leases, and by implication the existence of Hong Kong SAR, China, would go on beyond the date of June 30, 2047, which was the limit set for all new and renewed leases in the joint declaration and the Basic Law.

This sent a strong positive signal to both the business and residential communities about the future continuity of land rights in Hong Kong SAR, China. The new land policies ensured that the rights of leaseholders would continue to be protected under current legislation, that the transfer of land administration from the old to the new regime would be seamless, and that, via significant concessions, the rights and benefits of leaseholders after July 1, 1997, would definitely not be worse and in most cases would be significantly better than those prevailing before the handover.

The following are some important features of the current system:

• The execution of a land lease is regarded as a *private* transaction between the government and the lessee with appropriate contractual rights. As such, these transactions cannot be considered as performing an executive function and therefore are not susceptible to judicial review. For the most part, they are dealt with within the framework of private law and not public law.
• Land leases are allocated either by public auction or by private negotiation. As in other countries, negotiation is more appropriate where a

leaseholder has made a substantial investment and would risk losing it all if his lease were not renewed. See chapter 13 of this volume on the allocation of public land.

- Leases are freely transferable; leaseholders can sell their lease rights to a third party at the market price without further government approvals. The legal framework protects the interest of the lender if the leaseholder chooses to use the lease as collateral to borrow from banks. The mortgage on the lease can be properly secured, and, if necessary, the lease can be sold to a third party. On this issue, the rights of leaseholders and lenders are both clearly defined.

The clarity of lease conditions also plays an important role. Each lease defines the obligations and duties of the owner of the lease, as well as the planning, engineering, and development requirements that need to be met according to the nature and use of the lease. These usually include the following:

- Lease term, which is normally 50 years from the date of grant, with an annual rent assessed at 3 percent of ratable value
- Permitted uses, which generally correspond to the land use specified in the Lands Department's zoning plan. In residential zones, only private residential use is normally permitted. If the site is zoned for commercial and residential, then mixed use is permitted, and the user clause is usually written allowing nonindustrial use, with certain exceptions such as petrol stations. Industrial lots are usually sold allowing industrial together with *godown* (covered storage) use, but sometimes only the latter is permitted.
- Maximum building height
- Minimum and maximum gross floor area
- Maximum permitted site coverage
- The period required for construction, known as the building covenant; for most sites, 48 months are specified, although longer periods may be granted if appropriate
- The requirements of the layout master plan (for large schemes)
- Design, disposition, and height limitation
- Parking spaces, loading and unloading requirements
- Restrictions on vehicular ingress and egress
- Landscaping and environmental requirements, which are spelled out in the Lands Department Practice Note no. 3/94 for architects, surveyors, and engineers

- Recreational facilities, which are permitted in residential sites. The floor area for recreational facilities is not usually specified, but as a guideline, 3–5 percent of the residential gross floor area would normally be approved for recreational purposes, with each case being considered on its merits.

Conclusions and Lessons Learned

Facing up to the historical opportunities and challenges, authorities in Hong Kong SAR, China, have successfully put in place a long-term lease system that is transparent, stable, and predictable. The simplicity of the system has proved to be extraordinarily efficient in creating a fluid land market, despite the complex legal status of land resources, periodic political uncertainty, and occasional economic turmoil.

With a great appreciation for the interests of local business, authorities both before and after the transfer to China have consistently acted to standardize and stabilize the land market, to remove uncertainties as quickly as possible, and to adopt measures that are generally favorable to and protective of leaseholders. Although Hong Kong SAR, China, has undergone two major territorial expansions and a transfer of sovereignty, its policies toward private sector access to land have been remarkably consistent throughout its more than 160 years of existence and, on the whole, favorable to the lessees. There are many instances during its history where, given the choice, the courts and sovereign powers have come down clearly in favor of the leaseholders, thus maintaining a system that works well for them.

Therefore, although land policy has never been dictated by the need to attract investment, it has been hugely successful as a facilitator. The key aspects of the land regime in Hong Kong SAR, China, include the following:

- The land market is open and treats domestic and foreign investors equally.
- Land information is freely available, and land prices are determined transparently through public auction.
- The rules and regulations governing the acquisition and use of land are clear and stable.
- Leases are freely transferable, with leaseholders having the right to subdivide their land and to sublease portions of it.

- The legal system for upholding the law and handling disputes is well established and effective, so that the rights of leaseholders and the public are protected.
- Since February 1974, when the Independent Commission against Corruption was established to fight corruption in government, Hong Kong SAR, China, has developed a reputation as a fairly "clean" place to do business, where bribery and corruption are not endemic.
- The financial market is very well developed and able to finance the acquisition and development of land in the territory.
- Given the sound legal system for protecting leaseholder and creditor rights, as well as for handling disputes and upholding court decisions, banks are more than happy to provide financing for both the development and the purchase of real estate.

In sum, the experience of Hong Kong SAR, China, shows that freehold ownership is not the only way to provide private businesses with access to the land they need. A long-term leasing system has, and can, work very well. In Hong Kong SAR, China, long-term leasing has worked well over a long period of time—about 150 years and still counting—in spite of potentially serious problems:

- Merging of different territories, each with different previously existing legal systems and in particular land rights, ownership, laws, and systems
- Frequent economic and political turmoil and uncertainty
- A drastic change in sovereignty, from a British Crown colony to a part of China.

The following have been essential for the success of long-term leasing in spite of the problems just mentioned:

- A reasonably business-friendly attitude, consistently maintained throughout the period, with most unavoidable changes managed such that few, if any, private leaseholders suffered, while many benefited
- A respect for the rule of law and of legitimately granted prior rights in particular
- Clear, simple, flexible, easy-to-manage, efficient leasing systems
- A strong financial sector to finance the acquisition and development of land. This aspect has not been dealt with in depth in this chapter, as its importance is well known.

So, in addition to teaching us that long-term leasing *can* work, the experience of Hong Kong SAR, China, also teaches us much about *how* to make it work.

Of course, Hong Kong SAR, China, is a largely urbanized metropolitan area, not a country with vast rural lands or many cities. But this nearly unique characteristic does not seem to have been a necessary condition for the success of its land access system. Nothing that was done in Hong Kong SAR, China, could not be done just as effectively in a large, geographically diverse country.

Annex. Articles Relating to Property and Land Rights in the Basic Law

Article 6. The Hong Kong Special Administrative Region shall protect the right of private ownership of property in accordance with law.

Article 7. The land and natural resources within the Hong Kong Special Administrative Region shall be State property. The Government of the Hong Kong Special Administrative Region shall be responsible for their management, use, and development and for their lease or grant to individuals, legal persons or organizations for use or development. The revenues derived therefrom shall be exclusively at the disposal of the Government of the Region.

Article 120. All leases of land granted, decided upon, or renewed before the establishment of the Hong Kong Special Administrative Region which extends beyond 30 June 1997, and all rights in relation to such leases, shall continue to be recognized and protected under the law of the Region.

Article 121. As regards all leases of land granted or renewed where the original leases contain no right of renewal, during the period from 27 May 1985 to 30 June 1997, which extend beyond 30 June 1997 and expire not later than 30 June 2047, the lessee is not required to pay an additional premium as from 1 July 1997. But an annual rent equivalent to 3% of the ratable value of the property at that date, adjusted in step with any changes in the ratable value thereafter, shall be charged.

Article 122. In the case of old schedule lots, village lots, small houses, and similar rural holdings, where the property was on 30 June 1984 held by, or, in the case of small houses granted after that date, where the property is granted to a lessee descended through the male line from a person who was in 1898 a resident of an established village in Hong Kong, the previous rent shall remain unchanged so long as the property is held by that lessee or by one of his lawful successors in the male line.

Article 123. Where leases of land without a right of renewal expire after the establishment of the Hong Kong Special Administrative Region, they shall be dealt with in accordance with laws and policies formulated by the Region on its own.

Notes

1. Draft agreement between the United Kingdom of Great Britain and Northern Ireland and the Government of the People's Republic of China on the Future of Hong Kong, white paper (September 26, 1984), reprinted in *I.L.M.* 23, no. 1366 (1984).

2. Between 50.74 and 1,379.2 hectares of new land were granted annually from 1985 to 1997. The peak was recorded in 1994–95, with the new Chek Lap Kok airport (1,248 hectares).

CHAPTER 12

United States: Developing Tribal Trust Land for Native Americans

Ezra Rosser

On many Native American reservations, poverty is a fact of life, and the level of economic development is a fraction of that found off-reservation in the surrounding United States. Limitations and protections in the law regarding landownership and control play an important role in both shaping forms of growth and establishing how investors perceive the available opportunities. Native American nations are considered "domestic dependent nations" and generally enjoy all attributes of sovereignty that have not been expressly taken away by the U.S. government. But prior policies aimed at alienating Native Americans from their land, as well as the current protective trust status of reservation land, together make Native American land distinctly different from off-reservation private land that can be transferred through sale, used as loan collateral, and developed according to processes that are normal outside the reservations.

Native American nations, together with U.S. government agencies, have attempted to solve several land-related problems that have hampered development and limited investment within reservations. Staff shortages at the Bureau of Indian Affairs (BIA) as well as excessive tribal bureaucratic steps can make getting permission for development prohibitively expensive and time-consuming. Additionally, there are prohibitions on non-Native American ownership of reservation land and on the use of such land as collateral by non-Native Americans and Native Americans. These prohibitions serve the valuable function of protecting the Native American land base against further loss. But such limitations may also require complementary policies to ameliorate their negative effects on those whom they are meant to protect—complementary policies that would provide for long-term leases or alternative collateral approaches.

Some tribes have improved their development process by taking over reservation land registration systems from duplicative federal title search and approval processes. Other tribes have worked on providing regulatory clarity by formalizing land use rules for those seeking to conduct business on reservation land. There is no single answer to how Native American nations should regulate their land, and a single set of institutional changes will not necessarily lead to growth. Given the more than 550 federally recognized tribes with distinct histories, cultural values, and land-related challenges, a belief in a magic bullet is not only misguided but perhaps even counterproductive. What has become clear over the last 40 years is that tribal assertion of de facto sovereignty and tribal—as opposed to U.S. government—path setting are critical steps in the right direction.

Status of Native American Land

The power that Native American nations have to control and use their land has been limited by the doctrines and policies that have shaped the relationship between tribes and the United States. Racism, colonialism, and conquest combined to curtail the powers that Native American tribes had over their land before contact with European settlers. As the U.S. Supreme Court declared in 1823,

> The rights of the original inhabitants were, in no instance, entirely disregarded; but were necessarily, to a considerable extent, impaired. They were admitted to be the rightful occupants of the soil, with a legal as well as just claim to retain possession of it, and to use it according to their own discretion; but their rights to complete sovereignty, as independent nations, were necessarily diminished, and their power to dispose of the soil at their own will, to whomsoever they pleased, was denied by the original fundamental principle, that discovery gave exclusive title to those who made it (Johnson V. M'Intosh, 21 U.S. 543, 574 [1823]).

The century that followed would witness the continued systematic taking of Native American land, using a variety of legal means, all grounded in the assumption that Native Americans had lesser rights than non-Native Americans.

The treaty-based relationship between Native American tribes and the United States ended in 1871 and was replaced by an assimilative experiment—the breaking up of reservations into individual allotments. Although some tribes were spared allotment, most notably the Navajo Nation, many tribes are still suffering the consequences. The supposed goal of allotment was to turn Native Americans into small farmers by providing for individual ownership that would, after time, take the fee-simple form of ownership found off-reservation. But the sale of "surplus" land—reservation land that remained after all tribal members got their individual parcels—to non-Native Americans reflected the true goal: further diminishing tribal landholdings. When the sale of surplus land was coupled with the sale of land by Native American allottees, the reservation border no longer truly represented the line between Native American and non-Native American land. Instead of a single form of reservation land, a checkerboard pattern of alternating forms of landownership and jurisdiction developed (see figure 12.1).

Reservation land that was not simply taken by the U.S. government or allotted is subject to dual oversight and control. Native Americans were and still are considered "wards" of the U.S. government; consequently, there is a trust relationship between the U.S. government and tribes. In the context of land, this trust relationship involves the responsibility of the United States to protect the tribal land base. Trust land therefore is subject to overlapping administrative control—that of the particular tribe and, through the Department of the Interior, that of the U.S. government—with joint trust responsibility for the land and prohibition on alienation. As Professor Randall Akee writes, "Trust land provides significant protection for land, but it also adds to the complications for land investment" (Akee 2009, 395, 398). The result is predictable underdevelopment. Although off-reservation title searches can be accomplished quickly and without too great an administrative burden, getting a home-site permit, much less permission to start a business, often involves navigating the bureaucracies of both governments. Understaffing at the BIA only makes the red tape problems worse and expensive both financially and in terms of delay.

Outsiders and Sovereignty

Many non-Native Americans in the United States think of Native Americans as being remnants of the precontact period, and their continued sovereignty consequently comes as a surprise. While the success of Native American gaming, especially that of a few large casinos such as

Figure 12.1 Patterns of Tribal Land Tenure

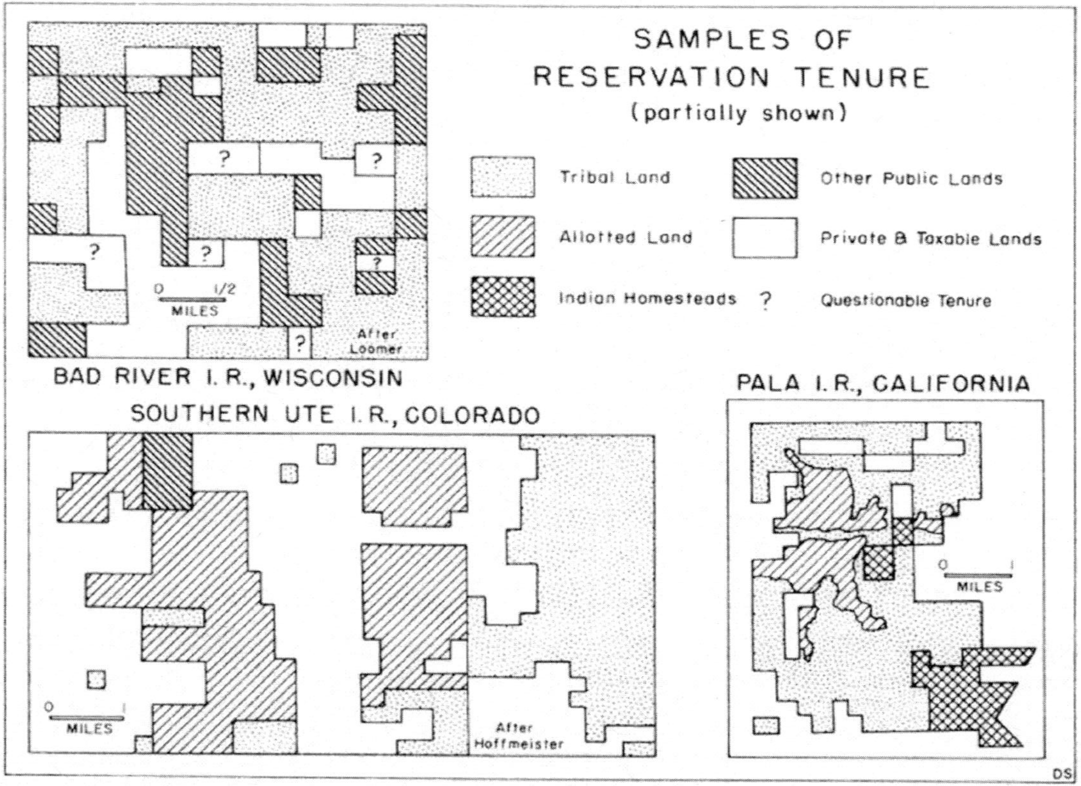

SAMPLES OF
RESERVATION TENURE
(partially shown)
Tribal Land
Allotted Land
Indian Homesteads
Other Public Lands
Private & Taxable Lands
? Questionable Tenure
0 1/2 MILES
After Loomer
BAD RIVER I.R., WISCONSIN
SOUTHERN UTE I.R., COLORADO
0 1 MILES
After Hoffmeister
PALA I.R., CALIFORNIA
0 1 MILES
DS

Source: Sutton 1975, 85.

Foxwoods, Mohegan Sun, and Turning Stone, has brought increased popular attention to the existence of Native Americans, gaming also distorts non-Native American understandings. Although gaming has made a few small tribes fabulously wealthy, reservation Native Americans remain far below the rest of the United States with regard to income, poverty rates, and most other socioeconomic indicators, from housing to health care. Limited experience of non-Native Americans visiting reservations and disproportionate media focus on gaming tribes are pushing below the surface the underdevelopment, high unemployment, and poverty that mark much of Native American country. Generally speaking, non-Native Americans are surprised that tribes may have "special rights"—including the right to engage in gaming—but know little about the contours of Native American sovereignty.

Tribal governance structures or the perception of such structures may contribute to fears among outsiders, whether justified or not, that reservation investment is particularly risky or uncertain. Tribal governments are not mere copies of state or municipal governments in their administrative structure, and these differences can make investors nervous. For example, by operating on a reservation, does a company become subject to tribal jurisdiction? Even though tribal courts may, in fact, treat non-Native Americans fairly, which early research suggests is indeed the case, outsiders may still be nervous about appearing before a Native American court and a jury not necessarily of their peers. Tribal courts are just the start: outsiders may be even more concerned about tribal taxation and land use regulation. Rumors also abound that tribal governments impose unpredictable costs on investors by changing the terms after an initial agreement has been reached because they mix politics with economic development. Even well-informed outsiders without prejudices against reservation investment may prefer the comfort of only being subject to more familiar non-Native American governments. Finally, the prohibition against non-Native American ownership of reservation land and the inalienable nature of trust land force those doing business on reservation land to obtain a lease and get business permits without being able to collateralize the land.

The best way to think about the powers of Native American nations is to remember that they are sovereigns predating the United States. Under U.S. law, Congress does have the power to take away tribal authority, but any powers not explicitly taken away by Congress remain within the tribal sovereign domain. Additionally, the Supreme Court has narrowed the authority Native American nations have over non-Native Americans and over fee-simple land located within original reservation boundaries. These limitations reflect the status of tribes as "domestic dependent nations," but focusing on the limitations risks obscuring the big picture. As Felix Cohen, author of the 1941 *Handbook of Federal Indian Law* and a Yale law professor, observed, "Indian tribes have been recognized as distinct, independent, and political communities, and, as such, qualified to exercise powers of self-government, not by the delegation of powers from the Federal Government, but rather by reason of their original tribal sovereignty" (Cohen 1941, 123). For entrepreneurs, whether Native American or non-Native American, considering on-reservation opportunities, tribal sovereignty and control over land will play an important role in shaping the economic environment and the risks involved.

Successful Tribal Approaches

Limitations on tribal authority owing to the pervasive role of the federal government in the regulation of reservation land use arguably play a significant role in reservation underdevelopment. For more than 20 years, the Harvard Project on American Economic Development has been exploring what leads to economic growth in Native American country. Led by professors Joseph Kalt and Stephen Cornell, the project has found that a successful nation-building approach has five characteristics (Cornell and Kalt 2007, box 1.4):

* Native nations assert decision-making power.
* Native nations back up that power with effective governing institutions.
* Governing institutions match indigenous political cultures.
* Decision making is strategic.
* Leaders serve as nation builders and mobilizers.

Asserting decision-making power involves both political and practical sovereignty, but it is practical, de facto, sovereignty that matters the most. Political sovereignty refers to the legal authority of tribes, and the extent of tribal political sovereignty is determined largely by federal Native American policy (Royster 2008). Focused on what a tribe actually does and its decision-making power in practice instead of simply on the legal structure that defines tribal authority, practical sovereignty refers to the degree of tribal self-rule or "actual on-the-ground governance" (Royster 2008).[1]

Most of the improvements in Native American country have not come from the federal government simply turning over governing authority. Rather, tribes have *asserted* their right to self-governance, sometimes with the blessing of, and sometimes in spite of, the federal government. In *Blood Struggle: The Rise of Modern Indian Nations*, Professor Charles Wilkinson presents story after story of tribes successfully asserting their right to determine their own fate and such assertions leading to victories for tribes that had been struggling for survival. And although "economists see the task of breaking from BIA control to tribal democracy as comparable to rebuilding the government-controlled economies of Eastern Europe," Professor Wilkinson concludes his opus by celebrating the "staying power" of Native American nations (Wilkinson 2005, 350, 383).

Specifically, assertion of decision-making power by Native American nations has helped tribes to improve their land policies. Lengthy title searches can take years for the BIA to complete, even though similar off-reservation title searches are simple and quick. These delays can have a tremendous impact on reservation economies (First Nations Development Institute and National Congress of American Indians 2009, 8):

> On a macro level, land title processing impacts the capacity of tribal governments to make and enforce their own decisions. . . . If the tribe wants to develop an enterprise, create a wildlife reserve, or change the designation of any tract of land at all, it needs to wait a considerable amount of time— sometimes years—before it can enact the plan. The above examples of the impediment to sovereignty also underscore the challenges to economic development. Tribal leaders and tribal members are frustrated by the lengthy and often unnecessarily complex process required to obtain a [title search report]. This frustration leads some, both leaders and citizens, to give up completely on dreams of homeownership for tribal members and successful economic development for the tribe.

Tribal takeover of land titling can not only ease the frustration but also permit economic development to occur that otherwise would be blocked by process delays. The Saginaw Chippewa Tribe of Michigan, a small tribe with less than 3,000 members and just over 3,000 acres of land, by taking over land titling from the BIA, managed to go from between a one- and two-year wait to a turnaround of 24 hours or less on title reports (First Nations Development Institute and National Congress of American Indians 2009, 23). Most important, this assertion of sovereign regulation of reservation land allowed tribal members better access to capital. Before, the only loans available were predatory loans tied to five-year balloon payments; now, 30-year fixed-rate loans are available from numerous reputable lenders (First Nations Development Institute and National Congress of American Indians 2009). In recognition of the transformative role that changes in land titling played in helping to bring lending, economic development, and the return of tribal members to the reservation who had been unable to get housing under the old system, the Tribal Land Title and Records Office of the Saginaw Chippewa Tribe was named a winner of the Harvard Project's "Honoring Nations" awards program.[2]

Another Harvard Project awardee, the Yakama Nation, had different, tribe-specific land challenges that it too addressed by asserting tribal control over their land and reservation.[3] Located in Washington State, the Yakama reservation today has only 90,000 acres held in trust, even though, according to the original boundaries, the reservation should have a total of 1.4 million acres. As a heavily allotted reservation, the checkerboard pattern of non-Native American and Native American ownership within the original reservation borders led the tribe into numerous jurisdictional disputes with state and county governments over everything from tax authority to environmental regulation. "These disputes, in turn, have slowed the progress of development, compromised the Nation's economic interests, and challenged its stewardship over the environment and local wildlife."[4]

The tribe formed a separate, quasi-governmental, enterprise tasked with consolidating the tribal land base and with land development operations. The tribal council approved the strategic plans that guide the Yakama Nation Land Enterprise, but day-to-day operations were deliberately separated from political involvement and pressure. What began with the goal of reducing jurisdictional disputes through land consolidation and purchases ended up doing far more than that, even attracting non-Native American businesses to the reservation and leading to a fivefold increase in lease income. By buying up checkerboard land, the tribe managed to reduce jurisdictional disputes, "regulate more land on its own terms," and generate land development opportunities.[5]

These are just a few of the creative solutions to the challenges of development in the context of tribal trust land that cannot be sold or used as collateral. A land market can support the efficient use of land, and some tribes have set up transferable use rights as a stand-in for market allocation. In line with Hernando de Soto's emphasis on reducing the red tape that poor people face when they seek to engage in small-scale business activities or attempt to get permission from the state to formalize their property interests, tribes have made efforts to reduce "red tape" in the tribal bureaucracy (de Soto 2000).

Efforts have also been made by tribes and the federal government to provide alternative forms of collateral—whether in the form of government guarantees or asset substitution—so that those seeking to develop trust land can have the same access to capital that is available off-reservation. Finally, tribal land values and level of development can converge toward that of surrounding private land when tribes or the federal government makes longer lease terms available for trust land (Akee 2009, 399–401, n. 90). Working to solve the problems of red tape, missing collateral, and lease terms reflects the Harvard Project's observation that successful native nation building requires that tribal assertions of decision-making power be backed up by effective governing institutions.[6]

Conclusions and Lessons Learned

The late Vine Deloria Jr., perhaps the foremost scholar on Native American life, law, and culture of the twentieth century, noted, "Among the more surprising elements of Indian land tenure is the aspect of continual experimentation with property rights which has been visited upon the individual tribes by Congressional fiat" (Rosser 2005, 276). But such experimentation is a history of failure: policies that looked good on paper from the standpoint of Washington politicians failed to generate predicted levels of economic growth and opportunity. Tellingly, although the ethos of the United States celebrates yeoman farming and individual ownership, Native American families remained impoverished and tribes affected by the policy witnessed tremendous loss of land. Native nations have faced and will continue to face development challenges, and the need for outside capital is likely to remain important if tribes are to narrow the poverty and employment gaps that exist between reservations and the rest of the United States. While what has been successful differs from tribe to tribe, the common denominator explaining successful reservation land policies and approaches is a commitment to tribal decision making and effective tribal government institutions.

Notes

1. See also Cornell and Kalt (2007, 18, n. 92), linking practical sovereignty and self-rule.
2. A description of the office's work and the reasons why the Harvard Project chose to give the honor to it can be found at http://www.hks.harvard.edu/hpaied/hn/hn_2006_TribalLandTitleandRecordsOffice.htm.

3. More on the Yakama Nation Land Enterprise's 2002 award and description of the tribe's work can be found on the Harvard Project's website at http://www.hks.harvard.edu/hpaied/hn/hn_2002_land.htm.

4. Harvard Project's website.

5. Harvard Project's website.

6. A more detailed discussion regarding creative approaches to the challenges presented by the status of reservation land can be found in Rosser (2005).

References

Akee, Randall. 2009. "Checkerboards and Coase: The Effect of Property Institutions on Efficiency in Housing Markets." *Journal of Law and Economics* 52 (2): 395–410.

Cohen, Felix S. 1941. *Handbook of Federal Indian Law.* Washington, DC: U.S. Government Printing Office.

Cornell, Stephen, and Joseph P. Kalt. 2007. "Two Approaches to the Development of Native Nations: One Works, the Other Doesn't." In *Rebuilding Native Nations: Strategies for Governance and Development*, ed. Miriam Jorgensen. Tucson: University of Arizona Press.

de Soto, Hernando. 2000. *The Mystery of Capital: Why Capitalism Triumphs in the West and Fails Everywhere Else.* New York: Basic Books; London: Bantam Press/Random House.

First Nations Development Institute and National Congress of American Indians. 2009. "Exercising Sovereignty and Expanding Economic Opportunity through Tribal Land Management: A Study Addressing the Range of Options to Expedite Land Title Processing on Indian Lands." First Nations Development Institute, Longmont, CO; National Congress of American Indians, Washington, DC.

Rosser, Ezra. 2005. "This Land Is My Land, This Land Is Your Land: Markets and Institutions for Economic Development on Native American Reservations." *Arizona Law Review* 47 (2): 245–312.

Royster, Judith V. 2008. "Practical Sovereignty, Political Sovereignty, and the Indian Tribal Energy Development and Self-Determination Act." *Lewis and Clark Law Review* 12 (4): 1065–101.

Sutton, Imre. 1975. *Indian Land Tenure: Biographical Essays and a Guide to the Literature.* New York: Clearwater.

Wilkinson, Charles. 2005. *Blood Struggle: The Rise of Modern Indian Nations.* New York: W. W. Norton.

PART 2

Lessons Learned: Technical Papers

CHAPTER 13

Improving State Land Approval Processes: From Administrative Simplification to Competitive Allocation

Stephen B. Butler

State control of land remains a reality in many transition economies and developing countries. Where land markets have not been developed due to political, economic, and historical factors, investors in those countries often have no choice but to apply to the government for the land they need to make their investment. Even in some countries where private ownership is relatively well established and there are relatively viable land markets, industrial and commercial developers may still have to deal with governments, often municipalities, because of the difficulty of finding or assembling appropriate sites in the market.

In this chapter, "state land" means land owned and controlled by governments, at both national and subnational levels. "Allocation" means the process by which state land is made available to citizens and businesses for various purposes, including businesses and housing development. Most of this chapter focuses on the techniques for allocating state land and *how* it can be done more equitably, efficiently, and transparently. This allocation is done through a variety of processes, which may differ in the details but which ultimately come down to two main approaches—application and negotiation, sometimes called administrative allocation, and competitive bidding, usually implemented through auction or public tender.

A more detailed discussion of the "what" of state land programs—including lease rights, rents and sale prices, development and other covenants and restrictions, and restrictions on transfer—is found in chapter 15 of this volume.

Other important, but more specialized, means of allocating state land are not discussed in this chapter. Examples include privatization of state land by conveyance to its current occupants and restitution of land by governments to former owners. Both of these approaches have been important to the divestiture or allocation of state-owned land to private sector users in many transition economies in recent years. Such processes are especially designed according to the historical settings and, for the time being, appear to be substantially complete in most states that have used them. Special economic and industrial zones are another major component of land policy in many countries today (for example, Bangladesh, China, India, and Vietnam, as well as an increasing number of African countries). There is an extensive literature on such zones (see, for example, Farole and Akinci 2011), and some of its relevance for this book is discussed in chapter 6 giving the example of Shenzhen special economic zone, China.

An important issue also beyond the scope of this chapter, but worth noting, is that, in many countries, allocation of state land is, in fact, reallocation of land. Most of the well-located and well-serviced land is already occupied and used. Vacant, well-serviced, state-owned land in good locations is relatively uncommon. Consequently, a good deal of land allocation done in emerging markets is, in fact, reallocation through compulsory acquisition. Even if the land is not owned by its occupants, most countries today require that some level of due process be provided and compensation paid for land taken from its occupants and given to another user. Acquiring the land for reallocation can be a major and controversial component of the state land allocation process, a topic that deserves discussion far beyond the scope of this book.[1]

Land Allocation by Administrative Process

Most developing countries allocate state land for business use through an application process. A distinction sometimes made is between "active" administrative procedures in which the state takes an aggressive and entrepreneurial approach to promoting land opportunities and investment and "passive" programs in which it reacts to requests and proposals but does not actively seek to market or even disseminate information about available state lands.

Another distinction among programs may be the extent to which the key terms of the land grant are flexible and subject to negotiation and those in which most key terms are predetermined by law or regulation. Most programs will probably fall in the middle of this spectrum, having some negotiable elements (for example, location and size) and some fixed elements (for example, price, rent, and maximum duration).

Even states that use competitive procedures for allocating land (discussed more specifically later in this chapter) may permit administrative allocation in some cases. The Russian Federation, for example, requires auction of land zoned for residential use but allows administrative allocation of other types. In Bangladesh the law requires competitive procedures for industrial land but uses lottery and first-come-first-served applications for residential plots. Hong Kong SAR, China, uses both auctions and administrative procedures. Australian states allow both procedures, but some erect a high threshold to prove that administrative allocation is in the "public interest."[2]

From an investor's perspective, allocation of land by administrative procedure has both benefits and drawbacks. One benefit is that the investor can apply at any time and is not subject to the schedule of state-sponsored auctions or limited to land sites selected by the state. On the negative side, again from the investor's perspective, compared to auctions the procedures for applying for a land allocation can be complex, time-consuming, expensive, and uncertain, although they do not necessarily have to be so if properly structured. A problem that investors may encounter is that administrative allocation can lack transparency, permitting the exercise of discretion by land officials, rent seeking, and favoritism. Administrative procedures also may provide more opportunity for the state to direct land resources to preferred investments and uses, a form of economic planning that may have poor outcomes and exclude investors who are not on the favored lists.

Improving Administrative Procedures for Land Allocation

In recent years, many countries have made efforts to improve their administrative processes for allocating state land, aiming to make it more transparent, reduce processing times, and eliminate unnecessary paperwork. The main approaches to improving administrative procedures for land allocation have included the following:

- *One-stop shops.* The pros and cons of the "one-stop shop" solution are discussed in detail in chapter 16 of this volume.

- *Simultaneous processing.* Cases in which commencement of one step in an application process must depend on completion of a prior step are relatively rare, and it is considered best practice to compress steps and make many of them simultaneous as far as is possible.

- *Mandatory review forums.* Simultaneous processing of applications among regulatory agencies can be facilitated by holding periodic forums at which responsible representatives of the agencies are required to appear in the presence of the applicant to comment on the application and identify further steps expected of the applicant. Minutes should be kept, and, in the absence of a change of facts or other extraordinary circumstances, comments and instructions made by reviewing agencies in such forums should be considered binding.

- *Standardization of application and documentation requirements.* Application requirements can be coordinated among reviewing agencies to determine if they are asking for the same information in different ways or formats, as is often the case. With the increasing use of electronic data input, analysis, and storage, this becomes more obvious and also easier. Unless there are compelling reasons to the contrary, all agencies should be required to accept applications and documents in a single standardized format.

- *Time-bound processing.* Reasonable time limits can be set on processing applications, although experience suggests that strict limits excluding an agency's input unless the time limits are met may be unrealistic and will, in most cases, be ignored, particularly if the result would be to allocate a state asset or avoid a legitimate health or safety regulation. Clear time limits established as part of agency performance standards also can be effective tools in staff evaluations and advancement and provide watchdog entities (including the press) a fair and objective measure against which to evaluate performance.

- *Delegation.* Some studies by the International Finance Corporation (IFC) have shown that a significant cause of delay in administrative processes is routing of applications through high-level officials, who can be bottlenecks in the process because they are few in number, tend to have other priorities, and are often less accountable than staff. Delegation of decision-making authority to lower levels with appropriate checks and balances can avoid bottlenecks and delays.

- *Clear instructions and guides.* Providing clear, comprehensive instruction and guidelines can avoid the delays caused by incomplete and otherwise defective applications and documentation. The absence of clear, published guidelines can facilitate rent-seeking behavior on the part of officials. Investor guides to land allocation processes can benefit both the land applicants and honest government officials.

- *Inventory and site selection.* The efficiency of a state land program may depend on how entrepreneurial the officials in charge are and how they perceive their role. If they view their role as gatekeepers and as, in effect, owners of the land, they may tend to hoard information, exercise tight control over the choices available to land users, and allocate land selectively. If they view their role as facilitators whose success will be evaluated on the basis of how much investment they can facilitate, it will be in their interests to advertise their product as widely as possible and respond generously to requests for information. As with promoting transparency of land allocation generally, the ability of businesses to find land can be facilitated by rules that require the maintenance of land inventories, disclosure on request of data on available land, mandatory advertising of state land offered for sale or lease, mandatory disclosure of alternative suitable sites, and investor choice of location.

Ameliorating the Risks of the Land Application Process

One of the risks of allocating land by administrative process is that the applicant may have to invest significant amounts of effort and money before receiving a binding commitment on the land. Public officials may be reluctant to make legally binding commitments until the entire process has been completed and all open questions resolved. The simple form of this risk is that the potential investor proceeds in good faith through a time-consuming and expensive process only to have his application rejected at the end for technical or policy reasons. But public officials may also reserve the right to award a land site to another investor or to offer the land by competitive process even after the application process has begun, in which case the investor has put his best ideas forward for possible use by others without compensation.

To encourage investment, a good process would seek to provide as much assurance to the investor as early as possible that the application process will be undertaken by the state in good faith and, barring extraordinary or unforeseen circumstances, that the land will be awarded to the applicant, provided all technical requirements are met. The following are some steps that might be taken to create this sense of good faith:

- *Transparent eligibility requirements.* Investors should know at the earliest possible time whether they and their projects are eligible to obtain the land. Eligibility criteria should be clearly expressed and objectively verifiable.

- *Transparent application requirements.* Clear application requirements provide assurances to the investor that his efforts and application will not be derailed because of vague technical requirements subject to a broad array of interpretations.

- *Early commitment subject to clearly defined reasons for termination.* The degree of commitment to the applicant can increase in stages, as issues are resolved and requirements are met. One approach may be to provide the investor with preliminary approval of an application at an early stage, which constitutes a representation of the government that the land site identified by the investor has not been committed to another; that the proposed project conforms essentially to local social, economic, and physical planning requirements; and that there is no objection to the investor pursuing the next steps of the application process. This can be followed by an agreement in principle or a letter of intent, which constitutes assurance that the requested land has been conditionally reserved for the investor and will not be allocated to another, provided that the investor diligently pursues and completes all further requirements of the application process within the time allowed. Upon issuance of the agreement in principle, the authorities should be committed to cooperate with the investor in good faith to complete the application. Even though these steps may not provide a legally binding commitment to the investor, they do place a burden on the state to act fairly in dealing with the investor's request.

Transparency

From the perspective of transparency and protection of the public interest, allocation of land by administrative procedure can be improved by a few steps, some of which can be viewed as converting from a "passive" land allocation program to an "active" one. In addition to keeping good and accessible inventories of available state lands, other steps can be taken to improve the transparency of allocation programs:

- *Advertisement.* A practice of regularly advertising the availability of state lands may induce demand, increase offers, create greater transparency, and level the playing field. As with the award of other public benefits, such as procurement contracts, it can be provided in law that no land may be allocated unless its availability is first widely advertised and offers or applications solicited.
- *Appraisal.* It is possible to require property to be sold or leased at the appraised market value, as established by one or more independent professional appraisals.
- *Publication of transaction data.* Light can be thrown on proposed or completed transactions with state land by requiring that the terms of the transaction be published in the press or official gazette prior to completion of the transaction—for example, a 30-day notice period before rights to the land can be transferred by the state.
- *Reporting by state agencies and subnational governments.* Any initiatives to increase the transparency of state land allocation should be imposed as well on subnational governments, which are often vested with authority to allocate land as agents of the state.

Simplifying Administrative Procedures through Process Mapping

Process mapping is a useful tool for analysis of many administrative processes. It is sometimes referred to as analysis of "administrative barriers." It has been used in land-related projects to assist governments to simplify and reduce the costs of their procedures, as well as to raise public awareness.

Mapping is a detailed investigation of the process, including its legal foundations, the agencies involved, and their interactions, the steps involved and time taken for each step, fees and charges (including taxes), and documents and other information required to be submitted by applicants. Figure 13.1 provides an example of the end product. Such a map can help governments to identify duplicative and unnecessary activities, procedural bottlenecks, and derogations from current best practice. Mapping can be particularly helpful in multiagency procedures to show the participating agencies the relationship of their roles and procedures to the activities of other agencies involved in the process, sometimes revealing opportunities for better coordination.

Depending on the needs and starting point of the country, process mapping can be a quick exercise or a substantial, detailed investigation using empirical methods such as survey research. Process maps are typically developed on the basis of reviews of the laws, regulations, and literature as well as discussions with selected public officials and private sector stakeholders, which can include businesses and other direct users of the land as well as land market intermediaries such as attorneys, consultants, brokers, and design professionals who assist others in obtaining land rights. Gathering information from administrators and users is necessary, as the written descriptions of procedures found in law and regulations often do not describe what happens in fact, due to interpretation and gradual accumulation of administrative practice over time.

As a rule of thumb, gathering detailed data on administrative procedures solely from business firms is not considered to be effective, given the fragmented experience of individual employees and the fact they are often assisted in the process by professionals. It has been found that private sector stakeholders serve as an important cross-check on the opinions of public officials who are responsible for managing administrative processes, particularly with respect to the amount of time a process takes, and professional land market intermediaries are a useful check on the opinions of business professionals, whose recollection of the details of land transactions is sometimes incomplete.

After a review of the laws and regulations, data for process maps can be gathered through in-depth interviews with stakeholders or face-to-face survey questionnaires, the difference being the type of data gathered and how they are reported. In-depth interviews tend to call for more open-ended responses and produce more opinion material, which is harder to aggregate and report, but which can add depth to the understanding of the process. It is not appropriate for large-scale surveys. IFC work on land process mapping in recent years has made use of both techniques, emphasizing practicality, reasonable costs, and quick completion of the work.

Figure 13.1   Process Map for the Allocation of State-Owned Commercial Land in Bangladesh

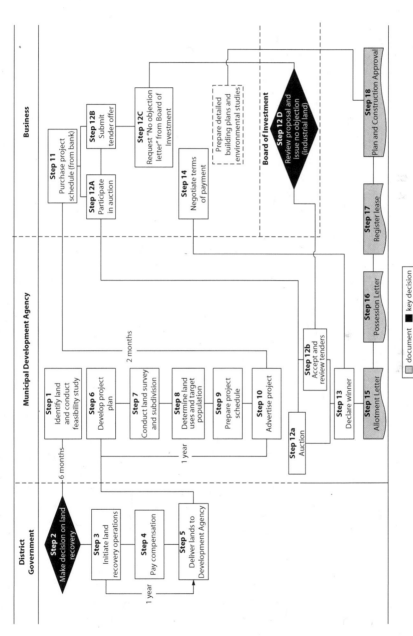

Source: Author.

Allocation of State-Owned Commercial Land

Step	Description	Legal basis	Institutions	Official fees	Required documentation	Processing time	
						Official	*Actual*
1	Development agency identifies land and conducts feasibility study	See generally, National Housing act of 2000 Town Improvement Act of 1953 (RAJUK enabling act) Rajshani Town Development Ordinance of 1976 Khulna Development Authority Ordinance of 1961 Chittagong Development Authority Ordinance of 1959 (1963)	Development agency			N/A	6 months
2	District government takes decision on land acquisition	Acquisition and Requisition of Immovable Property Ordinance of 1982	District government District commissioner and deputy commissioner			45 days	45 days – 1 year
3	District government conducts land recovery operations	Acquisition and Requisition of Immovable Property Ordinance of 1982	District government		Notice/ advertisement of acquisition		
4	Compensation of land owners	Acquisition and Requisition of Immovable Property Ordinance of 1982	District government	Compensation set by law—market value			

#	Activity	Legal reference	Agency	Notes	Requirement	Timeframe
5	Delivery of land to development agency	Acquisition and Requisition of Immovable Property Ordinance of 1982	District government Development agency	Development agency may be required to reimburse district government for acquisition costs	None	1 year
6	Development agency prepares project plan	See municipal development ordinances, generally	Development agency		None	
7	Site survey and subdivision	See municipal development ordinances, generally	Development agency		None	
8	Determination of land uses and target populations	See municipal development ordinances, generally	Development agency		None	
9	Preparation of project schedules	See municipal development ordinances, generally	Development agency		None	
10	Advertisement of project (newspapers)	Town Improvement Act of 1953 Dhaka Improvement Trust (Allocation of Lands) Rules of 1969 See municipal development ordinances, generally	Development agency	Notice of auction/tender	Published for minimum of 3 weeks	

(continued next page)

189

Allocation of State-Owned Commercial Land *(continued)*

Step	Description	Legal basis	Institutions	Official fees	Required documentation	Processing time	
						Official	*Actual*
11	Businesses purchase project schedule from banks	Town Improvement Act of 1953 Dhaka Improvement Trust (Allocation of Lands) Rules of 1969 See municipal development ordinances, generally		Approx. 1,000 taka	Project schedule (prospectus, offering memorandum, etc.)	None	
12A	Auction conducted	Dhaka Improvement Trust (Allocation of Lands) Rules of 1969	Development agency	Earnest money deposit; variable	Affidavit of no prior grant Other pre-qualification documentation as required	None	
12B	Tenders submitted and reviewed	Dhaka Improvement Trust (Allocation of Lands) Rules of 1969	Development agency		Affidavit of no prior grant Other pre-qualification documentation as required BOI no-objection letter	None	

	Activity	Law/Rule	Agency	Fee	Document	Timeline
12C	Business requests "no objection" letter from BOI	Dhaka Improvement Trust (Allocation of Lands) Rules of 1969	BOI		Request for no-objection letter	n.a.
12D	BOI issues/denies no objection letter		BOI			5–15 days
13	Winner of auction/tender declared	Dhaka Improvement Trust (Allocation of Lands) Rules of 1969	Development agency		Auction/tender protocol	30 days
14	Negotiations between winner and development agency		Development agency			
15	Allotment letter issued by development agency		Development agency		Allotment Letter	
16	Possession letter issued by development agency		Development agency		Possession Letter	
17	Land lease issued and registered		Development agency SRO Land Registry	Registration fee	Lease	
18	Plan and construction approval	Building Construction Act of 1952 Building Construction Rules	Development agency	Varies	Building Plans per Rules	30 days–1 year

Source: Author.

Note: BOI = Bangladesh Board of Investment; RAJUK = Rajdhani Unnayaan Kartipakkha (Dhaka Municipal Development Agency); SRO = sub-registry office; n.a. = not applicable.

Allocation of State Land through Competitive Procedures

Governments in many countries have in recent years seen many weaknesses of administrative modes of allocating land, with regard to both their own objectives and those of private business. These governments have therefore moved toward competitive allocation of state-owned land. Depending on the objective of the land allocation program or the type of land allocated, governments may choose competitive procedures such as lottery, auction, or tender. Lottery is not used for commercial and industrial offerings and can be excluded for purposes of this discussion. In recent years the practice of using auctions and similar competitive procedures to allocate land has become accepted, if not yet widespread, in emerging economies, particularly in countries with large state land sectors such as China and Russia, where reforms have proceeded to the point where it is mandatory today to offer certain types of state lands only through competitive bidding.[3] Jurisdictions that use competitive procedures either exclusively or for important components of their state land programs also include Australia; Bangladesh; Hong Kong SAR, China; India; Singapore; and Taiwan, China.

The objectives and potential benefits of competitive procedures are generally agreed to include greater transparency in the allocation of a public asset, creation of a level playing field for investors, and greater accuracy in pricing. From the investor's perspective, participation in auctions can be low cost, quick, and definitive, qualities often lacking in complex and drawn out application processes in which investors often do not receive a legal commitment of the land until after investing significant amounts of time and money in the process. Competitive procedures can be useful in establishing prices for land in markets in which land values are difficult to determine because of lack of market activity or the prevalence of unreported informal transactions.

Despite the growing acceptance of competitive bidding procedures for allocating land, there is not a great deal of compelling data that such procedures result in higher prices than would be achieved through other methods, such as advertisement and negotiation or simply listing the land with a competent broker. Given the nature of the activity and the difficulty of experimental controls, this is to be expected. What is frequently measured is whether the auction price exceeds the established starting or reserve price, but the significance of this figure depends on how that starting price is established; frequently it is set lower than the market price.

Two major types of competitive procedures are used today: open auction and public tender or request for proposals. (Sometimes procedures in which participants are requested by public advertisement to submit confidential, sealed offers for a property are referred to as "public tenders," but they are, in fact, much closer to the auction format.) Auctions and tenders serve different purposes, and each may be more applicable in different circumstances.

Auction

For a competitive offering to succeed, the product itself should be well located and have value; auctioning poorly located and marginal lands is unlikely to succeed. In addition, the state must be prepared to invest time and resources in preparing the land for sale, which would include selecting an appropriate land site, conducting a survey and town planning, investing in appropriate infrastructure, developing auction rules and documentation, and undertaking publicity and marketing of the auction. These costs can be recaptured in the auction price.

While any site can be auctioned, some sites are more suited than others to the auction technique. Smaller land sites with a wide range of permitted uses are most suitable. Large complex sites subject to specific public development objectives and constraints—or for which there are only a few potential developers with sufficient finance and experience—may be less suitable. Auction is not suitable if the landowner is uncertain about the development program for the site and is seeking proposals. A key to the process is that potential bidders must be able to value the land within a relatively short period of time, meaning that all of the development parameters and conditions are known.

An auction is a process usually governed as a form of contract by either the general civil law or a special law on auction.[4] By participating in the auction, the state agrees to transfer the land to the highest bidder, and other participants in the auction agree to pay for and take delivery of the land if they are the successful bidder. Upon successful completion, the auction creates a legal contract as binding as if the parties had negotiated and signed an agreement to transfer the land. Even if the basic rules of auction are established in the civil or commercial law, it may not be possible to dispose of state assets by auction unless specifically permitted by other laws on the disposition of state assets.

There are different formats for land auctions, but the most typical is the single-unit auction, where one object is offered for bid at a time, and the typical format is the simple first-price, sealed-bid auction.

The auction rules and procedures are essentially terms of the offer made by the state to grant the land to the highest bidder and are legally binding on the participants. Departures from the specified rules and procedures could be cause for challenging and nullifying the auction results. Unless auction procedures are sufficiently detailed in the applicable law, it may be advisable to adopt a detailed procedure in the form of a regulation for the disposition of state lands. The decision as to what belongs in law and what in regulation needs to be made in light of the requirements of the local legal system.

Provided that the auction is properly prepared and the information provided with respect to the land is accurate and comprehensive, there are few risks to the investor. From the investor's perspective, the key is that the permitted use of the land is known prior to the bid and he or she is not put in the position of acquiring the land and then slogging through uncooperative bureaucracies to obtain land use and building permits. This issue can be addressed by including land use rights in the terms of the auction.

This is not to say that auction procedures cannot be corrupted; auctions can be sham transactions intended to hide the fact that participation has been limited by administrative rules or compromised by private collusion enforced by agreement or intimidation. Assuring inclusive rules of participation and good publicity for the auction may be able to address some of these issues. From the state's perspective, good appraisal practice, reasonable reserve prices, and the willingness to reject unreasonably low bids may offer some protection against collusion.

Tender

Tender is the term sometimes used to describe a type of competitive land allocation procedure in which price is only one of the determining factors. Another term might be "request for proposals." Auctions and tenders are not alternatives, but may be appropriate in different circumstances. Tender competitions may be appropriate when a unique land opportunity is offered—for example, a prime site in the center city—and the authorities are genuinely open to suggestions from the private market regarding the best use of the land. It may also be appropriate where the public authorities are unwilling or unable to invest in planning and preparing the land for auction and where allowing planning proposals and complex pricing is in order. Public tendering is often applied to the development of special districts, the special rationale for and approaches of which are discussed in chapter 18 of this volume.

The tender technique is often more similar to an administrative allocation procedure than a competitive land auction. In addition to the prices offered by the participants, these competitions may be judged on factors that may include experience with similar projects, financial capability, proposed use of the land, and, in some cases, the quality of the land use plan and design aspects of the proposed project. Also, unlike simple auctions, tender competitions may allow far more complex pricing proposals, including, for example, deferred payment and profit participation by the state. (Auctions also may entail consideration of prior experience and financial capability through prequalification requirements by which only those meeting certain threshold qualifications are permitted to participate, but in such cases these determinations are made before the competition begins. This is not to say, however, that prequalification cannot and has not been used to manipulate the outcome of auctions.)

In some cases, tenders may have significant drawbacks from the perspective of the investor. Participation in a tender competition can be expensive, particularly if it requires development of planning or design materials. Moreover, once submitted, the investor is putting his best ideas on the table without compensation, free for the state, or anyone else for that matter, to use. Aggravating both of these conditions even further is that selection of a tender winner is essentially a subjective process requiring exercise of judgment by public officials or others and is consequently subject to corrupting or political influences. For all of these reasons, allocation by tender has sometimes been referred to as a "beauty contest."

Attempts can be made to reduce the severity of these problems by structuring the tender process. The following are some of the steps that might be taken:

- Focusing on a small set of selection criteria or variables
- Focusing on selection criteria that can be quantified to a significant extent—for example, prior experience with similar projects is largely an objective determination
- Clearly defining and assigning percentage weights to selection criteria; requiring selection panels to document scores and issue written reports
- For significant projects, placing selection in the hands of an independent panel that includes civic leaders and nongovernmental organizations; including design professionals in cases in which land use and design are important factors in selection

- Requiring a transparent formula for comparing economic proposals—for example, a discounted value of cash flows using a standard discount rate.

Summary

Administrative or negotiated procedures probably remain the predominant model for the allocation of state lands in developing countries today. While such procedures may pose certain risks to investors in terms of transparency, time, and costs, progress is being made in improving performance and transparency, including creation of accessible inventories of state lands available for investment, one-stop land allocation shops, and simplified application requirements. A key objective from the perspective of investors is to receive assurances that the state is acting in good faith.

A good place to start in assessing administrative land allocation procedures is with a thorough procedural mapping exercise, which can reveal bottlenecks and suggest ideas for simplification.

Use of competitive land allocation procedures such as auctions and public tenders is becoming more common in developing and transitional countries and may have certain advantages from the perspective of investors, including greater transparency, lower transaction costs, and a level playing field. Transparency is also an objective of the state, which may achieve higher prices for its land through competitive bidding.

Notes

1. There are many treatises on land expropriation and resettlement. For three of the guides on best practice in land expropriations under different conditions, see Asian Development Bank (1998), United Nations (1997), and World Bank (2001).

2. See, for example, New South Wales Crown Lands Business Directive for Commercial Leases and Licenses as Approved by the Director General, Department of Lands, September 7, 2004.

3. Under the 2008 amendments to the Russian Land Code, all publicly owned land intended for residential development must be allocated through competitive auction. In China all state-owned land must be bid through competitive auction. The Vietnamese Law on Land (Article 58) says that land for residential use, infrastructure development, and business or production purposes must be offered by auction, but this provision of the law

seems to be rarely enforced and, in an extensive 2007 survey of land allocation, the IFC found that few, if any, businesses in that country had acquired
land through an auction.

4. An example of a specific law on auction is China's Auction Law (adopted at
the twentieth Meeting of the Standing Committee of the Eighth National
People's Congress on July 5, 1996, promulgated by Presidential Order no. 70
on July 5, 1996, and effective as of January 1, 1997). Countries that address
auction procedures in a rudimentary way in their Civil Code include Russia
(Articles 447–48) and Vietnam (Articles 452–55). A modern civil law of
auction is found in the Civil Code of Quebec, Canada (Articles 1757–78).

References

Asian Development Bank. 1998. *Handbook on Resettlement: A Guide to Good
Practice.* Tokyo: Asian Development Bank.

Farole, T., and G. Akinci, eds. 2011. "Special Economic Zones: Progress, Emerging
Challenges, and Future Directions." World Bank, Washington, DC.

United Nations. 1997. *Comprehensive Human Rights Guidelines on Development-
Based Displacement.* New York: United Nations.

World Bank. 2001. "Operational Policy on Involuntary Resettlement (OP 4.12)."
World Bank, Washington, DC.

CHAPTER 14

Business Access to Land under Customary Use: How to Involve and Benefit Local Communities

Xiaofang Shen and Elizabeth Hannah

In many parts of the developing world, land use rights are determined by custom: the land and land-related resources are used and managed by the local communities according to their traditions. Such land covers 80 to 90 percent of Sub-Saharan Africa, and it provides the basis for the livelihood, as well as the social and cultural practices, of more than half of the population on the continent. In other parts of the world, ranging from the Pacific islands to the *ejido* communities in Mexico, customary land regimes also play a critical role. The people who inhabit customary land are for the most part indigenous to the land and are usually among the poorest of the poor in those countries.

For centuries, customary land has been used for community farming, grazing, hunting, gathering, and other traditional activities. However, this pattern has come under increased pressures to change in recent decades. Specific pressures vary from place to place, but generally include the following:

- *General economic and social development* has prompted many national and local governments to explore ways to use traditionally held land more productively. In many places where major roads and other infrastructural works have been carried out, new land use opportunities have opened up and land value has increased, attracting commercial interest.

- *Accelerated urbanization* in many countries, and along with it the urgent need to accommodate an ever-growing urban population with housing and job creation, has increased pressure on converting rural land— much of it traditionally held—to construction land.
- *Recent global food shortages and energy crises* have led to a significant increase in the interest in large-scale farming for food and biofuels. In some places, especially in Africa, this trend has caused a surge of large-scale acquisition of farmland, or a "land rush" as it is called, involving sovereign-backed funds and multinational companies.
- *Conservation.* Some customary land has valuable natural resources—for example, wildlife and nature—that are under threat of depletion. Many countries have designated such land as national parks for conservation purposes. As such, traditional activities such as hunting and gathering are no longer allowed inside these areas.[1]

These trends—with possibly the exception of the alarmingly large-scale acquisition of farmland recently taking place in some parts of Africa and elsewhere[2]—present potential, sometimes significant, opportunities to current users of customary land. For instance, roads and other infrastructure have brought market access closer to small landholders. They have also increased the market value of land, often the main asset that local communities have. In protected areas, conservation needs may force rapid, sometimes painful, lifestyle transformation among indigenous groups, but they also encourage the development of nontraditional activities—for example, ecotourism combining conservation with income generation. If well developed, such activities may bring alternative, and improved, livelihoods to the affected people.

However, none of these potential benefits can be realized unless the rights of the local communities are respected and protected. They also require that local communities be fully included in the development process as an equal partner. In cases where the loss of traditional ways of living is inevitable, fair compensation and resettlement assistance must be provided to the affected population. At present, the position of small landholders and indigenous groups in many places is frequently undermined by insecure property rights and policy procedures that neglect their needs. They often do not have either access to information or adequate institutions of their own with which to defend their interests. Most countries currently do not have social safety nets to protect the poorest and most vulnerable groups.

This reality has caused considerable concern within the development community that the acquisition of customary land for business purposes risks bringing detriments rather than benefits to the poor and vulnerable (Cotula and others 2009). Among the business community, there is also a growing awareness that inappropriate treatment of local communities can adversely affect their long-term business objectives.[3] Preventing these dangers through the use of specially tailored policy and institutional instruments has, thus, become a focus of both policy and business decision makers.

Understanding Customary Rights

The core of customary rights is the principle of usufruct. Whether based on statutes or traditions, local communities have a right to use the land and to retain the fruits of it. Traditionally and typically, they do not have the right to sell or even to lease such land to others; such limitations imply, among other things, that such land cannot be used as collateral for loans, which severely limits access to the finance usually necessary for developing any parcel of land. The traditions that govern use of this land, and access to it, range from the rules of families and villages to the politics of tribes and kingdoms. Customary rights are consistent with the traditional ways of living, but whether in this day and age such a structure protects the local communities or limits their development possibilities can be, and is, debated; in general, it does both.

During colonial times in Sub-Saharan Africa, customary land was frequently taken by the colonial government and allocated to new immigrant settlers, often without consideration of the local communities. After independence, many governments simply imposed state ownership on the basis that customary tenure was an inadequate legal framework for development.[4] Some even introduced new laws to enhance state power over customary rights. Consequently, many African countries today have national laws that place all land, including customary land, under the control of a "public trustee" (see tables 14.1 and 14.2). In many places, governments have introduced land reform programs to "regularize" customary rights with a view to reconciling the coexisting land systems and converting informal rights into formal titles, either freeholds or leaseholds.[5]

Table 14.1   Land Tenure Structure in Select African Countries

Country	Percent privately owned or leased and registered as such	Percent under customary use, recognized or unrecognized by law	Legislation vests all land interest in the state
Angola	0	95	Yes
Benin	1	90	Yes
Botswana	6	71	No
Burkina Faso	1	99	Yes
Cape Verde	—	—	Yes
Cameroon	—	—	No
Chad	—	—	Yes
Congo, Dem. Rep.	—	—	Yes
Eritrea	—	—	Yes
Ethiopia	—	—	Yes
Gabon	—	—	Yes
Gambia, The	—	—	Yes
Ghana	5	85	No
Guinea	5	90	No
Guinea-Bissau	—	—	Yes
Kenya	20	60	No
Lesotho	5	90	No
Liberia	—	—	Yes
Malawi	13	69	No
Mali	2	90	Yes
Mauritania	—	—	No
Mozambique	3	80	Yes
Namibia	44	43	No
Niger	—	—	No
Nigeria	10	80	Yes
Rwanda	1	80	Yes
Senegal	15	80	Yes
Seychelles	—	—	Yes
Sierra Leone	5	90	No
South Africa	72	14	No
Swaziland	27	73	No
Tanzania	5	80	Yes
Togo	40	—	No
Uganda	15	80	No
Zambia	14	80	Yes
Zimbabwe	41	42	No

Sources: Authors' compilation assisted by Ezra Rosser and Alex Bernshteyn of the International Legal Resource Center.
Note: — = Not available.

Table 14.2   Sub-Saharan African Countries with National Laws That Vest the Land Interest in the State

Country	Description of laws
Angola	The 1975 constitution (revised 1992) stipulates that the state shall be the owner of lands and that individuals are no longer able to buy private land, but can be granted "surface" or "possession" rights to the lands that belonged to the state.
Burkina Faso	The 1984 Agrarian and Land Reform Act established a national land domain over the entire national territory. Any previous land property or customary right was abolished; individuals and legal entities were entitled only to land use rights. The 1996 Land Law intended to modify the system has not produced the expected results in the field.
Cameroon	The 1974 Land Law abolished the recognition of customary land rights, imposed titling as the sole way for acquiring private property, and empowered the state as guardian of nonregistered land (national domain). Use rights of local communities were recognized on land in the national domain.
Cape Verde	The 1983 Agrarian Reform Law gave the state the option of expropriating unused land in order to allocate it to farmers without land who benefit from land use rights. Faced with many physical, technical, cultural, and financial constraints, this law was revoked in 1993.
Chad	Three 1967 laws organized the land tenure regime based on principles derived from colonial legislation, which upheld the principle of state monopoly over land. All unused land is considered as state property, including community-owned land. Although legislation recognizes indigenous land tenure systems, the state makes it impossible for local communities to benefit from recognition of their rights by requiring legal registration and titling and by denying collective property rights.
Congo, Dem. Rep.	The 1973 General Property Law (modified in 1980) stipulates that land is "the exclusive, inalienable property of the state."
Eritrea	The 1994 Land Proclamation says that all land is owned by the state and that the government may allow the lease of usufruct or similar rights over land and may provide preconditions and criteria pertaining to use of the land.
Ethiopia	Constitution (Article 40) vests all land in the state.
Gabon	The 1963 Land Law stipulates that all land belongs to the state.
Gambia, The	The 1990 Lands Act calls for converting customary tenure to leasehold tenure; the 1990 Land Acquisition and Compensation Act expands considerably the power of government to acquire and control development of land for a wide variety of purposes.
Guinea-Bissau	The 1998 Land Law maintains state ownership over land, but also acknowledges the existence of use rights for individuals.
Liberia	The constitution affirms a double land system by allowing descendants of the first occupants and so-called civilized groups to own a title issued by the government after approval by the head of state. All other land belongs to the state, and only the state can sell off the land.

(continued next page)

Table 14.2   *(continued)*

Country	Description of laws
Mali	The 2000 Code Domanial et Foncier and its applied decrees establish a national domain composed of all land on Malian territory, which includes land that belongs to the state as well as land that belongs to local communities or private individuals.
Mozambique	The 1997 Land Law stipulates that all land belongs to the state. The 1998 Land Regulation recognizes the priority use rights of state land by current land users, including customary users.
Nigeria	The Land Use Act of 1978 (revised in 1990 and 1997) vests all land in the territory of each state (except land vested in the federal government or its agencies) exclusively in the governor of the state. The governor holds such land in trust for the population and administers it on behalf of and for all Nigerians.
Rwanda	The 2005 Organic Law on Land requires all individual landholders, rural and urban, to register as holders of "lease contracts" of state land. The law allows such lease contracts to be turned into formal titles after 10 years of evident use of the land.
Senegal	The 1964 National Domain Law and the 1972 Rural Communities Act (applying to 95 percent of rural lands) define state lands as all lands that had not been registered prior to the 1964 law.
Seychelles	Immovable Property (Transfer Restriction) Act Cap 96 stipulates that access to all immovable property must have government approval.
Tanzania	Article 3(4) of the Land Act 1999 stipulates that all land interest is vested in the state.
Zambia	The 1995 Land Act stipulates that all land shall vest absolutely in the president and shall be held by him in perpetuity for and on behalf of all Zambians.

Sources: Authors' compilation assisted by Alex Bernshteyn of the International Legal Resource Center.

In spite of wide-reaching attempts to legislate state ownership of land, as illustrated by table 14.2, many governments have found it difficult to enforce such ownership on the ground. Efforts to "regularize" land tenure by converting customary rights into formal (state-owned) land use rights have failed in most places. Meanwhile, customary regimes continue to play a resilient role across the African continent. As a result, there is a dual system of land tenure in Africa today, wherein the de jure rights of the state and the de facto rights of the traditional users overlap. In recent years, more and more policy workers and scholars have argued that the role of customary rights needs to be formally respected and that a customary land regime needs to be recognized and incorporated in the land management system (Burns 2007).

Understanding the Stakeholders and Their Special Interests

Understanding the nature of customary rights helps to appreciate the sensitive issue of customary land use. It also sets the context in which three different stakeholders interplay when commercial use of such land arises, each with their own priorities and concerns.

Local Communities

Local communities, as the current occupiers of land, are a fundamental stakeholder in this process. As seen earlier, local communities are not monolithic, but include a variety of traditional land users ranging from individual small landholders and villages to tribes and kingdoms. Their needs may vary from place to place, but in general they share the following common interests and concerns.

First, while local communities are usually the poorest strata of society, they have the same ambitions as anyone else of improving their situation and are ready to welcome development that they believe will benefit them. When increased commercial interest raises the value of the land, especially in suburban and periurban areas, local communities respond to the market relatively quickly. Some community members may have reasonable expectations of deriving their fair share of the benefits of development through the partial sale or leasing of the land. Others may see the opportunity to turn the land they control into the capital to attract technology and management know-how, thereby transforming themselves into entrepreneurs.

This trend is evident in many places. Near Gaborone, the capital city of Botswana, where construction land is in high demand, villages place advertisements offering land for lease to industrial and commercial users. In northern Rwanda, where the volcanoes park and mountain gorillas are attracting a growing number of tourists, villagers are quick to embrace opportunities by embarking upon tourism ventures. Some are negotiating joint-venture agreements with brand-name hotel developers, land being their equity contribution; others are turning their homes into bed and breakfast accommodations for backpackers. In South Africa, the largest commercial demand for communal land use comes, in fact, from the community entrepreneurs themselves rather than from incoming investors.

However, in many places the absence of clear property rights for local communities and the lack of legal and institutional instruments to protect such rights impede the realization of potential commercial benefits for current occupiers. In numerous instances, the development process has moved forward without undertaking proper consultation with local communities or sufficiently compensating them for their losses; development that should represent a potential benefit for them in fact becomes a threat to their livelihoods. This inevitably causes social resentment and even unrest, which can backfire on the investors, as seen in China, India, and many African countries.

Furthermore, local communities generally lack information and experience in business dealings, and there is often no institutional support for their needs. This significantly weakens their bargaining position in the marketplace. Sometimes, lack of organized decision making and internal dissent present hurdles in commercial negotiations that are time sensitive and require clarity. In some cases, community elites have disregarded the interests of their own members, striking deals with governments and private developers for their own personal gain.[6]

Finally, in areas where land rich in natural resources has recently been converted into conservation areas, there is an acute need to support the indigenous people whose livelihoods depend on access to such land. When people are asked (or forced) to give up the land and their traditional way of life, some feasible alternatives to meeting their economic, cultural, and religious needs must be put in place. Otherwise, they face the danger of further impoverishment.

Investors

Investors seeking land for investment purposes are an equally important stakeholder.[7] They can be small or large, locals or outsiders; regardless of their size and origin, they share a common desire to generate profit. They require a high degree of clarity and security in terms of property rights to underpin their long-term investment plans and to use as collateral for bank loans. For commercial investors, timing is of paramount importance. To them, the speed with which their plans may be implemented is fundamental to gaining the advantage over competitors in a rapidly changing marketplace.

For these reasons, most investors may prefer to avoid customary land if they have other choices. Because it has not been demarcated or registered, such land represents high risk and low value to investors, since banks usually do not accept it as security for lending. Land that is remote from roads, power, or other infrastructure may also be less attractive, as it implies higher up-front capital costs for the investment projects. When considering such land, investors must consider the risks and costs and, as a trade-off, they expect higher than normal returns. This often makes otherwise commercially promising projects less viable. The need for definite timeliness and a reasonably foreseeable high return are some of the reasons why investors may appear impatient, and even greedy, at times in negotiations. Frequently, protracted negotiations simply lead investors to give up. This is especially true of external investors, who have more alternatives than their local peers. If the process drags on or gets too complicated, they may simply go elsewhere.

Investors, especially foreign investors, are sensitive to landownership issues when entering emerging markets. Many are prepared to work with a lease arrangement instead of direct ownership, as long as the terms and conditions of the leases meet their basic business needs. Such needs can vary. For instance, investors may accept relatively short terms for quick-turnaround crops, but may require longer terms for more capital-intensive investment such as perennial tree crops. The duration of the lease term is often a prerequisite to using the land as collateral for bank loans, so a sufficiently long term is always important to those who need to borrow from banks. See chapter 15 in this volume for a more detailed discussion of the general principles of long-term land leasing.

In general, investors are aware that it is in their best interests to act as "good citizens" in the geographic areas in which they operate. Most investors are prepared to comply with the existing laws and regulations designed to safeguard public interest, including necessary protection for weak and vulnerable communities. Investors, however, need clear guidance of what is required, what is encouraged, and what is prohibited. They respond best to laws and regulations that they find credible and to equal and consistent treatment of all parties. Companies also act in response to systemic awards and punishments based on their behaviors. It is therefore not a surprise that compliance is low where laws and regulations are confusing and poorly enforced.

Governments

Governments responsible for economic growth, social development, and environmental protection are an indispensable stakeholder in the process. Many parts of the government may exert influence. Line ministries responsible for rural or urban development, for instance, make policy decisions that can have a significant impact on customary land use. Land administration agencies specialized in land surveying, cadastre, and registration provide the services critical to establishing secure rights for communities and investors. Local government authorities responsible for planning, environmental protection, roads, and utilities hold the power that inevitably affects the status of traditionally used land.

More and more governments, anxious for job and income creation, have stepped up the effort to promote investment, particularly in sectors such as agriculture, tourism, and manufacturing. Sometimes, government intervention is deemed necessary to facilitate the strategic needs of such sectors (for example, consolidation of land, development of special infrastructure, and development of industrial zones). In other instances, they try to be the brokers of "anchor" investment projects in underdeveloped regions. In still other cases, they act as the facilitator to help investors to deal with numerous local parties, on the one hand, and to help inexperienced local partners to negotiate with large, powerful companies, on the other.

Governments also commonly exercise their regulatory power, through land access approvals, especially in countries where customary land is, by law, also "state land." In such places, investors seeking rural land are often not allowed to negotiate directly with local communities before obtaining government approvals. In others, investors and local communities can first reach an agreement that is subject to final approval by the government. As a general practice, land containing natural resources—such as forestry, minerals, or wildlife—is put under government control, and the use of such land typically requires government approval.

Although many government goals are intrinsic, the results of government intervention, at best, are mixed. One common problem is that many governments are not coherent players. Land decisions are made at national or local levels, by many ministries and agencies, without proper coordination. The lack of agreed priorities frequently leads to ad hoc and inconsistent interventions, while overlapping mandates of the various agencies cause turf struggles among bureaucratic agencies that impede the investment process.

Further, the desire of governments to promote investment is frequently not matched by the necessary knowledge and competence required for implementation. The wish to support business and market growth may be strong at the top, but low-level officials may not fully understand business needs, and some are still deeply suspicious about the profit-driven motives of investors. Moreover, there is a common lack of capacity among implementing agencies to provide the services needed, for example, to survey the land, adjudicate the boundaries, establish and maintain land registries, and so forth. Consequently, many government programs intended to promote investment instead become bureaucratic hurdles to investment.

Most problematic, government interventions suffer where laws and regulations are not clear about the rights of the state and the customary land users. In some situations, government officials anxious to promote investment act irresponsibly with regard to the rights of local communities. This sometimes helps to speed up the investment projects in the short term, but leaves behind long-term problems, including confrontations between the investor and the local community. In the worst scenario, excessive power in the hands of government officials simply encourages rent-seeking behavior, leading to losses on the part of local communities, investors, and the general public.

Toward a Solution

The stakeholder analysis above suggests that there is an important tripartite relationship, illustrated by the simplified diagram shown in figure 14.1, in which three key stakeholders are pivotal in the central play of commercial access to customary land. Although conflicting interests potentially exist that might complicate the process, complementary goals are also present to offer a basis for cooperation in order to develop win-win situations. The key to success, as in any relationship, lies in a process that supports open dialogue, consultation, and

Figure 14.1   A Tripartite Process Inclusive of All Stakeholders for Shared Interests

- Higher return from land
- Employment and income
- Social/cultural preservation

Local communities

Investors domestic and foreign

The government national and local

- Sustainable business
- Efficient and predictable process
- "Good citizen" status

- Strategic sector growth
- Investment and employment
- Environment protection
- Social sustainability

Source: Authors.

conciliation aimed at maximizing common interests and minimizing potential conflicts. Just as important, the analysis shows the presence of an asymmetrical power relationship in the triangular structure, with the local communities in a relatively disadvantaged position vis-à-vis the other two players. This suggests that some special assistance to the local communities is needed if the objective is to promote sustainable businesses that will ensure the trickle-down effect of economic development to the poor and the vulnerable.

This requires the commitment of all stakeholders, but the government must take the lead by providing the right policy and legal conditions under which a fair, inclusive investment process can take place and the interests of those who are less well placed to protect themselves are safeguarded. Among the specific conditions needed, three are top priorities: secure property rights, systematic social impact assessment, and good governance.

Secure Property Rights

Providing the customary land users with secure property rights is fundamental to empowering them and giving them a voice in the modernization process, which, in turn, provides the basis for equitable and sustainable development. Clear rights of tenure will provide customary land users with the incentive to invest in the land and will put them in a stronger position in any kind of business venture. A greater sense of ownership will motivate customary land users to take a long-term view, which will, in turn, generate an understanding of the need to conserve and develop the land and related resources. Needless to say, secure land rights will always be attractive to commercial investors, as they reduce the risks and raise the value associated with customary land.

Clear rights are not necessarily individually attributed rights, as some government programs have, rather unsuccessfully, tried to implement. Frequently, community structures and dynamics provide a degree of protection for vulnerable groups in traditional settings. Legislative efforts to recognize different types of rights that are appropriate in the context of traditional ways of living can be very useful (Deininger 2003). In recent years, quite a number of countries in Africa, Asia, and elsewhere have moved in this direction. In Vietnam, the government introduced in the 2003 Land Act a collective rights regime wherein villagers can register group rights. In Mexico, reforms in the late 1990s enabled the transformation of *ejido* land by allowing group registration and the registration of secondary rights under such group rights. Today, many African countries have enacted laws giving indigenous communities collective legal rights to forest reserves or ancestral lands.[8]

Although the implementation of collective rights remains inconsistent in Africa, some countries have reaped positive results from innovative approaches. In Namibia, as seen in chapter 3 in this volume, the introduction of the Nature Conservation Amendment Act no. 5 in 1996 gave indigenous groups the opportunity to register certain areas of land as "conservancies," which gave them the same legal rights to use wildlife resources for commercial activities previously available only to freeholder owners. The number of conservancies and the income from them have since grown rapidly. Similarly, the transformation of *ejido* land in Mexico shows that, by allowing collective rights for communities and secondary rights within communities, the country has succeeded in encouraging community groups to invest in land, which has led to maize yields of about 5 tons per hectare, more than twice the previous state average. Secure rights also put communities in a stronger position to do business with the outside world. To date, the *ejido* communities have signed some 3,000 commercial contracts, often with large firms (Deininger and Byerlee 2011).

The real difference in these cases lies not just in the enactment of appropriate laws but in the implementation of them, supported by follow-up initiatives to strengthen land administration. Typically, a problem with customary rights is that they are not conclusive, lack authoritative and consistent documentary support, and are subject to disputes within and among the local communities (Deininger and Byerlee 2011). A recent study by the World Bank found that, in Indonesia and Cambodia, where customary landownership is conceptually recognized in law, ultimately, those with formal documents evidencing their rights have been in a better position to defend or transact those rights than those with only general statutory recognition (Deininger and Byerlee 2011).

Complete implementation of property registration programs is often an onerous undertaking requiring resources that many developing countries simply do not have. In recent years, some governments have adopted a geographically phased approach in order to accelerate the process in areas where demand is evident. In Burkina Faso, as seen in chapter 1 of this volume, reforms of the registry system initially targeted the capital city and resulted in an increase in the number of new land titles from 15 to 2,030 in three years. In Rwanda, as presented in chapter 4 of this volume, the land registry program, which aimed to give small farmers and urban citizens clearer property rights, initially focused on four target areas. These pilots led to impressive increases in the number of new registrations and allowed the implementing agencies to gain experience and confidence. In both cases, the models created on the basis of successful pilots were then used to show the way for the rest of the country.

Systematic Social Impact Assessment with a View to Protecting Current Landholders

Governments sometimes need to acquire and consolidate land for more focused infrastructure development or more efficient use of limited land resources. The process, if not carefully handled, can have a devastating effect on the poor people whose only asset is the land they currently occupy. The repercussions on general society are also evident. Box 14.1 offers just one of many examples of how inappropriately forced relocation can perpetuate social problems for the local communities. Such a lack of respect for the rights of the local poor can seriously erode the confidence of investors. As a businessman once commented in a workshop in Nairobi, how the government treated the citizens currently occupying the land sent a signal to potential investors about how they might be treated in the future. This can be a particular concern for the smaller and less politically connected investors—if land may be given to them arbitrarily today, could it not be taken away from them arbitrarily tomorrow?

Box 14.1

Impact of Inappropriately Forced Relocation on the Poor and the Vulnerable

The Maroco community of Lagos (Nigeria)—some 10,000 strong—was first moved in 1960 from what is now the area between Victoria Island and Ikoyi to a swampy area, which is now the Victoria Island Annex. They lived there for about 30 years, until 1990, when they were told by the government to vacate the area. An announcement was made on the radio, giving them a notice of seven days. On the seventh day, they were forced out of their homes, and the buildings were bulldozed. A smaller group of them eventually moved to Ilasan Estate in Lekki corridor, where they were allocated unfinished, previously abandoned units. They have allocation letters showing their legitimate occupation of those apartments. However, now, after living there for 15 years, the government has come back to tell them to leave once again—for the third time.

Source: Mathema 2008.

Disrespect for local rights has backfired at investment projects in many places. The protracted difficulties in erecting a greenfield steel plant by Tata Steel in Orissa, India, due to its initial failure to carefully consult the local communities, is a well-known example. Similar lessons are learned from many instances in Africa, as box 14.2 illustrates. In many African countries, new national park laws that deny indigenous people their traditional way of life without providing them with viable alternatives simply lead to illegal hunting, high cost of policing, and an unsafe environment for conservation staff and tourists—all of which seriously impede the goal of conservation and ecotourism business development.

Putting human beings at the center of sustainable development is highlighted as Principle no. 1 of the 1992 Rio Declaration on Environment and Development. Over the years, increased recognition of the importance of

---

Box 14.2

Inappropriate Government Intervention and the Effect on Investment

In Mozambique, a local government eager to attract investment acted in haste to clear land for a foreign investor from South Africa. It posted a public notice of the land use intention in town hall offices for three months, to satisfy the regulatory requirement. However, local people, unaware of the intention to develop, did not travel to the office to see the notice during the period. When the deadline passed, the investor was given official approval. Initially happy, the investor recognized that he had a problem soon after starting construction. Local communities that had not been properly consulted resented the development and started to sabotage it by squatting and cutting the fences at night to steal the construction materials. The investor had to renegotiate with the locals to save his project.

In the Copperbelt of Zambia, the earlier decline in the copper market led to the reduction in mining employment and the spread of "informal" settlements of small-scale farming in the area. To restore the planned land use, the government and the mining company first tried police actions, which did not resolve the problem and instead caused more confrontations. A better solution was found for all parties involved only after CARE, a nongovernmental organization active in the country, acted as facilitator in bringing all parties to the table to negotiate an agreement giving the necessary consideration to the small farmers.

Sources: Authors' interviews in Mozambique in 2001; Steckley and Muleba 2001.

this principle has led several international initiatives by the Food and Agriculture Organization, United Nations Habitat, the World Bank, and others, to develop principles, criteria, and standards to guide governments facing the pressing need of development, which, if not carefully handled, could cause undesirable social impacts. These principles, first and foremost, require that governments use expropriation only as the last resort and only for true public interests, such as public infrastructure, environmental protection, and other publicly needed facilities. When expropriation is unavoidable, governments are required to develop relocation plans including sufficient compensation, assistance in resettlements, and other important measures for protecting and assisting the adversely affected population. Further, it has been recognized that a good stakeholder analysis up-front of development projects, leading to a systematic and transparent consultation process, is critical to success, both socially and economically (Vanclay 2003).

Some governments have taken decisive steps to involve customary stakeholders in making decisions that would affect their land, with encouraging results. The Ngamiland development in Botswana, described in box 14.3, is one such example. The country has established national laws by which decisions on any uses of land and land-related resources are decentralized to local land boards, which include local community representatives. Ministries and the government investment promotion agency assist investors in the process, but cannot intervene in the final decisions made by the land boards. This can sometimes take time, but once decisions have been reached, they are carried out faithfully. Over time, Botswana has earned a reputation among local and foreign investors as a fair and predictable place to do business (see box 14.3).

In most places where general laws and institutions are still missing, self-regulation by investors appears to be useful as the second-best solution. From the investors' perspective, spending time up-front to understand and accommodate the needs of the local economy may, initially, slow down project implementation, but such care can pay off well in the long run by increasing the possibility that such projects will succeed. The case study in chapter 2 of this volume is one good example in which a progressive investor in an acclaimed national park in Mozambique was able to turn an ecotourism project on the verge of conflict into a sustainable business by reaching out to the local communities and engaging them in mutually beneficial business development, despite the fact that the existing law requires the eviction of indigenous groups.

Box 14.3

High-End Ecotourism Investment Involving Local Communities in Botswana

At the outset of the Ngamiland hunting safari and lodging development project in 1995, there was a deep-seated suspicion on the part of local government and the indigenous community of the profit motive. There was little knowledge of how to make the foreign investor an ally in promoting public welfare and conserving biodiversity. Over time, however, joint efforts of the investor, the national nature conservation authority, local land boards, and the local community trust (representing five villages) managed to work out a series of measures to serve the minimum interests of all parties. By 2004, the business not only had proved to be sustainable but was expanding. In the meantime, several communities were starting to develop and run profitable enterprises, either on their own or in partnership with incoming investors in this otherwise remote area with limited alternative opportunities. The impact on conservation of the resource base was profound, including less poaching in the privately run hunting concessions than in other national parks and game reserves. The core of the Okavango delta, a world heritage site, is now more secure than it had ever been in the past century.

Source: White 2004.

To assist those companies in using self-regulation on social and environmental standards, several leading financial institutions have been developing a set of basic principles and guidelines. In 2003 the Equator Bank, a group of more than 70 private financial institutions, made a joint commitment to implementing a set of principles for social and environmental performance. In 2006 the International Finance Corporation (IFC), the private sector arm of the World Bank Group, further developed more detailed performance standards on social and environmental sustainability, to provide investors with specific guidance on how to avoid or reduce the risks associated with the acquisition of land in developing countries (see box 14.4).

Finally, the local communities themselves have an important role to play in ensuring that the voices of all members, especially the poorest, are heard and that the benefits of development are fairly shared among all. This can be challenging in places where the communities represent different groups but do not have clear institutional mechanisms to ensure

Box 14.4

IFC Performance Standard 5 on Social and Environmental Sustainability

IFC Performance Standard 5 focuses on "involuntary resettlement" with a view to preventing long-term hardship and impoverishment for affected communities. It supports the principle that involuntary resettlement should be avoided or at least minimized. However, where it is unavoidable, appropriate measures to mitigate the adverse impact on displaced persons and communities should be carefully planned and implemented along the following lines:

• To avoid or at least minimize involuntary resettlement wherever feasible by exploring alternative project designs
• To mitigate adverse social and economic impacts from land acquisition or restrictions on affected persons' use of land by (a) providing compensation for loss of assets at replacement cost and (b) ensuring that resettlement activities are implemented with appropriate disclosure of information, consultation, and the informed participation of those affected
• To improve or at least restore the livelihoods and standards of living of displaced persons
• To improve living conditions among displaced persons through the provision of adequate housing with security of tenure for resettlement sites.

Source: International Finance Corporation.

that help is available to all. In almost all countries where community landownership is recognized by law, the creation of a transparent structure of internal governance with adequate checks and balances is a formal requirement. The experience of the Makuleke community in South Africa (presented in chapter 5 of this volume) provides a good example of how communities and nongovernmental organizations can use self-help to improve a situation.

Good Governance

Weak governance of tenure discourages social stability, investment, and economic growth, and the impact can be particularly severe for vulnerable groups and women. Good governance is therefore the sine qua non of both enlarging the pie and assuring its equitable distribution. In the present context, it basically includes three elements.

First, governance includes the *content* of laws and regulations. Most countries in the developing world suffer from a mix of excessive regulation in some areas and inadequate or even no regulation in others. Many existing regulations serve no clear public interest; many have simply been there for ages—some have been inherited from colonial times! The outdated laws have become counterproductive to today's needs. Ironically, where regulation is needed, such as zoning, social, and environmental protection, it is often inadequate or entirely lacking. Both excessive (archaic) regulation and no regulation leave the system open to abuse by those who hold positions of authority within it. To address the problem, some regulatory simplification is required. A mapping process to serve this goal by identifying what is unnecessary, what is weak, and what is missing and designing solutions accordingly is described in detail in chapter 13 of this volume.

The second problem relates to *process and structure, particularly with regard to the central-local relations.* A common challenge in streamlining the bureaucratic functions is determining how to move public services closer to the users. Many countries maintain highly centralized land administration systems, which make things difficult for both the system users and the administrators. In Nigeria, for instance, initial land registration, transaction approvals, land use applications, and other land management functions are almost all dealt with at the state level. Users of the system from the rural areas must travel long distances, sometimes on foot, to the state capitals just to complete the paperwork; if on-site services (for example, surveys, inspections) are required, users have to wait even longer for the agencies responsible for such functions to send someone. Nigeria is not unique. The same problem is evident in Kenya, Mozambique, Zambia, and many other African countries.

The central-local administrative tug-of-war is sometimes reflected in government versus tribal power, especially in countries where a dual land system exists in which state rights overlap with customary rights. In such cases, long-established traditional land management arrangements for local communities can run into conflict with the land management systems of government agencies. In Liberia, for instance, the state and local communities constantly debate the legal rights associated with customary land (Deininger and Byerlee 2011). There have been numerous examples of government authorities and local community chiefs allocating the same land to different users.

Countries in Africa and elsewhere have tried decentralization as a way to deal with these kinds of problems. Decentralization has not been successful in many places, as it is not supported by the necessary resources and sustainable capacity-building initiatives at a local level. But, where the efforts are politically and financially supported, they have fared better. In Botswana and Namibia, for example, the effort to decentralize the administration of land led to the establishment of local land boards consisting of both local government officials and community representatives, as a means of keeping the system both unified and impartial. In Botswana, important decisions by the land boards are sometimes reviewed by an additional technical advisory committee, composed of officials of appropriate central government and district council departments, to ensure the balance of central-local government interests. There are also instances—for example, in South Africa—where decentralization has helped the local parties to deal with land disputes through alternative channels, such as mediation and local land tribunals, which are operated by community members (Wily 2000).

The third element of good governance lies in increasing the availability of *information, education, and capacity building.* Information and education are essential to increasing public awareness and improving transparency, but they require both political willingness and technical means. In many places, the required skills and expertise are not readily available among government officials and will have to be built up over time. This is an area in which civil society, international organizations, and donor agencies can help through both financial and technical assistance.

Conclusions

Investment that requires access to customary land raises multiple questions of a social, economic, and institutional nature, which are not always an issue in the context of other land regimes. For the most part, there are no off-the-rack solutions, as each parcel of land and each indigenous group has its own unique problems, potential, and aspirations. Finding workable solutions that meet the needs of each stakeholder requires a tremendous amount of goodwill and flexibility from all parties. A key role of government is to provide the policy, legal, and institutional framework in which the stakeholders are encouraged to work together for common interests.

At its heart, access to customary land for commercial investment must treat the local communities as an equal partner if the goal of development is to create sustainable opportunities for the majority of the people and to alleviate poverty. A fundamental way to achieve this goal is to empower local communities by providing them secure rights, through legal and institutional efforts. This should be a priority of governments, investors, and local communities themselves.

In dealing with investment transactions, a tripartite approach that involves all of the relevant stakeholders is particularly useful to develop solid business deals based on mutual interest and trust. Each of the stakeholders can make special contributions to the relationship. *Investors* can assume responsibility for maintaining high standards of social commitment when acquiring customary land. They should not omit direct dialogue with local communities even if government agencies promise access and offer to bear the responsibility for evicting the current occupiers of the land in question. In addition to simply abiding by existing laws, investors should attempt to understand the nature of customary rights and exercise social and cultural sensitivity with regard to the interests of local communities. In most cases, acquiring customary land may require more time and resources than acquiring other types of land, but the time and effort invested in building trust and relationships with local communities can pay off well in the long run.

Local communities can arm themselves with the knowledge of their rights and be active in exercising them through stronger institutional arrangements. Local communities should be aware of the potential benefits available to them through commercial activities. In particular, they should support their own people with entrepreneurial ideas through, for instance, entering agreements on what they, as a group, want to do with their land. They need to play by the rules that treat all members fairly, so that what is gained is equally shared. When looking for partnerships with incoming investors, local communities need to familiarize themselves with the terms and conditions essential to commercial transactions. In dealing with land leases, for instance, they need to recognize the importance of a sufficiently long lease term in order to access bank finance. In business negotiations, local communities need to be aware of the importance of time and compliance with the terms agreed with the business partners and clients.

Civil society and donor groups can contribute significantly by assisting local communities through education, consultation, and capacity building, especially in the initial stages. In many places, nongovernmental organizations are already playing the role of watchdog by holding both private companies and governments accountable for upholding local people's rights. Many have also assisted local communities in preparing commercial contracts, taking part in negotiations, and facilitating mutually beneficial agreements. Clearly, a lot more of such assistance is needed.

Governments hold the ultimate key to creating the legal and institutional framework to provide a platform for the interaction of all stakeholders based on the principles of equality, accountability, and efficiency. It is up to governments to ensure a regulatory and administrative system that is consistent and transparent and that incorporates effective enforcement mechanisms. Governments also have a special responsibility to protect the weak and vulnerable. Assistance to local communities through the provision of information, education, and organizational capacity building is especially useful.

Notes

1. According to one study, in the last 75 years or so, forests and woodlands amounting to more than 100 million hectares have been appropriated by the state from local customary ownership through the creation of forest reserves for the purposes of conservation and protection of the economic value of such areas. See Wily (2000).

2. The recent surge in large-scale farmland acquisition, for its sheer size and speed, has raised considerable questions within the development community about the adverse social and environmental impact it might cause. See "The Surge in Land Deals: When Others Are Grabbing Their Land," *The Economist*, May 5, 2011. Many of the problems related to this trend are being discussed at special forums. For a comprehensive discussion of the issues, see Deininger and Byerlee (2011).

3. IFC Sustainability Framework, http://www.ifc.org/sustainability/.

4. Kanyinga (2000) explains that in the 1970s the land tenure systems prevalent in Africa were blamed for the lack of economic development and agricultural growth. Africa's customary systems were regarded as incapable of harnessing modern methods of agriculture, and donors and governments have often aspired to reform land tenure systems. See Kanyinga (2000).

5. Wily (2000) reports that in 2000 only those states actually at war had not embarked on tenure reform.

6. In South Kivu, the Democratic Republic of Congo, for instance, traditional chiefs sold the land to traders and developers, leaving the Pygmies who had lived in the forests since time immemorial, landless overnight. "Increasing Number of Landless Farmers in DRC (Syfia Grands-Lacs)," *African Farm*

News in Review, May 24, 2010. http://weekly.farmradio.org/2010/05/24/3-drc-increasing-number-of-landless-farmers-in-drc-syfia-grands-lacs/.

7. Landholding speculation is sometimes considered to be a form of "investment." Our concern, however, is with those who need land for real productive purposes.

8. These include Kenya, Lesotho, Malawi, Namibia, South Africa, Tanzania, Uganda, and Zambia, among others.

References

Burns, Tony. 2007. "Land Administration Reform: Indicators of Success and Future Challenges." Agriculture and Rural Development Discussion Paper 37, World Bank, Washington, DC.

Cotula, Lorenzo, Sonja Vermeulen, Rebeca Leonard, and James Keeley. 2009. *Land Grab or Development Opportunity? Agricultural Investment and International Land Deals in Africa.* London: International Institute for Environment and Development.

Deininger, Klaus. 2003. *Land Policies for Growth and Poverty Reduction.* World Bank Policy Research Report. New York: Oxford University Press for the World Bank.

Deininger, Klaus, and Dereck Byerlee, with Jonathan Lindsay, Andrew Norton, Harris Selod, and Mercedes Stickler. 2011. *Rising Global Interest in Farmland: Can It Yield Sustainable and Equitable Benefits?* Washington, DC: World Bank.

Kanyinga, Karuti. 2000. "Re-Distribution from Above: The Politics of Land Rights and Squatting in Costal Kenya." Research Report 115. Nordiska Afrikainstitutet, Uppsala.

Mathema, Ashna. 2008. "Slums and Sprawl in Lagos: The Unintended Consequence of 'Well-Intended' Regulation." World Bank, Washington, DC.

Steckley, Gail, and Mike Muleba. 2001. "Facilitating Land Access for the Copperbelt's Peri-Urban Farmers: An Interest-Based Approach." CARE Canada; CARE Zambia.

Vanclay, Frank. 2003. "International Principles for Social Impact Assessment." *Impact Assessment and Project Appraisal* 21 (1): 5–12.

White, Richard. 2004. "Using Tribal Land for Tourism: Ngamiland, Botswana Case Study." Unpublished case study by the Foreign Investment Advisory Service. Washington, DC.

Wily, Liz Alden. 2000. *Land Tenure Reform and the Balance of Power in Eastern and Southern Africa.* Natural Resource Perspectives 58. Washington, DC: Overseas Development Institute (June).

CHAPTER 15

Making Long-Term Leasing Work for the Land Market: Principles and Techniques

Stephen B. Butler

The long-term land lease has become a key element of the land markets in many developing countries. Leasing has become important for several reasons, not the least of which is that in many emerging markets today (for example, China, Nigeria, and Vietnam), all land is state owned and a lease or its equivalent is the only form of tenure permitted. In many countries, even if ownership is permitted to native people, foreign investors or legal entities of any type may be subject to restrictions preventing them from owning land.[1] Finally, even if ownership is permitted by law, the municipalities and other government agencies that own and control land may decide only to lease it, which is the case in the Russian Federation, for example.

Long-term leasing of land can satisfy both public and private interests, provided that certain conditions are met. Those conditions include legal protection of the lease right; liberal rights of alienation and subdivision of the right during the lease term; unrestricted pledge of the right and good protections for mortgage creditors; and flexible rights of land use free of state interventions other than generally applicable development controls. These conditions may not exist in some countries and, in that case, the leasing sector may be subject to a level of legal insecurity not found in freehold ownership systems.

This chapter focuses on the type of long-term land lease that would be required for a medium-scale investment project, including, for example, industrial, office, retail, and housing facilities. Not discussed here are some types of very large-scale investment projects, sometimes called concessions, which include not only a lease of land but also rights to provide exclusive services such as, for example, port, trade zone, airport, or infrastructure facilities and services or which include rights to extract natural resources, all of which may entail more complex issues, terms, and conditions than the typical long-term land lease. Also not discussed here at any length are the small-scale land-leasing programs operated in some countries to provide small plots for homes, family subsistence, and household enterprises, which may have different social and policy objectives than the commercial leasing that is the focus of this chapter.

What Do Investors Want in a Long-Term Land Lease?

In general, ownership is perceived as a higher and more secure form of tenure than a lease. At the same time, not all investors need or want to own land. From an investor's perspective, the differences between leasing the land and owning it can be minimized. But state land leasing policy differs widely, and some leasing regimes are more friendly to investors than others. This section summarizes some of the issues, responses, and best-practice recommendations for land-leasing policy based on the experience of the Foreign Investment Advisory Service in several emerging land markets in recent years.

Duration

The term of a land lease should be long enough to assure that the investor can amortize his improvements and earn an acceptable rate of return. The term of the lease is also crucial to obtaining leasehold financing for land improvements. What is an acceptable lease term is a matter to be determined by the market. Maximum durations and rights of renewal for state land leases are often, but not always, specified by law. Terms typically fall in the range of 25 to 50 years, with the shortest being about 20 years and the longest being 99 years. The Sierra Leone Non-Citizens Interest in Land Act limits leases to foreigners to a term of 21 years in urban areas of the country, making most serious investment by foreigners infeasible. At the other end of the spectrum, Nigeria, in which the state owns all of the land, allows 99-year leases. Some countries—Rwanda and Vietnam are good examples—establish maximum terms for different types of investments (agricultural, industrial, and so forth) or provide longer durations for investments in economically marginal areas in which incentives are needed and obtaining a return on investment may take longer.

The right to renew or extend a lease term is sometimes provided by law, subject to certain conditions. Rights of renewal are attractive to investors even if, as is typical, rentals are renegotiated or increased to current market rates upon extension of the lease term. Different rights may attach to different types of leases, and the conditions of renewal are important. In Vietnam, for example, agricultural leaseholders are guaranteed a lease renewal, while other commercial users are entitled only to "consideration" of a request for renewal; in either case, renewal depends on the leaseholder having upheld the terms of the lease and the permitted use of the land remaining unchanged. A rule denying renewal if the lessee has violated the terms of the lease is problematic, as some violation is almost inevitable, given the long terms and complexity of the lease relationship. An objective of any leasing regime should be to clarify the conditions of renewal and to reduce subjective decisions by public officials. This can be achieved by stating the conditions of renewal in concrete, objectively verifiable terms to the maximum extent possible.

In most countries, statutory rules on the fate of improvements apply only if the contract fails to address the issue. Some countries—Russia and Sweden are examples—establish the default rule that, in the absence of a contrary contractual agreement, the lessee is entitled to compensation for the value of his improvements upon expiration of the lease term. Whether the investor is entitled to compensation for improvements and how much compensation may also depend on why the lease term ends; if terminated for violation of a lease covenant, for example, no compensation may be payable. Some laws provide that, in lieu of compensation, the lessee has the right to remove the improvements from the land; if the lessee fails to do so within a defined period of time, these improvements will become the property of the lessor, which may be possible in only a small number of cases. As a general rule lessees may not remove property in the nature of fixtures that would result in the remaining property being unusable for the intended purposes; that is, they are required to remove it all or leave it all. As with the right to compensation for improvements, most systems leave the issue of whether a lessee is obligated to remove improvements and restore the land to the agreement of the landlord and lessee, and in the absence of specific agreement no obligation of removal is usually implied.

Alienability of Lease Rights

Unrestricted alienability, meaning that a leaseholder is permitted to transfer his rights to another lessee without government consent, is an ideal condition of an efficient market in leasehold land rights. Completely unrestricted alienability is rare in most state land-leasing systems. More often than not, some administrative procedure resulting in state consent to transfer a lease is required, and these can range from a mere formality to an expensive, time-consuming process constituting an administrative impediment to efficient operation of the market.

Approaches to transferring lease rights differ widely among countries today. In Rwanda there is a relatively simple procedure that in a typical case can be completed in five or six working days and involves mostly verification of the original right and registration of the transfer. In Nigeria citizens hold rights of occupancy in the nature of leases, which may be transferred only with the consent of the governor. A Foreign Investment Advisory Service study of procedures for transferring land rights found that obtaining the governor's consent to transfer can take many months.

There are good arguments in favor of liberal rights of transfer. A restriction on transferring a land lease right is also, in effect, a restriction on transferring the land improvements and may decrease the liquidity of an investment and increase the risk to the investor. The ability to transfer land on market terms underlies the process of moving land from lower- to higher-value uses. Creditors are likely to be more willing to provide leasehold financing for improvements if they are certain that they will be able to acquire or transfer a lease right if necessary to protect their investment.

In private markets it is the rule rather than the exception that landlords reserve the right to consent to transfer a lease to protect themselves against the transfer of a lease to a financially unqualified lessee or to prevent tenants from speculating in the land right and capturing any increase in the value of the leasehold. Where state rents are implicitly subsidized or lag market values, which is often the case, lessees can capture value from state land by assignment or subletting, and it may not be unreasonable for the state to demand a fee for its consent. Fees and taxes for granting consent to assign a state lease are common and can range from nominal (Vietnam, less than 1 percent) to significant (Nigeria, 8–30 percent; Brazil, 7 percent).

In state land-leasing systems, the requirement of state consent to transfer the right is typically imposed by law and may grow out of these concerns as well as several others arising from the public nature of the leasing program, including assuring that state land is allocated to the categories of persons and firms that the law intended, preventing the accumulation of state land in a few hands, controlling the allocation of a scarce state resource, and collecting fees and taxes imposed on income or transfer of property rights. For example, in practically all countries, state consent to assign a state lease is conditioned on showing that land rents and taxes are current and, in some cases (for example, Nigeria), that the lessee's income taxes have been paid.

In both developing and developed countries, most state land leases for commercial development prohibit transfer of the lease right prior to the completion of promised improvements. Satisfaction of the lessee's "development covenant" as a condition of transfer (discussed further below) is to be expected and is a reasonable precaution against speculation in state lands. Prior to completion of improvements, transfer may be permitted in certain cases such as legal merger or succession, transfer of control of a public company, or enforcement of a creditor's mortgage rights.

A standard clause in private leases is that consent to transfer will not be "unreasonably withheld" by the landlord, and some countries (for example, Tanzania) carry this over into their state programs. This is not yet a common approach in state leasing systems, but any approach that approximates this concept can be useful. Long-term leases also should be transferable without the consent of the landlord in certain cases, including corporate reorganization, bankruptcy or liquidation, and change of control of a company by sale of publicly traded stock; in the case of family enterprises and sole proprietorships, leases should be transferable by devise and by inheritance without consent.

Subletting is a special case of transferring rights, and, as a general rule, subletting of constructed facilities should be freely permitted and no consent procedure should be required, particularly in the case of buildings with multiple tenants. Subletting of land for purposes of construction is another matter entirely and typically is not permitted.

Lease Financing

The right to pledge the lease is an important consideration for investors and financiers. Although creditors typically finance on the basis of the land improvements, not the land lease, they take a pledge of the lease to assure their access to and lien on the land improvements. They are exposed to whatever risks their debtor is exposed to concerning the lease and should be provided with at least the same protections as, and are often provided by creditors with greater protections than, the lessee as an inducement to lending for development of the land.

A lease right may be offered as collateral for financing by mortgage or pledge, and it is in the interests of the state to assure that leases are easily used as collateral for land improvement loans. Consent to pledge of the lease right is a subcase of state consent to transfer generally; time-consuming and expensive procedures for obtaining consent to pledge lease rights can be disincentives to investment. While a good law on state land leases would specifically provide that they may be pledged, the bare right to pledge the lease is not sufficient, and creditors will usually look for further protections of their interests.

The duration of the lease term affects significantly the ability to finance leasehold improvements. Creditors who require mortgage collateral obviously cannot provide a loan for a period longer than the term of the lease. As a rule of thumb, to finance leasehold improvements creditors will usually require a comfortable cushion of a lease term in excess of the term of the loan to protect against possibilities of delays in construction, defaults, and the need to find a replacement tenant to complete and operate the property. Thus, a loan repayable over 15 years may require a lease term of 25 years or more. The relationship between lease and loan durations is a matter to be settled in the credit market, but even in developed markets creditors may be reluctant to lend if the term of the lease does not exceed the term of the loan by a factor of 50 to 60 percent.

The law and lease documents should provide for the same notice to the creditor as is provided to the lessee before any lease is terminated for cause and at least the same opportunity for the creditor to cure any default of the lessee. In the best case the creditor would be given more time to cure the lessee's default, provided that the creditor delivers to the landlord a written undertaking to do so. The landlord should be obligated to accept performance of obligations by the creditor on behalf of the lessee.

A main concern of creditors is that they not be held liable for the obligations of their borrowers. A law or leasing policy should make clear that whether the creditor assumes or guarantees the obligations of the lessee is within the creditor's discretion and necessary only if the creditor seeks either to assume the rights under the lease or to transfer them to another user. Any obligation assumed by the creditor should terminate once the lease rights have been transferred to an acceptable new lessee.

Perhaps the most important concern of a leasehold mortgagee is the ability to enforce its rights against the lease. In the best case the leasing rules would permit the creditor to enforce its right through any method permitted by law and without the consent of the state, including by taking over the lease. Obtaining state consent to transfer a lease through enforcement of a mortgage or pledge can significantly complicate the procedure and lead to delays and uncertainty. Delays in enforcement can cause losses for creditors through missed interest payments, deterioration in the property and the financial condition of the debtor, as well as decline in market value of the property. The extent of the problem may depend on the nature of the enforcement procedures under local law. If the law gives to the creditor the power to sell the property through private negotiations or ultimately to acquire the lease itself, obtaining approval for transfer of the lease may be less of a burden than if the enforcement must be by auction procedures, which do not lend themselves to prequalification of bidders and which can experience problems if it is necessary to obtain state approval of the successful bidder.

Prices and Rents

Rents may be prepaid or paid periodically. Prepaid rent is the equivalent of purchasing the right to use the land for a term of years and may not be attractive to investors because it requires an initial outlay of capital that could otherwise be used for other business investment. Studies by the International Finance Corporation have suggested that few businesses prefer a prepaid lease if there is an alternative (see Butler 2006). Prepayment may decrease the risk to the lessee and can add to the financeable value of the leasehold right, but it diminishes one of the main benefits of leasing, which is the liberation of capital for other needs.

Countries that require prepaid rents may also require payment of a periodic rent. In such systems the periodic land rents may be nominal or holding rents in the nature of land taxes and not equivalent to market rents that would be paid for leasing equivalent property in the private market. In an efficient market the price bid for a right to lease would take into consideration the periodic rents payable over the term, so if increases in periodic rentals are not reasonably predictable, calculating the right bid price in a competitive procedure could be difficult. In such systems, predictability of periodic rentals can be achieved to some extent by establishing rents as fixed proportions of property value and tying property valuation to other reasonably predictable indexes such as cost of living or a reliable indicator of real property market value.

The methods for setting prices and rents for state leases vary among countries. Singapore and Hong Kong SAR, China, for example, use competitive bidding to approximate market value. Other approaches to setting prices and rents include market analysis, individual appraisal, and negotiation. Negotiated rents may also be based on appraisal. Many developing countries rely on setting prices and rents by administrative process. By law in some countries prices set administratively must have some relationship to market price, and there may be a requirement for periodic market studies by the authorities. How market rates are estimated may differ widely. A typical approach may entail some rudimentary market research and the use of statistical indicators, such as location, soil quality, and access to infrastructure. The level of accuracy of these programs in approximating actual market rates can vary widely among countries and may depend on how well the market and market information are developed to begin with.

A lessee under a long-term land lease may seem particularly vulnerable to unreasonable rent increases, but thus far there is little evidence that governments in emerging markets have overreached in setting and adjusting land rents. With respect to rent increases, the main concerns are transparency, some degree of predictability, and a reasonable relationship to underlying real property values. Rents can be fixed for extended periods or increased often, but rarely are they adjusted more frequently than annually. Periodic rent increases can be established by a uniform system or during negotiation of the specific lease. If determined by a uniform system, rent increases will be automatic and may be indexed to some economic indicator such as inflation or set normatively by an act of the authorities after some form of analysis and valuation. In Hong Kong SAR, China, for example, a "premium" or price must be paid for all land leases, which may be set by competition or appraisal and negotiation; thereafter, periodic rentals are set at 3 percent of the "rateable" value of the property, which is the value of the property as determined for ad valorem property taxes. Typically, increases in rents for state land are imposed in the same way on all state leases and according to the same schedule.

The best approach may be to tie rent increases to movements in land market values or rents as shown in reliable real estate market indicators, but not all emerging markets have such indicators. Moreover, markets move differently, and any system of indexing tied to general economic indicators such as inflation raises the possibility of "basis risk," whereby increases in the underlying indicator do not accurately reflect increases in property values. If authorities set rent increases by market assessment, it would, of course, be best if actual market studies were performed and if increases were imposed across all state leases of the same type and not imposed on an ad hoc or discriminatory basis.

It is not uncommon for governments to provide land at significantly discounted prices, sometimes even free, as an incentive to encourage investment, although there is some evidence that these concessions are usually available only to larger investors (see Butler 2006). This type of subsidy could be justified in some cases—for instance, when the land is undeveloped and the investor is expected to construct major infrastructure in order to make the land suitable for investment. Also, if the lease conditions include highly specified and inflexible uses, the land value can be significantly lower than otherwise.

Encouraging investment generally or in specific types of facilities may constitute legitimate objectives and uses of state resources, but significant undervaluation of state lands can have some detrimental effects, including incentives to speculate, land grabbing by elites, underutilization, and lack of budgetary transparency. When looking at any deliberate policy of undervaluation, it may be important to ask whether the land actually ends up in the hands of the targeted groups and whether it results in investment rather than speculation. A good way to throw some light on the issue of pricing may be to include the subsidy element of below-market rents in the state budget and to require that data on the allocation of state land leases be published in formats readily accessible to the press and the public. There are no cases where this is done today.

Lease Termination

Lease rights are less secure than ownership rights, as they may be terminated for a variety of causes. How events of termination are defined in the law and the lease may affect the security of the right. Broad and ambiguous legal grounds for state termination of rights might be abused and undermine property rights and willingness to invest. As a general rule, grounds for lease defaults should be objectively determinable and quantifiable. Defaults based on violations of laws should refer to specific laws and offenses, and the determination of a default should be based on final determination of a violation in a court of law.

Some breaches of lease terms are serious, and some are not so serious. Deliberate environmental degradation is serious. Occasional late payment of rent is not. This distinction can be captured in the concept of "materiality" of a lease violation—whether the lessee's breach is material to the landlord's receipt of the benefits it bargained for. This concept is specifically expressed in the laws of many developed economies and also in their contracts; it allows a court to deny a request for termination of a lease on frivolous, insignificant, and purely "technical" grounds. Many states have been reluctant to accept this concept or apply it to contracts with the state, and, in the absence of an established court doctrine of materiality, lessees could be vulnerable to abuse of their lease rights.

Perhaps the most important risk of termination is the failure to develop the leased land in accordance with the terms of the lease. Practically all long-term state land leases contain a "development covenant," a legally binding agreement of the lessee to invest in improvement of the land within a defined period of time, usually ranging from one to four years depending on the nature of the project. Leases may be terminated for failure to improve the property within the allotted time. Established by law or contract, the covenant is the main tool used to prevent private speculation in state land, but the extent to which covenants are actually enforced may differ among countries.

Compliance with development covenants can be measured by quantitative formulas such as construction costs, amount invested in the land, or square meters constructed; in the case of larger or more unique land sites, it is likely that the development covenant will be expressed in terms of a specific building program required by the terms of the land offer or proposed by the land recipient when requesting the site. Under the national land-leasing system of the Central American country of Belize, for example, the investment in the land required to satisfy the development covenant is specifically stated in the lease as an amount of money, based on formulas established for different regions of the country. The formulas are related to the value of the land as well as the costs of construction and materials.

The desire to prevent speculation is such that some systems will not issue a long-term lease to a landholder until all development obligations have been met. In this interim period, during which he may be acting diligently and making significant outlays, the landowner may hold a short-term land right such as a short-term lease or "right of construction" for the duration of the development period, which would be converted to a long-term lease upon satisfaction of the development covenant. While much may depend on the precedent of the legal system, by any objective standard this short-term right is less secure than a long-term lease, as it requires the state to determine subjectively that the development obligation has been satisfied and the long-term land right should be granted. Where development covenants are poorly defined or rent seeking by public officials is common, this may constitute a risk to investors, although there is little evidence that this is a regular occurrence. From an investment perspective, a good test of the security of the short-term land right is whether creditors are willing to finance improvements developed under the right.

A downside of development covenants is that the land right is conditional pending completion of the work, posing significant risks for creditors, who may have to take over the site and the obligation or at least find another tenant to complete the development obligation. Incomplete construction is a major headache for creditors, only made worse when the land right depends on completion. From the perspective of investors and creditors, some steps can be taken to reduce the burden of development covenants and their effect on property rights:

- *Transparent conditions of satisfaction of the covenant.* There should be objective standards against which compliance can be determined, and the means of proving satisfaction of the covenant should be clearly defined.
- *Flexible time periods tied to the nature of the project.* Time to satisfy the development covenant should be related to the characteristics of the local market; one size does not fit all.
- *Force majeure and other reasonable grounds for extension of periods.* Extensions of the development period should be required for any unforeseen events or conditions affecting completion of the project.
- *Issuance of a lease at commencement of the work.* Rather than a short-term right pending satisfaction of the development covenant, investors would be better protected by a full-term lease subject to termination in the event that the covenant is not satisfied. This approach would have several benefits for investors, including (a) putting the state in the position of having to take affirmative steps to terminate a lease rather than simply refusing to issue the new right, which may prevent ill-considered actions by state officials, and (b) giving the investor the benefit of any procedures for termination included in the law or final lease document. In most places the state has sufficient legal tools for enforcing the covenant and preventing speculation if it has the political will to use them.
- *Recognition of creditor rights.* Creditors should have the right to "step into the shoes" of the lessee to complete the improvements or find someone else to do it.

While most state land leases require the lessee to develop the land, few subject the lessee to "continuous use" covenants, which require the lessee to continue to use the land for productive purposes after the improvements have been completed. This sort of provision is more likely to be found in a lease of agricultural land or in important urban projects. The laws of many countries provide for recapture of abandoned state lands, but enforcement is often lacking. The upshot may be that productive use of the land may be abandoned at some point while the lease right continues, in effect removing the land from the market and allowing speculation. If land rents approximate market rates and land taxes are significant, there should be little financial incentive for a lessee to underutilize the land once the investment has been completed, but in some markets these costs may be insufficient to prevent abandonment, underutilization, and speculation.

In most systems, taking land improvements for state purposes is subject to compensation. A state land lease is a property right, and as such a termination of the right for state purposes should be subject to the rules of compensation. Some emerging and transitional countries do not recognize the asset value of the state lease for compensation purposes, but under a system that uses market rents and adjusts them frequently the lease right may have limited present asset value in any case. However, values such as the costs of improvements, the growing of crops, and the prepayment of rents are usually recognized. Also compensable may be the costs of relocation and the costs associated with locating a replacement site and obtaining a new lease.

Because holders of long-term land leases are typically obligated to develop and maintain the property, destruction of the property by natural or man-made hazard can be a significant event, but it is not cause for lease termination. Leaseholders should be given the option of redeveloping the land, and time to do so should not begin to run until all insurance matters have been settled.

In the typical private sector lease, voluntary surrender of lease rights is not permitted: the lessee may not simply turn back the property and walk away from the lease obligation; the lessee remains obligated for payment of rent and maintenance of the property, no matter what. This may or may not be true in the case of long-term state land leases, and some laws have specifically addressed the issue of surrender of lease rights as a means of terminating the lessee's obligations. This option would be very unlikely where there is more than a nominal rent obligation or in the case of important and visible projects; regardless of what the state allows, creditors holding mortgages on leasehold improvements will contractually prohibit voluntary surrender or termination of the lease by the lessee.

Terminating a lease should be subject to procedural protections that recognize the significance and vulnerability of the lessee's investment and the disparity in power of the lessee and the state. Leaseholders should be entitled to written notice of an alleged lease violation that sets out in specific terms the nature of the violation and the steps that should be taken to correct it. This is a standard provision of the lease law and administrative procedures law in most places.

Many lease violations are inadvertent or beyond the control of the lessee. The objective of the law and leasing practice should not be to punish violations, but to correct them. Upon receipt of a notice of lease violation, a landholder should be given a reasonable amount of time to correct the violation. Except in extreme circumstances, rights to cure a lease violation should be extended so long as the leaseholder has begun steps to cure the violation and is pursuing them diligently and in good faith.

Summary eviction and equivalent terms refer to procedures whereby a landlord may remove a tenant from a property quickly upon a simple allegation. Considering the relative size of the land lessee's investment in the property and the objective of promoting investment, a good land-leasing regime would not seek shortcuts in removing tenants from the property and would insist on normal judicial procedures, including imposing a burden on the state to prove a material violation. Appeals of lower court decisions on removal of the lessee from the property should be appealable to higher courts, and lessees should be entitled to remain in possession of the property pending final judgment and completion of appeals.

Summary

To recap, the typical investor mostly wants the same level of transparency and predictability in lease relations with the state as would be found in the private market. Most investors will ask the following questions about state land leasing:

- Is the lease term sufficient to amortize an investment, and are the conditions of renewal clearly defined?
- Can the lease right be transferred, if necessary, without inappropriate interference from the state?

- Can the land right be pledged to construct improvements on terms acceptable to creditors?
- Are rents and rent increases predictable and market based?
- Is the right protected by reasonable provisions on default?
- Are the investor's development and use obligations clearly specified and objectively determinable?
- Will the investor receive fair compensation in the event of expropriation?

Many investors will look beyond the mere letter of the law and obtain professional advice that the practice and precedent in the country regarding state leases reflect a respect for the rule of law and lease contracts.

Note

1. According to a recent World Bank survey, among foreign-owned manufacturing firms in 87 countries, about one-quarter of the surveyed countries prohibit foreign firms from owning land, but all countries allow foreign firms to lease land (World Bank 2010).

References

Butler, Stephen. 2006. "Critical Review of Laws and Regulations of Viet Nam Affecting Business Access to Land." Report prepared for the Vietnam Ministry of Natural Resources and Environment on behalf of the International Finance Corporation and Australian Agency for International Development (April).

FIAS (Foreign Investment Advisory Service). 2008. "Nigeria: Land Market Reform Implementation, a Key Component of Improving Investment Climate." FIAS, Washington, DC.

World Bank. 2010. Investing across Borders, 2010: Indicators of Foreign Direct Investment Regulation (database). World Bank, Washington, DC. http://iab.worldbank.org/.

CHAPTER 16

Using One-Stop Shops to Facilitate Access to Land: Its Pros and Cons

Jacqueline Coolidge

The concept of using a one-stop shop (OSS) to facilitate the procedures required to access land sounds very appealing. On the one hand, a large number of public agencies are usually involved, and an effective OSS can, under the right circumstances, become a very useful part of a reform package. On the other hand, also due to the large number of public agencies involved, making an OSS effective can be very difficult, sometimes impossible; at worst it can lead to the creation of a wasteful and frustrating "one-more-stop shop." Therefore, it is important to understand when and how it is possible to ensure a useful one.

Variations on the idea of an OSS have been tried with varying degrees of success in many countries. At a minimum, it is usually possible to develop an OSS for *information* on all the procedures for acquiring land in a particular jurisdiction. In this case, a desk at a city administration or investment or development agency and a Web portal can provide an overview of all the procedures and agencies involved in the process, including necessary authorizations and approvals, associated fees, and estimated time required to complete the process. It should also be possible to pick up application forms for all relevant procedures at the OSS.

A minimal-information OSS can be useful to investors who are not familiar with the procedures and can help to improve transparency and accountability. It can usually be organized by one agency (for example, the investment agency) that assembles the information and summarizes it in a user-friendly manner. The main challenge is to keep it up to date, as procedures and fees may be subject to frequent change.

If possible, an information OSS for land should also include basic information about land parcels that are available for purchase or long-term lease by investors, including information about each parcel's location, size, connections to infrastructure or public services (water and sewerage, electricity, and roads), and zoning designation (agriculture or commercial). While designing, compiling, and managing a comprehensive database of all available land parcels might be a significant challenge for low-capacity countries, at a minimum an inventory of the public land that is available should guide investors' initial efforts to identify and compare possible sites.

A more ambitious OSS is one that allows an investor to *complete all or most land-related procedures* in one location. This is much more convenient and efficient for an investor, saving a lot of time and energy that otherwise would be spent visiting many different agencies in different locations. If well organized, it can also help public agencies to cooperate better with each other. For instance, the agency responsible for allocating state land plots may require preapproval from the agency responsible for land use planning or zoning, whereas the latter may precondition its approval on the consent of the agencies responsible for power allocations, road connections, and so on. This functional interdependence, compounded by weak interagency communication, can significantly complicate the project approval process. When the sequence of these approvals is not clear to either the applicants or the various agencies, as is often the case, a lot of paperwork has to travel back and forth among these agencies before the final approvals can be obtained. In worse situations, different agencies may make different decisions, causing frustration to both the applicants and the agencies involved.

However, ensuring that staff members in the OSS who represent the various agencies involved actually have the information and the authority that they need to give approvals is often more difficult than it appears. Each individual agency wants to keep full control over its own procedures and to ensure efficiency and convenience from its own point of view (which is usually quite different from the point of view of the investor or even other agencies). Even in the case where political will and cooperation are sufficient to support an OSS, if the volume of work at the OSS is too low, the home agencies will complain that it is wasting valuable staff time.

Each agency may prefer to have several layers of approval internally and may resist sending one or two staff to a different location with delegated authority for approvals. The need to work in cooperation with other agencies may give rise to "turf battles."

The most successful examples of an OSS improving the land acquisition process are usually in countries or jurisdictions with high-level political commitment to improving and streamlining the procedures and making them more friendly to investors. Thus, a mayor who wants to encourage investment in his or her city may encourage and facilitate cooperation between agencies and put pressure on bureaucrats who resist reform.

Another key ingredient in the success of an OSS is when it is established as an integral component of a larger reform process designed to streamline and rationalize procedures. Otherwise, organizing many inefficient procedures in one geographic location will yield only minor improvements (and may even cause new problems, if staff in the OSS do not themselves have authority for approvals and have to spend time securing them from a different location). See box 16.1.

An OSS can also be created for construction permits, which might or might not be combined with an OSS for access to land.

Many countries have been experimenting with the OSS approach to land procedures in recent years, usually where the existing situation is very difficult and where more fundamental improvements would take

Box 16.1

One-Stop Shop for Investors

The idea of a one-stop shop is to have a single government agency to which investors can go for information and assistance in obtaining all the secondary approvals (that is, licenses and permits) pursuant to establishing a business. Various institutional structures for one-stop shops have been used around the world. One approach seeks to centralize some or all parts of the approval-granting process. Variations include a single autonomous agency with strong delegated powers in decision making, a permanent interministerial setup making decisions on a collective basis, or simply a single roof under which all ministries involved have a desk or space from which to process investment projects. All of these approaches emphasize the effort to draw the necessary resources from different authorities to a single central point.

(continued next page)

Box 16.1 *(continued)*

An alternative approach stresses having a central point for the *facilitation* of approvals, but not for the approvals themselves, which remain the responsibility of the various ministries and agencies. Under this approach, the institution functions as an intermediary, using its knowledge and contacts in the public sector to satisfy the requirements of the investors. How much assistance an investor may need depends on the complexity of the underlying procedures themselves. Agencies also need to ration the amount of highly personalized time and attention they can give. In this sense, the size and strategic importance of an investment or investor will guide an agency in allocating time.

When procedures are complex and not transparent, a facilitation agency has (a) to provide intensive assistance to investors, often on a one-to-one basis, and (b) to assist investors in obtaining all of the necessary government approvals and clearances. Even in countries where procedures have been reformed and simplified, having a single account executive to work with an investor in all stages of the investment process is desirable. In addition, the agency may help an investor to network with other public and private parties according to each individual investor's other needs—a role that is often important, for example, during an investor's site search or in negotiating access to public utility services.

For this reason, one-stop shops appear to be more helpful for investors with large strategic projects than for average investors with small and medium projects. Also, the facilitation activities of one-stop shops are perhaps more needed during the transitional stage when the overall business environment remains difficult. In the long run, efforts are required to improve the overall environment for all applicants. Put in different words, better organization may help, but for basic improvements deregulation is necessary.

Source: FIAS 2004.

considerable time. OSS seems to provide a quick way to start some useful reforms, with tangible benefits for investors. World Bank reports on the creation of an OSS for access to land have been written for Burkina Faso, Serbia, Georgia, the Russian Federation, and Sudan, helping to illustrate the challenges and opportunities in this approach. This chapter highlights the key features and lessons drawn from those experiences.

In all cases, procedures for access to land prior to introduction of the OSS were very complicated and confusing for investors and notoriously slow and frustrating.

Burkina Faso

In the case of Burkina Faso, the creation of an OSS was one part of a set of reforms designed to streamline procedures for access to land (for a full description of the OSS experience in Burkina Faso, see chapter 1 in this volume). These reforms included the creation of an OSS to bring all the land distribution and transaction procedures under one roof, accompanied by efforts to simplify operations and delegate authority.

The reforms were launched in 2008. One of the first reforms enacted was to eliminate the need to receive an authorization from the municipal government in order to transfer property rights, a step that used to take an average of about 45 days.

Other specific reforms followed, including the creation in 2009 of a table of property values for different zones in the city of Ouagadougou, which is now used to calculate the land transfer tax. A new table of revised values was slated to be published in 2010. In addition, a desk was set up in the same building as the Land Registry to facilitate the payment of transfer taxes.

New regulations were issued that set statutory time limits for processing land registry requests. Unfortunately, there was no enforcement mechanism for the statutory time limits. Although there has been some improvement in the overall time required to complete the procedures, many agencies have refused to comply with the statutory time limits.

The reforms, although limited, did have a positive impact. The number of new land titles soared, the time required to process new land title requests decreased steadily, and the cost of obtaining land titles dropped.

Serbia

In Serbia, at the level of local government, similar challenges were addressed with a similar set of solutions (for a full account of the Serbia experience, see Kocevic 2009). As one official put it, "Urban planning and permitting remain one of the last bastions of the old bureaucracy" (Serbia Local Government Reform Project 2008, 15).

A key issue is the need to involve agencies that report to different levels of government (national, provincial, and local). Thus, a mayor has strong influence over agencies within the local administration, but not necessarily higher levels of government. Conversely, if constitutional governance structures involve a substantial amount of decentralization, then even a strongly reformist national government may find it difficult to secure the cooperation of subnational bodies.

In such a setting, it is often best to start from the local level, initiate sound reforms within a few pilot municipalities, and try to facilitate or strengthen "networks" of officials at different levels (including ministries and mayors) to help to build interest in successful reforms. In the Serbian case, a two-pronged or "bottom-up, top-down" strategy was applied with assistance from the International Finance Corporation: (1) working at the national level on reforms to simplify and streamline regulations and (2) working at the subnational level to test the implementation of simpler regulations, starting with a few pilot municipalities. These efforts helped to build momentum for reforms and contributed to capacity building critical to sustaining the reform (Thomas, Cordova-Novion, and Batic 2010).

Development of an OSS for granting building permits benefited from a strong effort at public relations and outreach, including keeping the public informed through the media, inviting them to participate in workshops and through the Internet, and distributing pamphlets and display posters presenting information about the permitting process, steps, approvals, and fees.

Creating a customer-friendly institution and set of procedures was a major goal. For example, reformers strove to overcome the old problems of "applications spending time behind closed doors in some department while the clients wait endlessly without knowing about the status of their permit application" (Thomas, Cordova-Novion, and Batic 2010, 53).

The Serbian municipalities therefore benefited from the use of information technology that helped to track the progress of application forms, improving both transparency and accountability.

Separately, another group of municipalities in Serbia is developing "one-window" service for construction permits. These offices are being authorized to "acquire conditions and approvals from the utility companies and . . . cadastre for investors. This would enable businesses to . . . avoid visits to more than 10 institutions" (Kocevic 2009).

However, reformers in the four cities faced the same challenges as those in other locations: a lack of cooperation from the involved institutions. One city, Vranje, managed to secure the necessary cooperation and arranged a memorandum of understanding between the involved agencies. It is hoped that this will provide a positive demonstration effect for other cities in Serbia.

Georgia

In the case of Georgia, the government created the State Department for Land Management (SDLM) to manage the process of land privatization in 1996 (for a full description of the OSS experience in Georgia, see Fidas and Nicholas 2007). However, the mandate of the SDLM overlapped with that of other agencies: it was officially responsible for designing and implementing programs for land valuation, land statistics, land registration, and the cadastre; managing state control of land use and natural resources; developing state land management policies and legislation; undertaking reform; and resolving land disputes. Other agencies were responsible for critical pieces of the process, further complicating land records and registration procedures and providing space for conflicts of interest and corruption. The Ministry of Agriculture and Food managed agrarian land reform. The Ministry of Urbanization and Construction shared responsibility for land use planning and formulating policies. The Bureau of Technical Inventory kept urban real estate records, and the State Department of Geodesy and Cartography regulated surveying and mapping. The Chamber of Notaries was responsible for issuing non-encumbrance certificates. The separation of records, duties, and fee collection among the various agencies caused confusion, conflicting data on ownership, and a complicated system that was vulnerable to rent seeking.

In 2004, following the Rose Revolution, President Mikhail Saakashvili took office on a platform including land reform and anticorruption. The political will of his government would be a strong force in the bold reforms to take place. The government sought to guarantee efficiency and transparency by creating a single agency to manage the most important aspects of land administration. The entire process took about two years to complete (see figure 16.1).

How did the government achieve such a dramatic reform in such a short time? Several tactics were keys to its success:

- *The old agency (SDLM) was dissolved in favor of a new agency—the National Agency of the Public Registry (NAPR).* An overhaul of the SDLM would have failed—it was too rigid and slow. New institutions with new mandates changed operations and mentalities—both the services employees expected to provide and the services customers expected to receive.

- *Information from the previous institutions was transferred to the new agency.* This was important to avoid losing any records on ownership and beginning the process of consolidating all information into a single property information file.

- *Personnel reform.* The management of the SDLM was fired. Employees were allowed to transfer to the NAPR, but they had to reapply for their

Figure 16.1 The Reform of Property Registration in Georgia

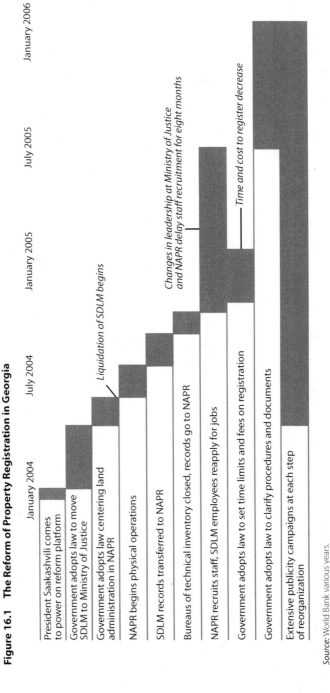

Source: World Bank various years.
Note: SDLM = Georgian State Department for Land Management; NAPR = National Agency of the Public Registry.

jobs and sit for qualification exams. The staff was also reduced—from 2,100 at the SDLM to just 600 at the NAPR. Salaries grew 20-fold. And the Tbilisi office established an incentive system for good performance, including bonuses.

- *Raising public awareness to increase usage of the new agency.* Broad public information campaigns educated people about the benefits of property registration. Trusted community leaders and nongovernmental organizations spoke out, wrote newspaper articles, and distributed flyers to encourage use of the NAPR. The result was an increase in the number of registrations.

- *Self-financing.* A new fee structure and retention of the funds at the registry led to significantly higher revenue for the NAPR. Revenue from the increased registrations was used to pay higher salaries to the employees. The NAPR became self-financing in 2006.

Russian Federation

In the case of Russia, government reform efforts started at the regional level in the early 2000s. With assistance from the World Bank Group, enterprise diagnostics were carried out in 20 of Russia's regions, which identified "business access to land" as the most severely problematic of all administrative procedures for businesses (for whom the procedure was relevant). Most urban land suitable for commercial use continued to remain in state ownership, untouched by the mass privatization of other business assets in the early 1990s. The land title remained with the state, and firms were using land mostly under indefinite and insecure "use rights."

The federal government became increasingly concerned about the inefficient use of the largest and most valuable public asset available for business growth—land. Soon after enacting the Land Code in 2001, the federal government, with the World Bank's assistance, prepared a cross-regional survey of land and real estate transactions covering 15 regions to identify the bottlenecks in state land management. The findings of the surveys provided input valuable to preparation of the new federal law in July 2006, which aimed to transition urban land, through either sale or lease, to private businesses and citizens and to use market price mechanisms when doing so.

To support implementation of the OSS concept, a pilot focusing on simplifying administrative procedures for business access to land at the municipal level was begun in 2008 in one of the advanced regions, the republic of Tatarstan, and in one of the most reform-minded municipalities, the city of Almetyevsk. Besides being the most reformist, Almetyevsk was lucky to have significant oil deposits in its territory, meaning that the municipal budget was receiving enough fiscal revenues to support changes in information systems and software applications.

Consolidation and streamlining of procedures were needed at both subnational levels—municipal and regional. The pilot for the capital city of Tatarstan was designed as follows:

- Establish a "single window" in each agency dealing with land allocation for construction
- Put all concerned agencies into one place, offering investors an opportunity to meet face-to-face with representatives of each agency involved in the process
- Create a stand-alone and independently functioning one-stop shop for land allocation in which representatives of agencies delegated to the OSS have all required information and, more important, authority to make decisions regarding cases.

The design at the local level looked somewhat different, since there were fewer agencies to coordinate and it was easier to line them up if a municipality was reform oriented. Usually the OSS concept was implemented at weekly meetings of the land planning and use commissions (in the city of Almetyevsk) or at a specially dedicated day (Wednesday) in a special economic zone (city of Yelabuga), when heads of all communal services and utility units (or their deputies) were present to sort out the pipeline of logged land allocation and construction-related cases and decisions were made on the spot.

The major challenges were procedures related to (a) making transparent a *closed* list of documents required to process applications for land allocation and (b) enforcing the statutory time limits in processing applications. Investors typically complained that regulators could ask for an unlimited number of "additional" documents. This was why the statutory time limits could not be enforced, since the application was deemed "accepted" only if and when all required documents had been submitted. Since nobody had been able to specify what a complete set of documents must look like, the application might be in "preparation" status for years before it would be accepted as complete; only then would the clock start ticking for the 30-day period legally mandated for processing the application.

By its Decision of October 15, 2009, the Ministry for Land and Property Relations of Tatarstan determined statutory deadlines for a variety of standard cases in land allocation procedures and established a *closed, exhaustive, and complete list of all documents* required for each standard case (housing construction, commercial). Of course, some investors still might submit an incomplete application. If so, they are given seven days to complete the file before their application is legally rejected. The required documents are clearly described in the *public service standards* adopted by the ministry and other agencies dealing with land allocation and construction in the republic.

In the city of Yelabuga, which is a free economic zone, the municipality-level one-stop shop is providing primarily an informational service, which is the minimum level of service. In a big hall at the headquarters of the zone, representatives of 14 municipal, republic, and federal agencies are available at the same time in their cubicles (with clearly written names on the top) and must spend the whole working day there. Interested investors can meet with them and collect information regarding procedures applied by each of these 14 agencies; they can even receive standard forms to write an application, but they cannot conclude a transaction because these clerks are not delegated such authority. The most they can do is to accept the application and suggest when and where the applicant should return after it has been processed.

Compared to the single window in Kazan and the informational one-stop shop at Yelabuga, the OSS in Almetyevsk has been much more effective. There, the mayor, a political heavyweight, calls weekly meetings of the Land Planning and Use Commission with all municipal, republican, and some federal bodies present in the town; reviews issues related to spatial development and land use; and makes a preliminary decision that should be examined and documented by the local Land and Property Chamber. The new procedure was started with Mayor's Decision no. 3029 of December 12, 2008, on the adoption of the public service standard (*reglament*) on allocation of a land parcel, which appointed the chamber as the focal point where decisions are prepared for later approval by the mayor.

With this high-level support in the city of Almetyevsk, the number of days to complete the procedure after introduction of the full-service one-stop shop was reduced from 730 to only 45. The processing of similar cases in Yelabuga (informational OSS) was also drastically reduced, but only from 654 to 98 days. In Kazan the ministry deals with nonmunicipal land, and outcomes are yet to be seen, because the single-window approach requires concerted efforts on the part of not only one ministry, but also other ministries and agencies as well.

Conclusions

Many of the various one-stop shops have been helpful in consolidating information and procedures to reduce the time and effort needed to gain access to land. However, this institutional approach works best as part of an agenda of broader reform aimed at streamlining procedures and improving transparency and efficiency. A common obstacle is resistance from individual agencies that oppose reform and do not want to cooperate with other agencies. In such situations, which are quite frequent, strong political leadership is needed to overcome resistance and put in place tangible incentives for cooperation. Ultimately, both counterproductive red tape and rent-seeking behavior by government officials can best be eliminated by deregulation. Better organization can help, but it is not sufficient. Box 16.2 lays out some guidelines for a successful OSS.

Box 16.2

Dos and Don'ts for OSS

Do manage expectations. Make it explicitly clear to the public what the OSS can and cannot do. If it is primarily an OSS for providing information, advice, and access to all the relevant application forms, call it a "one-stop information shop."

Do take advantage of the OSS to encourage more effective integration of the relevant agencies. The OSS should bring together representatives of all the relevant agencies. While not all of the representatives may be fully vested with decision-making authority, their interactions can help to identify opportunities to avoid unnecessary duplications and interactions and to streamline procedures.

Do try to get top-level leadership to push meaningful reform. If necessary, "bang heads together" and force necessary decisions (for example, in cases of duplication, decide which agency will take responsibility and which will cede it).

Don't "oversell" the capacity of the OSS. Many applicants expect that the OSS can obtain all of their approvals without any further effort on their part. If they are frustrated in their expectations, the resulting cynicism may hamper further efforts at reform.

Don't set up a "one-MORE-stop shop." The OSS should be set up only if it brings clear, tangible benefits to its constituents in the form of fewer steps or less time.

References

FIAS (Foreign Investment Advisory Service). 2004. "Botswana: Further Improving the Regulatory and Procedural Framework for Encouraging Private Investment." FIAS, Washington, DC.

Fidas, Penelope, and Jim Nicholas. 2007. "Need Land Administration Reforms? Start a Revolution." In *Celebrating Reform 2007: Doing Business Case Studies.* Washington, DC: World Bank.

Kocevic, Sladjana Karavdic. 2009. "Construction Permit Reforms: Helping Investors Obtain the Necessary Documents without Losing Their Money—or Their Minds." In *SmartLessons: Real Lessons, Real Development,* 1–5. Washington, DC: International Financial Corporation (November).

Serbia Local Government Reform Project. 2008. "Guidelines for the Implementation of One Stop Permitting Centers." DAI Washington, Bethesda, MD.

Thomas, Margo, Cesar Cordova-Novion, and Ana Batic. 2010. "Art or Science? Measuring the Impact of Business Environment Reforms at the Sub-national Level." In *Investment Climate SmartLessons: Real Experiences, Real Development,* 50–53. Washington, DC: International Finance Corporation.

World Bank. Various years. Doing Business (database). World Bank, Washington, DC. http://www.doingbusiness.org/.

CHAPTER 17

Applying Land Information Systems to Assist Business Access to Land

Mathew Warnest and Xiaofang Shen

Jack Walvin, a private property consultant in the United Kingdom, describes the complex need for land information that private developers typically face when choosing a site for investment:

> A wealth of information must be gathered, and it takes time. The board of directors must be convinced—site potential, market trends, pedestrian flows, utility connections, environmental risks—that the land beneath is unencumbered, and clean, and that they won't find an ancient roman chariot below when construction begins! The board wants to know what conditions and constraints local authorities will impose, before they demand it![1]

Such a need is similar anywhere in the world. Even in an advanced country, where information of all kinds is relatively available and accessible, accessing it can still be a laborious process for the developer. The situation is much worse in the developing world. Land information is scarce, outdated, and difficult to assemble. Land records are kept primarily in paper form, supported by inadequate resources and human capacity. Land management functions are fragmented among agencies that are poorly coordinated. As a result, investors, or citizens with a need to build, have to carry the burden of visiting the various ministries and agencies to gather the required information. Too often, they find that the data they need are incomplete, inconsistent, or simply unavailable. This adds significant risk and cost to doing business in developing countries.

The lack of an adequate system for sharing information and keeping records is also a common source of frustration for the large number of public agencies involved in land administration. It is difficult to track land transactions when the site- and owner-related records are separated. Property validations for legal or financial purposes are hard to conduct when paper-based records are in a dire state of neglect. Agencies responsible for land use planning, zoning, infrastructure, and many other important public services duplicate the information they all need. Agencies run the risk of contradicting rather than reinforcing each other in the absence of a coherent system for sharing information. The lack of interagency coordination leads to the waste of public resources and disrupts the project approval processes that investors and citizens depend upon when building needs arise.

Land Information Systems

Information and communications technology (ICT) has grown quickly over the past few decades and been widely deployed around the world to assist business and support socioeconomic development. The new technology has also caused rapid changes in the concept and practice of maintaining a land information system (LIS)—the way in which data about land are generated, integrated, and used. This trend offers the potential to improve significantly the amount and handling of information pertinent to the investment climate. Many governments worldwide are recognizing the potential of emerging ICT and modern land information systems.

Applying ICT to the compilation and integration of land databases started as early as the 1980s in several advanced countries, including Australia, Canada, and the United States. The "database" concept provided an excellent resolution of the many deficiencies of the cumbersome paper-based land information system. The 1990s saw the further integration of geographic (spatial) information with land records, leading to digital cadastral databases and multipurpose land information systems. Further technological improvements and new approaches in the twenty-first century, such as spatial data infrastructure, allow the new generation of LISs to integrate the many layers of land information, including cadastre, land use, town planning, environment, roads, utilities, and others.

Today, ICT-based LISs have become commonplace in the developed world—agencies and their data management information systems, document-tracking applications, client services, and payment systems can all be interconnected through Web-based technologies.

As the technology becomes increasingly available and affordable, countries in the developing world are recognizing the opportunity, and some are acquiring and employing it. China, Nigeria, Rwanda, Turkey, and many others have already commenced ambitious LIS programs aimed to create, visualize, analyze, report, and publish land-based data as needed by private and public users. In some places, the programs are geared to online integration of the multiple public functions carried out by otherwise segregated agencies, thus creating electronic government, or virtual "one-stop shops," that improves efficiency and transparency.

Although LIS programs serve many purposes, governments have been drawn to the potential "win-win" benefits of applying LIS to the investment climate. On the one hand, faster and more consistent information and service delivery make the investment climate more attractive to investors. On the other hand, developers, real estate brokers, lawyers, banks, and other business people are eager users of the system and often willing to pay for quick, reliable information and services received. Therefore, making quality information and services available to investors not only helps to attract private businesses but also can generate income to recover the costs of developing and operating the LIS.

Applying LIS to improve the investment climate requires targeted efforts to tailor the packaging and delivery of information to investors' needs. Modern LISs have the potential to contain limitless data that need to be carefully selected and packaged for special uses. Table 17.1 suggests a set of data that would be of most interest to investors. Such information provides the basis for business analyses to support the selection of investment sites. Packaging the needed information in one place—say, a specially designed portal for investors—gives users a path to making a faster and better-informed investment decision.

The starting point for applying LIS to the investment climate has varied among regions and countries. In many Asian and Eastern European countries, digital land databases and even integrated LISs have already been developed, so applying the available data and system to the investment climate is truly a "low-hanging fruit." Governments can draw relevant data from the available sources, upload them on portals designed to guide and facilitate investors, and provide links to connect investors with the appropriate ministries and agencies. Singapore's LandNet, which can

Table 17.1   Typical Data Sets Critical to Investors

Subject	Example
Land availability	Public and private land inventories: location, size, use rights and conditions, and land value by districts
Land tenure	For publicly owned land: transfer methods and conditions, use fees, incentives, procedures; for privately owned land: transaction procedures, costs, property rights
Land development conditions	Definition of urban and rural land; zoning and urban plans; parks, recreation, and open spaces; environmental information; flood areas and polluted locations; population and census data
Transportation and utilities	Roads and traffic; transportation routes and ports; power and energy; water and sewage; telecommunications; waste management and disposal locations

Source: Authors.

be accessed via online portals INLIS (www.inlis.gov.sg) and SPIO (www.spio.sla.gov.sg), is a good example of how land information service portals are designed. Similar websites containing useful information on location and links to land administrations are also available for the Czech Republic, Poland, Slovenia, and many others.[2]

In countries where ICT development is less advanced or a comprehensive LIS is not feasible for the near future, some digital data components may be available and can be used to enhance the investment climate. Many African countries, such as Nigeria and Sierra Leone, offer the opportunity to bring together the few agencies that have acquired some limited forms of digital data for the test of a "limited LIS model." In Kano and Lagos, two important states of Nigeria, the governments have long-term plans to develop comprehensive LISs, and they are aware of the time and resources that will be required for full development of such a system. Just to develop a consensus among 15 to 20 major stakeholders can be a daunting task. Therefore, in parallel with their long-term plans, the governments see the immediate value in pursuing "limited LIS pilots" focusing on the few agencies whose data and functions are most critical to investors and that are ready to work with each other. Such pilots are much more manageable and, if successful, provide immediate value to investors, while showcasing an example of interagency collaboration for other ministries and agencies.

Many of the goals for implementation of an investment-focused LIS go well beyond disseminating information on available land. With the appropriate technology, investors' portals can be further developed to accommodate online applications and approvals. Singapore's LandNet is already functioning as a virtual one-stop shop, with a developed "back office" in which officers of the various agencies do not need to be physically together but are still well informed of each other's status and actions when performing their respective functions.

Such an option is not limited to advanced countries. Several developing and emerging countries are catching up fast, with strong government commitment to technology, investment, and development. In China and Turkey, the advent of new-generation computing, digital mapping, fiber-optic networks, and wireless technologies is rapidly transforming how information is generated, shared, and made available. The new technology offers unprecedented potential to validate applicants or landowners: land registries can now be connected to the system of births, deaths, marriages, and business registries; financiers can automatically query mortgage systems; utilities can notify other referral authorities of new installations; and developers and architects can readily inspect planning controls and zoning restrictions in any one location.

Even some latecomer countries in Africa are moving up fast. In Rwanda, the government has been aggressively modernizing the various components of land information in the last few years, including a computerized land registry, improved processing of land transactions, digital mapping, and national spatial planning. In the meantime, the government, through the Rwanda Development Board (RDB), is developing the concept of electronic government to support investors' needs by offering efficient and transparent interagency services. Based on these two pillars, the Rwanda government is now looking at how to integrate further the various components of land information and management and to develop a world-class LIS that will better serve the needs of investors and all citizens to identify available land for development and to navigate the planning approval process. Figure 17.1 presents a conceptual framework for the next step forward.

Broader Needs for Effective Implementation

A land information system can be a practical tool in providing information that a potential investor will use to make decisions on investment opportunities. However, the extent to which a LIS can benefit users depends on the quality and availability of up-to-date land information. Installing a modern electronic system is not enough. The data inputs,

Figure 17.1   The Concept for Online Land and Property Information Services for Investors

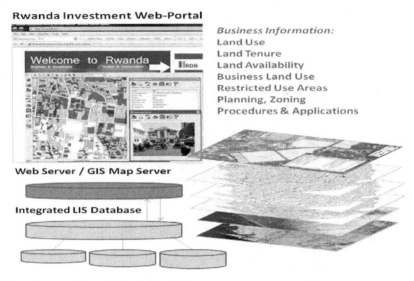

Source: Investment Climate Advisory Services 2010.
Note: GIS = global imaging system.

ICT infrastructure, and skilled staff to build and maintain the system are the foundation of the services.

Although development or investment promotion agencies often lead the development of investors' portals where useful information can be readily accessed, the supporting data are generated and integrated by teams of LIS specialists who are usually housed in the land administration. This process can involve the collective efforts of many specialized agencies including land registry, spatial planning, infrastructure, environment, roads, and utilities. In other words, investment promotion agencies themselves do not need to be LIS experts, but they do need smart "vendors" who know how to package special information and services to the investors who are their clients. However, unless quality data are available from a well-implemented foundation and supported by an effective transmitting system, investment promotion agencies will not be able to deliver quality services to the end users, in this case investors.

It is thus no surprise that the biggest challenge is achieving interagency collaboration. Just as the largest benefit of the LIS lies in the integration of multiple agencies, the biggest challenge to implementation is in multiparty participation. The information-producing model emphasizing "collect once, use many times" may be accepted by all in principle, but is hard to follow in practice. Agencies responsible for collecting, recording, and storing particular data tend to think of themselves as custodians of the data and are resistant to changes that suggest a loss of control. To overcome the barriers, it is essential to secure high-level support and political buy-in up front regarding policies, administrative structures, and organizational responsibilities.

Countries may start to develop a LIS from different levels, but they all benefit by following some general principles and approaches. These principles and approaches have been discussed extensively in the ICT and LIS literature (ECA 2008; ECLAC 2003). In general, a two-step methodology is recommended. Step one should start with a careful analysis aimed at understanding the priority needs of clients and the existing capacities and constraints. This should be followed by step two, which includes a series of feasibility studies focusing on determining the technical, economic, and organizational conditions that will have a significant impact on the system. While many issues should be carefully addressed at the design stage, the following deserve the highest attention:

- Interagency coordination
- Availability of existing data (paper-based or digital)
- Availability of skilled staff
- Availability of ICT infrastructure
- Cost of information technology (IT) systems, software, and licenses
- System and data maintenance and backup
- Data security and privacy.

Many efforts are required to implement the LIS and apply it successfully to the investment climate. The following are the most important: obtaining political support and institutional commitment, managing land information resources, simplifying procedures and modernizing administration, selecting the right technology, ensuring proper training of the workforce, and ensuring the privacy and security of data.

Political Support and Institutional Commitment
Making a political decision to pilot an integrated land information system will be a crucial first step in initiating implementation of the LIS. Successful LIS programs are often championed by political leaders at the highest level, considering the multiple ministries and agencies involved.

The potential of the system must be recognized by the whole government in order for it to work. In some places, a push from investment agencies works well, as investment generation and job creation are often top priorities on the agenda of political leaders. In other places, the land authority or government ICT body may advocate progress, especially when such progress is likely to enhance the collection of property tax revenue, which, in return, justifies the financial decision to develop the LIS.

The high-level decision to commence the program should be followed by an institutional awareness campaign to help the concerned ministries and agencies to see the value of participating. Efforts are also needed to establish a tiered management structure involving the appointment of a high-level LIS executive committee to provide interagency representation and oversight. The committee may need to appoint a LIS taskforce including policy, legal, technical, and institutional expertise required to design and implement strategies and to structure implementation of the system. Investment and development agencies should play an active role in this stage, ensuring that clients' needs are injected into the development of the LIS or targeting a pilot project to the information and service needs of business communities.

Management of Land Information Resources

The aim of land information management is to ensure the following:

- Land records are complete and updated.
- Duplicate processing of data is eliminated or reduced.
- Data are more readily available and accessible (through digitization).
- Potential revenues from land information services are realized.

Efforts at several levels are required to achieve the goals. Each agency responsible for certain types of data generation and record keeping must complete and update the data and, in many cases, convert data into digital form. Across agencies, preferably at the national level, data transfer standards must be developed and implemented to guide all institutions and ensure that data processes are consistent and accurate. There is also the need to establish the rules and mechanisms required to safeguard legitimate needs for privacy and confidentiality.

Land information management has tended to involve the private sector in recent years. The public-private partnership option is especially attractive in areas that consume both time and resources, such as acquisition of spatial data, conversion of paper-based records, and management and maintenance of data. Contracting these technical tasks out to private sector providers frees up government officials to regulate and protect the public interest. The data generated must remain the property of the government, and mechanisms for securing the privacy of these data are required.

Simple Procedures and Modern Administration

Simply computerizing old systems without rationalizing procedures will just transfer the duplication and inefficiency of existing procedures and, likely, compound errors without taking full advantage of modern technology. Excessive paper-based records and approval steps are often the result of attempts to provide appropriate checks and balances in the era prior to computing. New ICT and LIS are effective tools for accommodating a much simpler process, as well as effective for tracking files and offering virtual one-stop shop communications.

As desirable as it may be, procedural simplification itself requires policy decisions. Interagency collaboration, virtual or not, still depends on institutional willingness and agreements. In some places, modernization of the land information system has been seriously hindered by the existing legal framework. In Sierra Leone, the ambitious commencement of a program to build a new electronic land titling system quickly ran into conflicts with the existing deeds registration system.

Ideally, regulatory and procedural reforms can be carried out in parallel with the task of converting paper records, training staff, and developing the IT systems and LIS, so that by the time new LIS programs are up and ready, supporting laws and procedures have also been streamlined. A balance must be struck between what is possible through technological advancement and what is allowed by law. If well planned and implemented with a realistic vision and schedule, legislative and administrative land reforms and the technical integration of data for land use, planning, and natural resource management with the LIS can be mutually supportive and reinforcing.

Technology Based on Long-Term Objectives

Some developing nations are presented with an opportunity to make a technological leap, but significant challenges arise because technology, software, and imagery are expensive. Converting and validating existing records and detailed mapping are costly and time-consuming. Before making a decision, responsible agencies should ask the following questions:

What are the technological options? Is there the human and institutional capacity to maintain the new system and keep the data up-to-date? How long will it take to deploy the system, and how much will it cost? Will the technology pay for itself eventually, and when? Can the private sector help? Is there political will to commit to maintaining the system in the long run when the project ends?

One important need, which should never be overlooked, even at the design stage, is that of long-term maintenance of the system. Governments often rush into technologically savvy programs without long-term financial planning. Such programs stop running as soon as the start-up funding dries up. Complex IT-based systems require robust, ongoing project management. Again, strong political will and long-term institutional commitment are essential to success.

Human Resources and Capacity

Technology can perform miracles, but only if people know how to use it. For LIS efforts to be successful, education and training are paramount. As changes in computer hardware and software are fast-paced, so must be the upgrading of staff skills and expertise.

Building local capacity is critical to long-term success. Many low-income countries lack qualified land information and IT specialists. Some governments become overly dependent on using external contractors to fill the gap. This not only raises the costs, but also presents the danger of losing the technical know-how entirely at the end of the contracts, especially if such contracts fail to include local capacity building. Being aware of this danger, some governments have emphasized the use of local talent wherever possible.

In Kano State, Nigeria, the design and deployment of the LIS program has been led by a group of young IT specialists in the Land Ministry, with international funding and technical support. The result is encouraging—not only does the program's design reflect both international best practice and local needs, but the IT team is also expanding local capacity on the ground. Today, the team regularly trains officers from other ministries and organizations based on their needs. Kano is also facing higher demand for training from its neighboring states. Many governments, including those of Kano, Lagos, and Rwanda, have made further efforts to work with universities and other relevant educational bodies to institute programs that assure the long-term supply of much-needed professionals. And retention of employees must be improved by improving salaries, working conditions, and other measures to increase the satisfaction of the staff.

Privacy and Security

Security of the IT system is important to prevent illegal access to information, both physically and electronically. The system must include well-defined rules and protocols for accessing a variety of information. The technical and administrative staffers who interact with the system must follow the rules, and database administrators must be tough on enforcement. Pirated software, weak antivirus safeguards, and misuse of portable storage devices can quickly disable an entire LIS, corrupt the data, or result in a complete loss of records. Equally, laws must be enacted to penalize offenders for illegally accessing personal information or mishandling records. In turn, individual agencies must adopt internal IT use and information management policies coincident with the overarching legal and national policy framework.

Conclusions

Using ICT-based land information systems is another win-win situation. The government gets a more efficient system that can do a better job of protecting the public interest, and the private sector gets much less red tape and better ability to identify, access, register, and develop the land that is needed to carry on their businesses. Investors are always attracted to locations that provide the best services. They are also willing to pay for the services they appreciate. Thus, the provision of integrated land information that meets the expectations of investors is likely to help governments to attract investment and to make the LIS operation financially viable at the same time.

Behind the scenes, a LIS application tailored to connect the multiple land management functions online is a powerful tool providing more efficient and transparent land approval procedures—another great service that is highly valued by investors. Online coordination among agencies can greatly speed up the development approval process and delivery of services. LIS further enables monitoring and evaluation, which feeds back into the planning and decision-making process of government.

Achieving this win-win situation requires a tremendous legal, technical, and financial effort. Institutional collaboration is perhaps the biggest challenge. It can be met only by a high-level political commitment and the willingness of all participating agencies. In this sense, focusing on the investment climate is helpful to implementing a land information system, because it is likely to attain visible economic benefits in the near future, possibly generate incomes for the agencies based on quality and timely services they provide, and thus rally political and institutional support for sustainable, ongoing implementation.

Notes

1. Author's interview with Jack Walvin.
2. The Czech Republic: http://www.czechinvest.org/en; Poland: http://www
.paiz.gov.pl; Slovenia: http://www.investslovenia.org/.

References

ECA (Economic Commission for Africa). 2008. "Land Management Information Systems in the Knowledge Economy: Discussion and Guiding Principles for Africa." United Nations, Science and Technology Division, ECA.

ECLAC (Economic Commission for Latin America and the Caribbean). 2003. "Road Maps towards an Information Society in Latin America and the Caribbean." United Nations, ECLAC, Regional Preparatory Ministerial Conference of Latin America and the Caribbean for the "World Summit on the Information Society," Bávaro, Punta Cana, Dominican Republic, January 29–31.

Investment Climate Advisory Services. 2010. "Business Access to Land in Rwanda: Issues and Recommendations." Investment Climate Advisory Services, World Bank Group, Washington, DC.

CHAPTER 18

Reconciling Public and Private Interests in Urban Land Development: An Integrated Approach to Urban Design

Ray Gordon with Zaki Ghiacy and Xiaofang Shen

Mathema (2008) describes the problem with urban land development as follows:

> Lagos State, Nigeria, has a population of 15 million, growing annually at a rate of approximately 5 percent. Its metropolitan area, the home to 90 percent of the State's population, displays a severe symptom of a problematic urban housing and land market: a rapidly expanding demand coupled with a stagnating supply of residential and commercial housing, which has resulted in disproportionately high prices of housing unaffordable even by middle-income households. To own a home, Lagos citizens face the cost that is comparable to prices in the US, about USD150,000–250,000 for a typical 2- or 3-bedroom unit. To rent, they typically pay the landlords 2–3 years of rent up-front, without guaranteed basic service. Currently, an estimated 70 percent of the population lives in slums which are characterized with extremely high densities, poor housing conditions, and little or no access to basic infrastructure like water or sanitation.

Lagos faces problems that are typical of many cities in the developing world, both Africa and elsewhere. Explosive urban growth in developing countries, the many issues surrounding it, and the many problems created by it have been around for many decades (World Bank 2008). Both population and economic activity are increasing rapidly, creating the need for land for more housing and for more commercial and industrial uses. In the context of very low personal incomes, as well as very limited government capacity in terms of both the budget and human resources, the usual results include lots of slums, effectively unregulated business locations, and the too many, too familiar problems associated with both.

Myriad books and papers have been written on the various dimensions of this set of problems, and we make no attempt to summarize them here. Rather, this chapter focuses on one approach that can improve the efficiency of both the land being developed and the limited budgets, time, and skills of the responsible public agencies, while also incorporating the need for private sector commercial and industrial development that provides the jobs, incomes, and higher productivity that are the essence of economic development.

Governments have a range of tools at their disposal, at least in principle, for managing urban growth. These include land use planning, zoning, environmental protection requirements, building codes, provision of infrastructure services or the lack thereof, and other policy and regulatory instruments to guide, regulate, and facilitate private development. But in practice several problems arise:

- The resources to use the tools—budgets and skills at the government agencies that are supposed to use them—are too limited to deal with the magnitude of explosive urban growth.
- There is often a gap—usually an enormous gulf—between planners, on the one hand, and businesses seeking land, on the other. The two talk different languages and rarely even try to speak with each other on a strategic level.
- There is often another gap, similarly unbridged, between any master plans that may exist (whether on the national, regional, or urban level), on the one hand, and the tools being used to guide the development of specific parcels of land that may be sought for housing or business sites. The master plans are not practical, and the practice is unplanned.

The Role of Urban Design

Urban design is—among other things, to be sure—one way to deal with these problems: to economize on the limited resources of municipal and regional planning, zoning, and permitting authorities and to bridge the gaps between micro project design and macro planning and between public sector agencies and private sector business development. Urban design, if properly implemented, helps to fill the gap between the public policy goals of planners and the desire of private developers to maximize profitability, making the two complementary rather than confrontational. It is a way to try to turn conflicts into win-win cooperation. As illustrated by figure 18.1, successful urban design is guided by the vision of regional or city development planning, while incorporating input from a wide range of public and private stakeholders, including local communities. Through emphasis on the creation of mixed uses, density requirements, building and street harmonization, and other key elements of the urban environment, urban design helps to achieve more efficient land use and more cost-effective construction, thus providing higher financial returns to private developers and end users.

As shown in the figure, the end product of urban design is often a set of mandatory building guidelines (or design codes). These codes incorporate the outcomes of consultations with relevant stakeholders and, once

Figure 18.1   The Elements of Urban Design

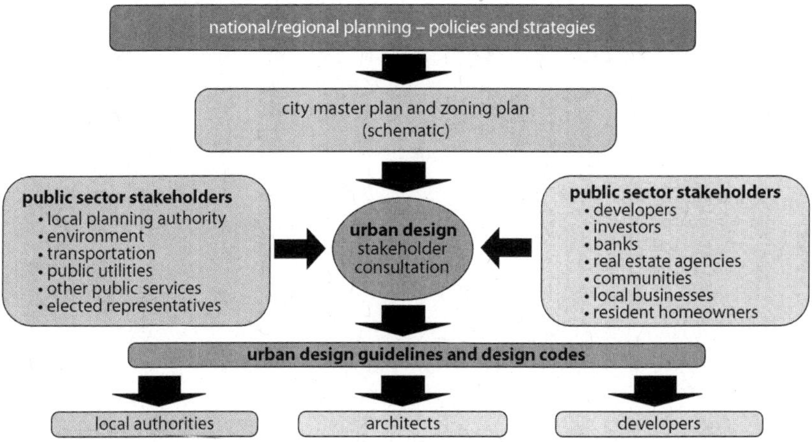

Source: Authors.

adopted by the city governments, become mandatory requirements for both private developers and public agencies. As long as the requirements are fulfilled, the guidelines often allow developers and architects sufficient flexibility to explore innovative and original designs. In special cases, the design guidelines can be used to encourage developers to invest by increasing densities, relaxing onerous regulatory requirements, and offering other incentives to make the projects economically worthwhile for investors and developers.

As an "overlay" on existing zoning designations, the urban design guidelines need not require a rewriting of existing land use regulations. This allows for the benefits to be implemented in a relatively short period of time, thus accelerating investment in priority locations.

The other aspect of the urban design approach that is key for our concerns here is that it deals only with limited areas—presumably priority areas for development—and thus allows the planning and regulatory authorities to concentrate their limited resources. Although urban design can be applied to quite large areas, in most cases it has been used most effectively on specific targeted locations within a city. In the United States, United Kingdom, and other European countries, where urban design has become popular over the last few decades, municipalities have been using it to engage the private sector in revitalizing commercial, residential, and recreational areas of cities facing special needs or challenges. The annex to this chapter provides two renowned examples, the Battery Park City project in the Lower Manhattan area of New York City and the Hammarby Sjöstad project in Stockholm. In both cases, city governments succeeded in applying innovative methods of urban design to achieve more efficient and sustainable urban expansion and revitalization.

Over the past decade some localities in developing countries, such as Shanghai (China) and Baja California (Mexico), have been attracted to these approaches for similar reasons. In Shanghai, the municipality has quickly adopted international practices to fast-track the modernization of its oldest shopping districts, with a view to upgrading retail businesses while providing residents and tourists with much more attractive spaces for urban entertainment and living (see chapter 6; McKinsey 2010). In Baja California, local governments and landowners in farming communities responded to the challenge caused by the depletion of freshwater aquifers by joining hands and using principles of integrated area design. They managed to transform the region from a dying agricultural focus to a dynamic aquaculture-based economy, with revived housing and commercial development (see chapter 8).

Challenges in Urban Design

The urban design process is inevitably complex. It requires the participation of a large group of public agencies, private developers, community representatives, urban designers, legal experts, and other technical land professionals. These players must address a comprehensive set of development issues including land use, density, demographic trends, property rights, job generation, utility services, transportation, environmental impact, and perhaps other concerns. This implies a huge task of reconciling many interests, some of which are often conflicting.

In cases of private sector commercial or industrial development, these difficulties may be compounded by what we might term "more than is necessary" frictions in public-private sector cooperation. On the one hand, government agencies are sometimes overly cautious when dealing with large, complex private development projects, being afraid of making serious mistakes. On the other hand, officials may exert undue influence in selecting sites and developer candidates, therefore emphasizing the need to have adequate checks and constraints. There is potential for the process to proceed so slowly that it drives away investors or, at the other extreme, to move too fast and be open to corruption, ignoring public interests.

The lack of government agency experience and capacity can also be a significant hurdle to the implementation of urban design. Local governments in developing countries are commonly constrained by limited resources and lack of relevant expertise. Government officials sometimes look for shortcuts by recreating models that may have worked elsewhere but are not appropriate for local needs and conditions. For example, in Kano, Nigeria, a well-intentioned government initiative to attract new investment and renovate the city's former central business district, complete with a detailed physical model, failed to incorporate critical factors on the ground, including sensitive issues related to relocating some of the existing land users, acquiring private properties for new infrastructure, and satisfying the requirements of financial feasibility and funding to implement the plan. It should come as no surprise that the model simply sat in a conference room, gathering dust as the project languished.

There are many cases in which governments are overly ambitious with regard to the scale of projects, failing to pay sufficient attention to market demand or infrastructure support. In such cases, projects end up with large vacant tracts, ill-serviced and unwanted. In some cases, projects become functionally obsolete even before they are completed. In Calabar,

Nigeria, a large-scale development including a shopping mall, recreational areas, and various waterfront facilities was rushed into implementation without carefully examining the potential needs and concerns of the local communities. The resultant building complex remains largely vacant several years after completion. Good public-private sector collaboration usually forestalls such fiascos, as private investors are unlikely to participate without studies of demand and other aspects of financial feasibility.

Prerequisites to Successful Implementation

Experience has shown that six prerequisites are particularly important:

- *High-level political will.* Successful urban design projects are possible only when they fit the government's vision and strategy and have the support of local political leadership, such as mayors or governors. This high-level political support is also critical to ensure the cooperation of the relevant agency directors, both during the initial stages and down the road.

- *Institutionalized agency coordination.* Government must put in place the necessary institutional mechanisms to assure cooperation among the various development agencies involved in the complex process. This can take the form of an official directive from decision makers or a steering committee of some type that regularly brings together the stakeholders to set overall goals and monitor progress.

- *Transparent procedures.* Transparency is the key to preventing abuse of power and ensuring that legitimate public and private sector interests are addressed. There are systematic ways to achieve this goal, which are elaborated later in this chapter.

- *Professionalism.* Urban design requires a strong understanding of private sector needs and an understanding of the objectives of developers, architects, and financiers. Successful projects are universally the product of city governments that designate professional teams whose members are familiar with laws, regulations, development needs, architectural design, and business procedures. In most cases government does not have all of these skills in-house, but draws from the expertise present in other public and private professional institutions.

- *Financial commitment.* An important goal of focused support for prioritized development is to create models of success. This requires governments to allocate sufficient resources to fund proposed projects, including staff resources, a budget for infrastructure improvements, and, where appropriate, incentives for developers such as tax relief or other regulatory benefits in return for the construction of projects within designated special districts.

- *Information availability.* Good urban design is based on a thorough understanding of the relationships between the various elements that contribute to a well-built environment. Because urban design synthesizes information from various sources, it is imperative that the various local government agencies make relevant data available to urban designers during their consultations.

A Four-Step Process

Having a systematic process is critical to ensuring the success of any sustainable development work. Urban design is no exception. There can be many steps, depending on the size, needs, and existing conditions of each project. Nevertheless, there are four essential steps that all governments should carefully consider using as a basic guide. One of the keys to success here is the concept of "think big, start small": the actual design may cover only one district in one urban area, but it must be consistent with plans and prospects for the entire city and often a larger region.

Schematic Master Plan

A logical first step might be to develop a master plan for the region or the metropolitan area. In this step, what is called a "schematic" master plan may be the best strategy. Conventional master planning, focusing on one or several decades and often extrapolating past data, is expensive, is often impractical, often misses the impact of technological advances, and, perhaps most important, often uses tools that are not sufficient to capture the entire range of how market forces affect the urban landscape. In too many places, plans developed in this manner become quickly obsolete—some even before they are completed. The city of Kano in northern Nigeria, for example, has a master plan prepared more than 40 years ago, a plan that was never substantially implemented. Similar problems are found in many East European cities, where governments are still using obsolete plans inherited from the previous communist regimes, which cause serious difficulties in obtaining construction project approvals for both private developers and responsible government authorities.

Schematic master plans are a more flexible approach that allows broader-brushed planning, leaving sufficient flexibility for cities to incorporate new technologies and the organic growth of development patterns. They are developed faster and at lower cost. With sufficient political support and technological help, a schematic master plan can be created in about one year. Active collaboration by all stakeholders, including private business and commercial leaders, is a necessity. Good schematic master plans follow the principles summarized in box 18.1.

More Specific Regulations within Each District

A logical second step, with a schematic master plan in place, is for municipalities and districts to create (or update) regulations for the legal disposition of urban land and to establish controls on the physical development of properties within their jurisdictions. Singapore, for instance, divides the city-state into 55 planning districts, ranging from downtown centers to new town neighborhoods to small islands, and requires each to develop zoning guidelines and regulations tailored to their specific social, economic, and environment needs (Yuen 2010). To make the regulations effective, local governments need to strengthen compliance and monitoring systems, which are often weak or nonexistent.

Definition of Priority Districts

The third step is to identify priority areas for deeper focus. These could be areas that have the biggest economic opportunities or the most pressing

---

Box 18.1

Elements of a Schematic Master Plan

- Policies on land use allocation
- Projections on housing and employment levels
- Social and economic trends in development
- Strategic directions for growth and regeneration
- Strategic growth of roadways and public transportation systems
- Incorporation of established government programs in business development, housing, education, health, and environmental protection
- Analysis of various plausible urbanization patterns for future growth
- Strategies to address alternative growth scenarios.

socioeconomic needs. Such areas can be commercial districts, low-income residential communities, industrial parks, or tourism destinations. They can be large or small; public, private, or jointly owned. Although still government-led, this step requires significant participation by the private sector. Government planners at this stage must think creatively and closely follow market forces (or, at the very least, take them seriously into account) in determining new development priorities. Among the many criteria to be used to select priority areas, a critical one is the attractiveness of the sites to potential developers.

Deeper Analysis of Priority Districts

Once the priority areas have been identified, the next step—again with all stakeholders actively involved—is to conduct a deeper analysis of each priority area. In general, this should include the following elements:

- *Land valuation.* A primary factor in the viability of urban projects is the value of land itself. In well-established economies, these values can be derived from their location, historical sales patterns, and the existing values of adjoining properties. However, in many developing countries, land valuation is more difficult, due to lack of market indicators or distorted land prices as a result of government allocation of land at below-market prices. In such cases, governments might consider using infrastructure cost recovery as one criterion in establishing a minimum land valuation.

- *Economic development and financial analysis.* Rate of return and other economic analyses are crucial to establishing the basis for development decisions. Both direct and indirect costs of proposed development programs can be compared to the potential economic benefits to the local economy. It is not enough for a development project to have lofty goals that serve the public good; projects must be economically and financially viable to attract private investment and to sustain government funding contributions. Private developers will not participate in development projects unless there is a reasonable prospect of attaining an acceptable return on their investment. Public investment must also be allowed an adequate return in order to be sustainable, even though government may gain from other aspects, such as generation of new jobs and higher tax revenues. This kind of analysis should not be taken either as gospel truth or as firm plans; it requires many assumptions about unknown quantities and uncontrollable future events. Rather, it should be used to filter out any schemes that are highly dubious and to indicate directions for fruitful promotion of investments in the area.

- *Zoning analysis.* Obsolete or inappropriate land use regulation can stymie private investment in urban areas. Taking into account the possibilities that have been explored, the team should review existing zoning and density regulations, if any, and modify these (or create new ones) to facilitate the development being envisaged.

- *Environmental impact analysis.* All development has an impact on the physical environment. An assessment project's environmental impacts should commence well before development planning is completed. Any significant impacts can then be identified and mitigated before they have an adverse effect on the local population. A comprehensive environmental impact analysis has the economic benefit of minimizing costly mitigation measures that are all too often identified after construction is well under way. A development that has a positive environmental impact often provides the added benefit of creating a more efficient project that uses less energy, creates fewer vehicular trips, and protects valuable natural resources. Modern environmental impact analysis includes detailed studies of short-term construction impacts, traffic patterns, service delivery, water consumption, subsurface water quality, waste generation, noise, air quality, water- and waste-recycling options, flora and fauna, estimated energy use, and prior land uses that may have introduced hazardous materials to the soils. Taken together, these studies result in sustainable and efficient use of land, with minimal long-term adverse impacts on the environment and the local population.

- *Social impact analysis.* Social impacts are closely associated with the environmental and economic aspects of any development. Good social impact analysis is essential to ensuring the lasting success of development projects. Therefore, it is important that policy decision makers, regulatory authorities, and developers work together to conduct good analysis so that the costs borne by people and the society (both present and in the future) are adequately taken into account. Through social impact analysis, social sustainability can be measured by the effects on people's way of life, including property rights, community culture, safety, fire protection, and health, among others. Such studies can also identify locally produced sources of construction materials and raw materials. A comprehensive social impact analysis should also identify the employment and economic development opportunities of a proposed project, including the availability of local workforce resources for construction and permanent employment, as well as long-term spin-off economic benefits for local businesses and suppliers.

With this process it should be possible to define a strategy to achieve good business and socioeconomic benefits for the selected industrial areas, commercial districts, or residential communities.

Summary

Where urban design is implemented properly, it brings many benefits to local governments, investors, and urban communities. For investors, it can break logjams of zoning, permitting, and accessing utility services that might otherwise be intractable—and do so in ways that also enhance the public interest. It is a win-win approach.

Urban design is likely to play a more important role in the next stage of urban growth in both the developed and developing worlds. This is because it allows governments to focus their limited resources on high-priority areas facing rapidly growing development needs. Urban design encourages government planners to consider a more pro-business approach and collaborate with private sector partners in seeking more efficient economically and financially viable development solutions.

Urban design also requires governments to listen to communities closely and to promote district development that is more environmentally friendly, better supported by infrastructure and other public services, and more attractive for work and living.

Finally, urban design provides local governments the opportunity to introduce new science, technology, and urban development concepts and practices, such as renewable energy systems and new building materials in developing the cities of the future.

However, urban design is not a panacea—it is useful only when the important prerequisites are in place. Above all, political will, a clearly defined development vision, genuine interagency cooperation, and active participation of all stakeholders are essential. The approach requires a strong commitment to cooperation between the public and private sectors, so that each can learn to see each other's priorities and find ways to support each other's functions. Finally, strong ethical standards and a genuine desire to serve the public are keys to the successful application of this process.

Annex. Examples of Successful Urban Design Projects

The two examples presented here applied innovative methods of urban design to achieve more efficient and sustainable urban expansion and revitalization.

Battery Park City, New York City: Developing Sound Design Guidelines to Support Integrated Urban Development

New York City is one of the front-runners in using urban design to deal with the multiple challenges of rapid urban growth, including an ever-increasing demand for commercial and residential space, the availability of developable land only in former industrial tracts and abandoned waterfront properties, a deteriorating infrastructure, and congested transportation systems.

Battery Park City, a 40-hectare landfill along the Hudson River in Lower Manhattan, adjacent to the world-famous Wall Street financial district, is a successful, high-profile urban design project. It demonstrates how a city government can take an integrated approach to bringing together economic, social, and environmental inputs to create more efficient and sustainable development.

The Battery Park City property was created from material excavated during construction of the World Trade Center's foundations. It was expected to be developed into a mixed-use residential and commercial community. But before the urban design project was introduced in 1980, the original plan failed to envision its potential to be a valuable extension of the nearby financial district. The plan used a traditional street grid with minimal public amenities. Without standards for building design, setbacks, or massing, all of the individually developed buildings were isolated from each other. There were minimal open spaces or commercial areas for public sharing. Moreover, there was no consideration for providing easy public access to the riverfront, and, in many instances, future buildings could easily block the view down streets from the interior of Manhattan.

Dissatisfied with the plan, the New York City government decided to launch a new urban design project using a more integrated approach to plan, design, and develop the area. The government established the Battery Park City Authority to manage the project. Throughout the project, the New York City Planning Department, urban designers, private developers, architects, lawyers, and other economic development experts worked closely as a team to craft a new set of design guidelines and associated district zoning regulations, aimed at providing the maximum value of space utilization, neighborhood integration, and attractive urban environment.

Based on the new guidelines and regulations, the entire district plan and block layout were revised, view corridors to the riverfront were provided, and central office complexes and interior plazas were integrated—all of which helped to harmonize the use of space and maximize the value of the land. Moreover, residential neighborhoods focused on publicly shared open spaces, with the waterfront, a boat marina, and other important public facilities accessible to all. The design project included a mile-long pedestrian esplanade, an interior winter garden, several plazas, and more— all of which contributed to a more efficient use of the shared space and created the attractive look of an established New York community.

The New York City government benefits from the project financially. The Battery Park City Authority, which continues to manage the project, makes significant annual contributions of more than US$200 million to support low-income housing in other parts of New York City, including the Bronx and Harlem.

Hammarby Sjöstad, Stockholm, Sweden: Minimizing Adverse Environmental Impact for Sustainable Development

Hammarby Sjöstad in Stockholm, Sweden, is a good example of how developments can minimize adverse environmental impacts and create a modern, sustainable neighborhood by adopting an integrated approach to urban design.

Hammarby Sjöstad is a 200-hectare brownfield development planned to expand the inner city and convert the old industrial and harbor area into a modern neighborhood. Approximately 10,000 people live in the area, and the project aims to create 9,000 homes and up to 10,000 jobs by 2015. The scheme epitomizes carbon-neutral development, has attracted international acclaim, and has become the benchmark for many similar developments around the world.

The Hammarby Sjöstad development uses urban design as the main tool for creating a natural extension of Stockholm's inner city that works well with the historic landscape and waterfront. Density, mix of uses, street dimensions, block lengths, and building heights are all carefully designed to ensure similarity with the surrounding area and successfully reflect the urban form of inner-city Stockholm. Trams, cycle lanes, ferry links, and pedestrian routes have been conscientiously built to provide integrated transportation links to Stockholm's existing infrastructure network.

Hammarby Sjöstad is particularly well known for its close attention to environmental sustainability. As an integral part of the urban design project, the public and private sector participants are encouraged to make extensive use of green roofs, solar panels, eco-friendly construction, car pooling, and a fully integrated underground waste collection system known as the Hammarby Model. Many places around the world are now learning from this example.

References

Mathema, Ashna. 2008. "Slums and Sprawl in Lagos: The Unintended Consequence of 'Well Intended' Regulation." World Bank, Washington, DC.

McKinsey and Company. 2010. "Shanghai's Road to Prosperity." http://www.mckinsey.com/aboutus/whatwedo/followateam/shanghai/index.asp.

World Bank. 2008. *World Development Report 2009: Reshaping Economic Geography*. New York: Oxford University for the World Bank.

Yuen, Belinda. 2010. "Guiding Spatial Changes: Singapore Urban Planning." In *Urban Land Markets: Improving Land Management for Successful Urbanization*, ed. Somik V. Lall, Mila Freire, Belinda Yuen, Robin Rajack, and Jean-Jacques Helluin. Washington, DC: World Bank; New York: Springer.